Immanent Materialisms

Must a philosophy of life be materialist, and if so, must it also be a philosophy of immanence? In the last twenty years or so there has been a growing trend in continental thought and philosophy and critical theory that has seen a return to the category of immanence. Through consideration of the work of thinkers such as Giorgio Agamben, Catherine Malabou, François Laruelle, Gilles Deleuze and others, this collection aims to examine the interplay between the concepts of immanence, materialism and life, particularly as this interplay can highlight new directions for political inquiry. Furthermore, critical reflection on this constellation of concepts could also be instructive for continental philosophy of religion, in which ideas about the divine, embodiment, sexual difference, desire, creation and incarnation are refigured in provocative new ways. The way of immanence, however, is not without its dangers. Indeed, it may be that with its affirmation something of importance is lost to material life. Could it be that the integrity of material things requires a transcendent origin? Precisely what are the metaphysical, political and theological consequences of pursuing a philosophy of immanence in relation to a philosophy of life?

This book was originally published as a special issue of *Angelaki: Journal of the Theoretical Humanities*.

Charlie Blake is currently visiting Senior Lecturer in Digital Culture at the University of West London and Lecturer in Philosophy at the University of Brighton, UK. He has published most recently on the topology of serial killing, ahumanism, music and hypostition and the greater politics of barnacles, bees and werewolves.

Patrice Haynes is a Senior Lecturer in Philosophy at Liverpool Hope University, UK. She publishes in the area of continental philosophy of religion, feminist philosophy and, recently, African philosophy. She is currently working on her second monograph, provisionally titled *Animist Humanism: West African Religious Traditions and Decolonising Philosophy of Religion*.

Immanent Materialisms
Speculation and Critique

Edited by
Charlie Blake and Patrice Haynes

LONDON AND NEW YORK

First published 2018
by Routledge
2 Park Square, Milton Park, Abingdon, Oxon, OX14 4RN, UK

and by Routledge
711 Third Avenue, New York, NY 10017, USA

Routledge is an imprint of the Taylor & Francis Group, an informa business

© 2018 Taylor & Francis

All rights reserved. No part of this book may be reprinted or reproduced or utilised in any form or by any electronic, mechanical, or other means, now known or hereafter invented, including photocopying and recording, or in any information storage or retrieval system, without permission in writing from the publishers.

Trademark notice: Product or corporate names may be trademarks or registered trademarks, and are used only for identification and explanation without intent to infringe.

British Library Cataloguing in Publication Data
A catalogue record for this book is available from the British Library

ISBN 13: 978-1-138-30189-4

Typeset in Bodoni MT
by RefineCatch Limited, Bungay, Suffolk

Publisher's Note
The publisher accepts responsibility for any inconsistencies that may have arisen during the conversion of this book from journal articles to book chapters, namely the possible inclusion of journal terminology.

Disclaimer
Every effort has been made to contact copyright holders for their permission to reprint material in this book. The publishers would be grateful to hear from any copyright holder who is not here acknowledged and will undertake to rectify any errors or omissions in future editions of this book.

Contents

Citation Information vii
Notes on Contributors ix

Introduction – Something in the Air: An Introduction to Immanent
Materialisms and the Unbounded Earth 3
Charlie Blake and Patrice Haynes

1. Spirit in the Materialist World: On the Structure of Regard 15
   John Ó Maoilearca

2. Contingency without Unreason: Speculation after Meillassoux 33
   Joshua Ramey

3. Religious Immanence: A Critique of Meillassoux's "Virtual" God 49
   Jim Urpeth

4. The Profanation of Revelation: On Language and Immanence in the
   Work of Giorgio Agamben 65
   Colby Dickinson

5. Idealism without Idealism: Badiou's Materialist Renaissance 85
   Frank Ruda

6. Prolegomena to a Materialist Humanism 101
   Michael O'Neill Burns

7. Mere Life, Damaged Life and Ephemeral Life: Adorno and the Concept of Life 115
   Alastair Morgan

8. Creative Becoming and the Patiency of Matter: Feminism, New
   Materialism and Theology 131
   Patrice Haynes

9. Nature Deserves to be Side by Side with the Angels: Nature and
   Messianism by Way of Non-Islam 153
   Anthony Paul Smith

10. The Art of the Absolute: Relations, Objects, and Immanence 173
    Benjamin Noys

Index 187

Citation Information

The chapters in this book were originally published in *Angelaki: Journal of the Theoretical Humanities*, volume 19, issue 1 (March 2014). When citing this material, please use the original page numbering for each article, as follows:

Introduction
Editorial Introduction – Something in the Air: An Introduction to Immanent Materialisms and the Unbounded Earth
Charlie Blake and Patrice Haynes
Angelaki: Journal of the Theoretical Humanities, volume 19, issue 1 (March 2014), pp. 3–14

Chapter 1
Spirit in the Materialist World: On the Structure of Regard
John Ó Maoilearca
Angelaki: Journal of the Theoretical Humanities, volume 19, issue 1 (March 2014), pp. 15–32

Chapter 2
Contingency without Unreason: Speculation after Meillassoux
Joshua Ramey
Angelaki: Journal of the Theoretical Humanities, volume 19, issue 1 (March 2014), pp. 33–48

Chapter 3
Religious Immanence: A Critique of Meillassoux's "Virtual" God
Jim Urpeth
Angelaki: Journal of the Theoretical Humanities, volume 19, issue 1 (March 2014), pp. 49–64

Chapter 4
The Profanation of Revelation: On Language and Immanence in the Work of Giorgio Agamben
Colby Dickinson
Angelaki: Journal of the Theoretical Humanities, volume 19, issue 1 (March 2014), pp. 65–84

CITATION INFORMATION

Chapter 5
Idealism without Idealism: Badiou's Materialist Renaissance
Frank Ruda
Angelaki: Journal of the Theoretical Humanities, volume 19, issue 1 (March 2014), pp. 85–100

Chapter 6
Prolegomena to a Materialist Humanism
Michael O'Neill Burns
Angelaki: Journal of the Theoretical Humanities, volume 19, issue 1 (March 2014), pp. 101–114

Chapter 7
Mere Life, Damaged Life and Ephemeral Life: Adorno and the Concept of Life
Alastair Morgan
Angelaki: Journal of the Theoretical Humanities, volume 19, issue 1 (March 2014), pp. 115–130

Chapter 8
Creative Becoming and the Patiency of Matter: Feminism, New Materialism and Theology
Patrice Haynes
Angelaki: Journal of the Theoretical Humanities, volume 19, issue 1 (March 2014), pp. 131–152

Chapter 9
Nature Deserves to be Side by Side with the Angels: Nature and Messianism by Way of Non-Islam
Anthony Paul Smith
Angelaki: Journal of the Theoretical Humanities, volume 19, issue 1 (March 2014), pp. 153–172

Chapter 10
The Art of the Absolute: Relations, Objects, and Immanence
Benjamin Noys
Angelaki: Journal of the Theoretical Humanities, volume 19, issue 1 (March 2014), pp. 173–186

For any permission-related enquiries please visit:
http://www.tandfonline.com/page/help/permissions

Notes on Contributors

Charlie Blake is currently visiting Senior Lecturer in Digital Culture at the University of West London and Lecturer in Philosophy at the University of Brighton, UK. He has published most recently on the topology of serial killing, ahumanism, music and hypostition and the greater politics of barnacles, bees and werewolves.

Michael O'Neill Burns is Senior Lecturer in the Department of Philosophy at the University of the West of England, UK. He is the author of *Kierkegaard and the Matter of Philosophy* (2015) and is in the early stages of a long-term project developing a systematic theory of materialist humanism in dialogue with recent European philosophy.

Colby Dickinson is Associate Professor of Theology at Loyola University, Chicago, USA. He is the author of *Agamben and Theology* (2011) and *Between the Canon and the Messiah: The Structure of Faith in Contemporary Continental Thought* (2013); and the editor of *The Postmodern "Saints" of France* (2013) and *The Shaping of Tradition: Context and Normativity* (2013).

Patrice Haynes is Senior Lecturer in Philosophy at Liverpool Hope University, UK. She publishes in the area of continental philosophy of religion, feminist philosophy and, recently, African philosophy. She is currently working on her second monograph, provisionally titled *Animist Humanism: West African Religious Traditions and Decolonising Philosophy of Religion*.

Alastair Morgan is Senior Lecturer at Sheffield Hallam University, UK. He is the author of *Adorno's Concept of Life* (2007); and the editor of *Being Human: Reflections on Mental Distress in Society* (2008) and *Values and Ethics in Mental Health: An Exploration for Practice* (with Anne Felton and Bill Fulford, 2015).

Benjamin Noys is Professor of Critical Theory at the University of Chichester, UK. He is the author of *Georges Bataille: A Critical Introduction* (2000), *The Culture of Death* (2005), *The Persistence of the Negative: A Critique of Contemporary Continental Theory* (2010), and *Malign Velocities: Accelerationism and Capitalism* (2014); and editor of *Communization and Its Discontents* (2011).

John Ó Maoilearca is Professor of Film at Kingston University, London, UK. His authored books include *Bergson and Philosophy* (2000), *Post-Continental Philosophy* (2006) and *All Thoughts are Equal: Laruelle and Nonhuman Philosophy* (2015); and he is the editor of *Laruelle and Non-Philosophy* (with Anthony Paul Smith, 2012) and *The Bloomsbury Companion to Continental Philosophy* (with Beth Lord, 2013).

NOTES ON CONTRIBUTORS

Joshua Ramey is Assistant Professor in Philosophy at Grinnell College, IA, USA. He is the author of *The Hermetic Deleuze: Philosophy and Spiritual Ordeal* (2012) and *Politics of Divination: Neoliberal Endgame and the Religion of Contingency* (2016); and the co-translator of *François Laruelle's Non-Philosophical Mysticism for Today* (with Edward Kazarian, 2016).

Frank Ruda is a Researcher at the Collaborative Research Center 626 at the Free University, Berlin, Germany; Visiting Lecturer at the Slovenian Academy of Arts and Sciences, Ljubljana, Slovenia; and Visiting Professor at the Bard College, Berlin, Germany. He is the author of *Abolishing Freedom: A Plea for the Contemporary Use of Fatalism* (2016).

Anthony Paul Smith is Assistant Professor in Religion at La Salle University, Philadelphia, USA. He is the author of *A Non-Philosophical Theory of Nature: Ecologies of Thought* (2013); and translator of *François Laruelle's Future Christ: A Lesson in Heresy* (2010), *Struggle and Utopia at the End Times of Philosophy* (2012), *Principles of Non-Philosophy* (2013), and *Intellectuals and Power: The Insurrection of the Victim* (2014).

Jim Urpeth is Senior Lecturer in Philosophy at the University of Greenwich, UK. He is the editor of *Nietzsche and the Divine* (with John Lippitt, 2000) and has published a number of papers on themes in the thought of Kant, Nietzsche, Bergson, Bataille, Heidegger and Deleuze, among others, focusing mainly on topics in the fields of aesthetics, philosophical naturalism, and the philosophy of religion.

Matter and meaning are not separate elements. They are inextricably fused together, and no event, no matter how energetic, can tear them asunder.
Karen Barad[1]

When immanence is no longer immanent to something other than itself it is possible to speak of a plane of immanence. Such a plane is, perhaps, a radical empiricism: it does not present a flux of the lived that is immanent to a subject and individualized in that which belongs to a self. It presents only events.
Gilles Deleuze[2]

Intelligent idealism is closer to intelligent materialism than is unintelligent materialism.
V.I. Lenin[3]

Immanence and materialism: two notions that have, of late, established a newly extensive resonance, repertoire and mobility across the tangled narratives and evolving protocols of disciplinary, inter-disciplinary and trans-disciplinary engagement. Just to note the comparatively recent flurry of publications on new materialism, for example, or on new materialisms, or material cultures, or material feminisms and the new materialities[4] (and the differences between the singular and plural forms here are, of course, significant) is to observe also the ways in which the materialist concerns of its authors mingle promiscuously with or parallel or stand resolutely opposed to a range of other urgencies. We might list such materially inflected urgencies and their points of advocacy, or a fair selection of them at least, as follows: neoliberalism (rarely pluralized), gender and sexuality, race and ethnicity, human or non-human

INTRODUCTION

charlie blake
patrice haynes

SOMETHING IN THE AIR
an introduction to immanent materialisms and the unbounded earth

demographics and ethology, geopolitical atrocity and transnational trauma, potlatch and parasitics, transhuman, posthuman and ahuman theory, media ecologies and archaeologies, animal or animality studies, post-secularity studies, geotraumatics, the bio-circuitries and extinction mechanics of the so-called Anthropocene and its disputed territories, ecosophy and ecoclasm, complexity studies, and neo-accelerationism[5] – not to mention the more traditional disciplinary terrains of theology, ontology, aesthetics, ethics, musicology, film, literature, geography, economics, legal theory, anthropology, ethnology, art history, visual culture and political philosophy. What we have here, then, is not so much a conflict of faculties, or a conflict between or even within faculties, as a carnival of faculties, both traditional or emergent, shot through with the collective memes of materialism and materiality.

As is often the case in times of intellectual and political ferment (and the second decade of the twenty-first century CE is undoubtedly that), a dominant narrative will tend to evolve in intellectual circles and academic networks to explain why a particular strand of thinking involving a particular family or pack or swarm of concepts might be gaining momentum against and then accelerating above and beyond other possible strands. In the case of the new materialism(s), the story often told in the past decade or so – a story which might seem somewhat parochial to those involved in, say, pure mathematics, or the more meticulous procedures and quotidian realism of the natural sciences, or even the consistently bracing outlands of analytic and post-analytic philosophy – is a story nonetheless pertinent to anyone involved in the arts, humanities and social sciences who has ever been touched by what in the anglophone world has come to be known as "Continental philosophy" or in its more mobile form, simply "theory." This story has various guises, forms and variables, but the underlying elements tell of an historical process which leads from an anglophone fascination with the worldly subjectivities and authenticities generated by existentialism and phenomenology in post-war France of the 1950s, through various structuralisms and anti-humanisms in the 1960s, and then, via post-structuralism, deconstructionism, certain philosophies of desire and the superfluities of postmodernism in the 1970s and 1980s, to a general collapse of consensus on theory itself in the 1990s. It is a process paralleled, moreover, or possibly even constituted by, an insidious institutionalization of text and language as the arbiters of all our realities, the production of a textual idealism, in effect, which displaced a more vigorous and politically engaged materialism, and thereby, however inadvertently, reflected, abetted and indeed accelerated the neoliberal ascendancy taking place in the material world outside – at least it seemed outside for a while – the sacred groves of the academy.[6]

In this narrative, both the preoccupation with the text over the referent or the materially bodied agent in so much (so-called) post-structuralist discourse, or with the mode of consumption (or viewer/reader/consumer) over the mode of production (or artist/writer/activist/citizen) in so much textualist and performative theory – had led institutional and unwittingly institutionalized intellectuals into the very malaise so famously specified by Karl Marx and Friedrich Engels in *The Communist Manifesto* when they wrote – contra both idealism and capitalism – of a state of affairs in which all

> [...] fixed, fast-frozen relations, with their train of ancient and venerable prejudices and opinions, are swept away, all new-formed ones become antiquated before they can ossify. All that is solid melts into air, all that is holy is profaned, and man is at last compelled to face with sober senses, his real conditions of life, and his relations with his kind.[7]

However often cited, this passage retains its power to shock us back into consideration of the very material forces that constitute our selves and our social relations as selves, our embodiment as flesh as much as our constitution as packets of information flowing at the speed of light through the seemingly dematerialized networks of twenty-first-century capitalism. Whether or not we are able to "face with sober sense" the results of this materialist epiphany amidst the accelerating "ecstasy of communication," as Jean Baudrillard once described it, is one of the questions which initially prompted this collection.[8]

Of course, the story of materialism in the late twentieth and early twenty-first centuries is a great deal more complex than the account here above allows, and it might well be contested that the reductive narrative relayed represses some of the more emancipatory aspects of that which certain aspects of new materialism, network theory and ontology have lately sought to criticize or condemn. This, indeed, is one of the strands of thought that runs through this collection, where the question of materialism is addressed from a number of different perspectives and theoretical contexts and in relation to a range of adjacent or available terms that alter its meaning and effect in the world. The other main term of our title – immanence – is, in this sense, equally contestable, profligate and fluid when left in isolation. For, as our opening contributor to this special issue put it in his seminal study of post-Continental philosophy from 2006: "Immanence is everywhere, but its meaning is completely open [...]"[9] – unless, that is, it is tethered, positively or negatively, to adjacent or differentiating concepts such as, for example, monism, realism, transcendence, qualities, or indeed itself, as Gilles Deleuze prefers.[10] As a consequence, and to borrow from the incipit of a recent and highly influential volume on negation and acceleration by our final contributor in this special issue, who himself borrows from Giorgio Agamben, who

> [...] suggests that [modern post-Kantian philosophy] is divided between two lines: the line of transcendence, which starts with Kant and culminates in Derrida and Lévinas, and the line of immanence, beginning with Spinoza and passing through Nietzsche to Deleuze and Foucault[11]

... we are, as theorists, forever straddling or flitting between these two lines of descent in our realisms, materialisms and idealisms. Our writer continues, however, by noting that the

> [...] contemporary dominance of affirmationism in Continental theory can be read as a sign of the triumph of the second line of immanence, which has become correlated with the political ability to disrupt and resist the false transcendental regime of capitalism.[12]

Along with those terms collecting around the concept of a resurgent materialism, this tradition of affirmationism and its relation to immanence is certainly highly charged, and from that charge (whether sparked by contest or accommodation) emerges yet another strand in the essays that follow, traversing and weaving around the first via a range of knots and contingencies and putative negations or lines of flight. Of the two further terms in our subtitle, speculation and critique, we will say little here, except to note that their inclusion resulted from a conversation over the central concepts and *differends* driving the brief ascendancy of the school of speculative realism, and in particular the appropriation and development in this network of Quentin Meillassoux's notions of materialism, realism, correlationism and contingency, of Bruno Latour's critique of critique, and, most notably, Alberto Toscano's eloquent response to these various themes in *The Speculative Turn*, in an essay entitled: "Against Speculation, or, A Critique of the Critique of Critique: A Remark on Quentin Meillassoux's After Finitude (After Colletti)."[13]

Another contributor to that earlier volume, Ray Brassier (who quickly distanced himself from speculative realism), also had a part to play in the origins of this current collection. In particular, the general sense drawn from his argument in chapter 7 of his *Nihil Unbound: Enlightenment and Extinction*[14] and especially around Jean-François Lyotard's notion of solar catastrophe – and with apologies to the detail of that argument here – remains a sobering reminder that it is against the horizon of human extinction, and not only human extinction but also solar and even cosmic extinction, that our grasp of immanence and transcendence must finally be given scale in terms of our own materialism and materiality, not to mention our grasp of notions of the absolute and hyperchaos, and notably in several of the essays here, of God and re-visioned theology, post-Meillassoux. Thus it is, the editors contend, and by way of an overall context for this collection, that in the midst of tectonic shifts in the human system that may well turn out to be auto-apocalyptic in several senses, in the midst of a growing global awareness of collapse and connectivity and the massive economic asymmetries which to a large degree have driven that collapse and new connectivity, that hyper-connectivity of the neural web spreading across the increasingly unbounded Earth, striated, nonetheless, by material, legal and political enclosure, and with all the affective consequences of accelerated sensational overload and libidinal disinvestment this implies, in the midst of all this there is undoubtedly "something in the air." This "something" is identified here as a sense of intellectual urgency and vibrancy that hovers around its terms and concepts impatiently, but of current necessity, at least, returns again and again to those ancient and modern questions of materialism, realism, monism, nominalism, immanence, transcendence, spirit, contingency, necessity, negation, speculation and critique.

Our collection opens with John Ó Maoilearca's elegant summary and weaving together of a number of themes touched on above, organized here around the problems of monism and the horror of/in philosophy. Amongst other targets, this paper questions provocatively, for example, the commitment to ontological monism ("everything is ... x [e.g., Life, Matter, Affect, Number]") in certain materialist or ostensibly materialist strands in recent Continental thought. Materialist monisms here typically seek to explain the dualistic *appearance* of reality – for reality never appears as one thing – as no more than illusion, error, misrepresentation or anthropomorphization, which theory must then eliminate. However, a genuine immanent materialism, Maoilearca argues, must admit dualities such as "spirit" and "matter," "manifest" and "scientific," "living" and "dead" or even "illusion" and "reality" as realizations of the Real's *resistance* to any one theory or explanation. In developing a revisionary metaphysics informed by the writings of Henri Bergson and François Laruelle (both of whom can be seen as espousing a "non-philosophy" in this sense), Maoilearca reconsiders and re-visions the monistic ontologies advanced in the works of Alain Badiou, Gilles Deleuze, Quentin Meillassoux, Ray Brassier and Graham Harman, amongst others. In the light of his re-view of the mind–body problem – where he maintains that consciousness need not be construed as the ghost in the machine, ultimately reducible to matter, but as a product of the Real – Maoilearca suggests that philosophy does not begin in wonder but rather in horror at the object that shows us that "it too is alive and thinks." He concludes by considering the ethical consequences of monism: the violent crushing of other modes of thinking and living in the attempt to define the Real in terms of a single, privileged philosophical orientation.

Our second contribution, from Joshua Ramey, offers a compelling critique of Meillassoux's "principle of unreason" via notions of divination. Drawing on the work of Charles S. Price and Avicenna, Ramey first analyses the concept of contingency in order to show that it cannot simply be equated with the abstract possibility to be or not to be, to have been otherwise – which is Meillassoux's claim in *After Finitude: An Essay on the Necessity of Contingency*. The trouble is, as Ramey points out, that if contingency demands the "principle of unreason," as Meillassoux's holds, then it can bear no workable relation to the actual. Accordingly, and from this fundamental criticism, it is Ramey's contention that, instead, contingency is continuous with the actual even if this continuity is often enigmatic and fleeting. In a strikingly original move, which takes and hones its cues from a variety of sources including Deleuze, Giambattista Vico and anthropological studies more generally, Ramey proposes the idea that divinatory practices can be understood as that set of practices which provide "a kind of immanent reason *for* contingency" (our emphasis). Indeed, and as Ramey suggests in concluding his paper, we can thereby view divination as a speculative practice that is not mere wish-fulfilment but a peculiarly rational method that uses actual elements – tarot cards, yarrow stalks, coins, runes, entrails – in order to activate chance (throws, spreads, casts) and thereby see contingencies pregnant in the actual.

Our third paper, from Jim Urpeth, gathers various strands and weaves them more directly into questions of theology/atheology and the philosophy of religion, and in particular the relations between immanence, contingency and the absolute. Here, Urpeth provides an incisive appraisal of Meillassoux's appeal to divine inexistence – that is, the possibility of a God still to come, a contingent and virtual God fully compatible with an ontology characterized by necessary contingency. Urpeth explains that while Meillassoux attempts to elaborate a non-metaphysical conception of the divine, his motivation for this – namely, an all-too-human desire for justice in the face of so many pointless, "terrible deaths" – betrays a sensibility still wedded to transcendent religion. For immanence, on this account, cannot be wholly affirmed within this universal context. Meillassoux's virtual God is a response to the demand that injustice should not be. A thoroughgoing religious immanence, Urpeth argues in agreement with Friedrich Nietzsche, refuses the negative evaluation of any aspect of immanent life, which is entirely self-justifying and thus does not face the "problem" of redeeming senseless deaths – in other words, the problem of evil that perennially haunts religions committed to divine transcendence. Through an analysis of the concept of religion and its relationship to immanence, Urpeth highlights how Meillassoux's ontological picture contains insights promissory for the articulation of a religious immanence, even if Meillassoux himself does not pursue this particular path.

Colby Dickinson's paper moves from the consideration of Meillassoux's contingency to another seminal thinker of immanence for contemporary theory, Giorgio Agamben. Titled "The Profanation of Revelation: On Language and Immanence in the Work of Giorgio Agamben," Dickinson's essay carefully explores the ways in which Agamben's work makes important interventions in contemporary theology – interventions we might think of – and which he names – as profanations. Dickinson begins by outlining Agamben's account of language, particularly with respect to the mystical and the question of naming God. According to Agamben, mystical traditions assume a gap between name and thing, between language and being-in-the-world, which produces the very structure of transcendence and its attendant political and onto-theological notion of sovereignty. By contrast, Dickinson explains, Agamben argues that language is that in which we dwell. But it is precisely the attempt to articulate such a dwelling that invites appeals (both theological and philosophical) to the mystical and the transcendent. Dickinson moves on to discuss how Agamben attempts to rethink language beyond the mystical, clarifying his understanding of the task of profanation and its implications for theology. While Agamben's anti-representationalism – a consequence of his insistence on profanation – may seem at times to deliver what is ultimately a form of political nihilism, Dickinson argues that, instead, his project offers no less than a revelation of an immanent absolute, which is not simply revelation of the sacredness of the world after the death of God but rather the revelation of its profane character. The prospect of an immanent theology, Dickinson suggests, is thus signalled in Agamben's work, one which carries considerable import for philosophical thought on language, life, subjectivity and politics.

Noting with Herbert Marcuse that "the democratic framing of life leads to an absence of dialectics," Frank Ruda, in his paper titled "Idealism without Idealism: Badiou's Materialist Renaissance," turns to Badiou's attempt to rethink a materialist dialectics – for it is such a dialectic that will facilitate an alternative vision of what it means to live today. While the contemporary philosophical situation can be characterized by the death of God and, with this, the death of idealism, Ruda argues that the split between idealism and materialism re-emerges within materialism itself. Contemporary materialism, Ruda suggests following Badiou, can be understood on the one hand as a democratic materialism (namely, a materialism without idealism whereby only bodies and languages exist, in relations of equivalence), and on the other as a materialist dialectic, which is at once an "idealism without idealism" (whereby only bodies and languages exist, except for those truths which subtract themselves from the hegemony of equivalence exchanges). After considering the relationship between philosophy and materialist conceptions of change, by highlighting three main ways in which Marx's famous eleventh thesis on Feuerbach has historically been read, Ruda then shows how Badiou offers a fourth reading of Marx's text. The important upshot of this reading is that, precisely because of its uselessness today, idealism is precisely that which enables a renewed affirmation of an immanent materialist dialectics beyond the parameters of a tenacious democratic materialism.

Badiou's materialist dialectic is also the topic of our next paper, by Michael O'Neill Burns, titled "Prolegomena to a Materialist Humanism." In this paper Burns addresses, through an engagement with Badiou's work, the problems raised by contemporary materialist (and immanentist) accounts of the subject. Burns traces the systematic development of Badiou's theory of the subject in his major works: *Theory of the Subject*, *Being and Event* and *Logics of Worlds*. While sympathetic to Badiou's project, Burns argues that there is a troubling tension in his work in so far as he asserts both that: (i) the subject is purely formal, collective, political and anti-humanist; and (ii) the subject is capable of affective responses to external events. This tension can be expressed, argues Burns, in terms of the internal (formal)/external (affective) problem of materialist subjectivity. The problem is, Burns explains, that Badiou fails to show how the subject as a "purely formal structure" is capable of feeling affects – affects that are notably human in character (terror, anxiety, courage and justice). In seeking to address this difficulty, Burns directs his attention to the work of Catherine Malabou who, by creatively engaging with neuroscience, articulates a theory of (internal, that is, neuronal) subjectivity that is both material and dialectical. Thought alongside Badiou's theorization of the subject, Malabou's neuronal subject offers "a sort of pre-eventful internal subjectivity which would subsequently explain just how it is that this pre-eventful internal subject can materially respond to the affects accompanying an event." Burns concludes his paper by defending, in dialogue with Meillassoux's materialist philosophy, "a minimal form of humanism" as a prerequisite for any immanent and materialist theory of subjectivity that is to be politically efficacious. The disavowal of anything so much as resembling humanism, warns Burns, is to the detriment of any contemporary immanent materialism.

Alastair Morgan's elegant contribution elucidates how we might speak of transcendence as an *experience*, a metaphysical experience, in the context of Theodor Adorno's negative dialectics. Indeed, Morgan asks how transcendence can even emerge given a negative philosophy that refuses to betray the immanent context of damaged life – namely, life that does not live. Morgan first considers Adorno's concept of transcendence in terms of pure possibility, something very much akin to Kant's regulative ideal. But he rejects such a reading of transcendence in Adorno's work in so far as it cannot be adequately reconciled with the latter's commitment to materialism. In order to show that an alternative account of transcendence, or metaphysical experience, is available in Adorno's philosophy – namely, through careful attention to "ephemeral and damaged objects" – Morgan goes on to discuss three concepts of life, which he identifies in Adorno's work: mere life, damaged life and ephemeral life. By distinguishing between these three notions of life, Morgan is able to develop a speculative materialism whereby it is a certain cognitive attitude, a mode of "contemplation without violence," that can enable an experience of transcendence – one that illuminates the possibility of something different, precisely by tarrying with the fragments of damaged, suffering life in capitalist societies.

Patrice Haynes' paper is titled "Creative Becoming and the Patiency of Matter: Feminism, New Materialism and Theology." Haynes' consideration here is of the emergence of "new materialist" approaches in feminist theory, particularly as these emphasize the agency of matter and so more treat matter as something other than a mere blank slate for socio-cultural determinations. Haynes welcomes this reconception of matter as that which is lively and generative since it helps to undermine the classic depiction of matter as passive, dumb, inert thingness typically associated with the feminine. However, and as she points out, there are dangers here in that the new materialist's vision of agentic matter might also be charged with an unwitting perpetuation of the masculinist and humanist norms it seeks to supersede. Accordingly, Haynes turns to the work of Claire Colebrook, who, in response to similar concerns, develops the idea of a "passive vitalism" informed by the immanent materialism advanced in Deleuze and Félix Guattari's co-authored works. Contrary to traditional forms of vitalism – forms which have become particularly appealing to feminist thinkers wishing to do justice to agentic matter – she argues that passive vitalism stresses matter's capacity *not* to actualize form, thereby remaining within itself and wholly unproductive. While appreciative of Colebrook's insights, however, Haynes aims to show how a theological materialism can affirm both the agency and patiency of matter without the latter pointing to a material immanence "perpetually at odds with itself" – a criticism directed at passive vitalism. The appeal to divine transcendence, Haynes suggests, may better support the integrity of matter than a wholly immanent materialism, and thus need not be automatically dismissed by new materialist feminists.

Anthony Paul Smith's contribution to *Immanent Materialisms* is the angelically inclined "Nature Deserves to be Side by Side with the Angels: Nature and Messianism by Way of Non-Islam." Here, Smith, emboldened by the methodology of Laruelle's non-philosophy, offers a non-theological conception of nature which enables him to "disclose a messianicity that runs through the immanental creature." Through a fascinating discussion of the angelology articulated in the works of Christian Jambet and Guy Lardreau, and with reference to Henry Corbin, Smith rethinks nature by way of what he calls the "theo-fiction" that is the angel. In doing so, Smith maintains that a truly immanent materialism can be developed whereby "nature is not reducible to matter and matter is not reducible to the idea of matter or the natural." Instead, reductive materialism, idealism and theological materialism stand in a certain immanent unity given their relationship to the immeasurable Real. When considering the messianism of nature, for instance, Smith's important and distinctive move is his turn to the Ismaili Shi'a Islam's conception of the One which approaches the non-philosophical concept of the One more closely than Christianity. Indeed, Smith argues that it is Islam – in its uncomfortable status as "pariah" in Europe – that provides the material "for the construction of a true non-theology." And it is a non-theology of nature that offers a way to think through the pitfalls of both analogical transcendence and absolute immanence, such that nature becomes the condition by which messianic divine potential can appear in ways that always depend on the Earth.

The last paper in our collection comes from Benjamin Noys, and broaches the question of the relation between immanence, materialism, antagonism and recent and contemporary developments in art theory, and in doing so unsettles immanence in a number of significant ways. Noting that "immanence implies a superior plane that exceeds specification or determination," and also that it allows us to "trace the problem of capitalism as an horizon of immanence that threatens to absorb any such excess, whether artistic, political or ontological," Noys tracks the problem *of* immanence to show how that problem itself relates *to* immanence qua immanence. Using the work of Deleuze he proceeds to analyse this relation as existing in the tension between a moment of excess, often theological, and an immanent relation or fold. Returning specifically to Deleuze's use of the early Jean-Paul Sartre he then argues that Sartre offers a subtly different thinking of relations and immanence through exploring how we are cast out amongst relations and objects. He subsequently deploys two of Sartre's later essays on art to examine the latter's development of a "situated absolute" – understood as the artwork positioned as the site which condenses and gathers the contradictions of relations and objects into itself, precisely refusing immanence. This move, Noys argues, offers the key to unsettling the coordinates of contemporary art theory by reinstating a thinking of the absolute as positional and at once immersed and antagonistic.

Finally, we are delighted to include photographs of a small selection of the artworks that Simeon Nelson[15] has been producing in two and three dimensions over the past decade. These are images, objects, designs, notions and projects which – artist and editors concur – correlate, reciprocate and enter into a range of mutually productive relationships with the essays in this special issue, conceptually, affectively and in the spirit of its genesis and development.

notes

1 Karen Barad, *Meeting the Universe Halfway: Quantum Physics and the Entanglement of Matter and Meaning* (Durham, NC: Duke UP, 2007) 3.

2 Gilles Deleuze and Félix Guattari, *What is Philosophy?*, trans. Graham Burchell and Hugh Tomlinson (London: Verso, 1994) 47.

3 V.I. Lenin, "Conspectus of Hegel's Book 'Lectures on the History of Philosophy,' Volume XIII, Volume I of 'The History of Philosophy'" in *Collected Works*, trans. Clemence Dutt (Moscow: Progress, 1930) 272.

4 The number of articles, texts and blog postings and discussions devoted to some version of new materialism or materiality or the more anthropologically based field of material cultures is vast and growing across the disciplines, but to indicate just a few of the more seminal printed moments within the broad field of recent "theory" see, for example, Stacy Alaimo and Susan Hekman, eds., *Material Feminisms* (Bloomington and Indianapolis: Indiana UP, 2008); Jane Bennett, *Vibrant Matter: A Political Ecology of Things* (Durham, NC: Duke UP, 2010); Diana Coole and Samantha Frost, *New Materialisms: Ontology, Agency and Politics* (Durham, NC: Duke UP, 2010); Graham Harman, "Realism without Materialism," *SubStance* 40.2 (2011): 52–72; Rick Dolphijn and Iris van de Tuin, *New Materialism: Interviews and Cartographies* (Ann Arbor: Open Humanities, 2012); Joshua Simon, *Neomaterialism* (Berlin and New York: Sternberg, 2013).

5 Good general surveys or discussions of at least some of these areas may be found in: Rosi Braidotti, *The Posthuman* (London: Polity, 2013); Patricia MacCormack, ed., *The Animal Catalyst: Towards Ahuman Theory* (London: Bloomsbury, 2014); Jussi Parikka, *What is Media Archaeology?* (London: Polity, 2012); Anthony Paul Smith and Daniel Whistler, *After the Postsecular and the Postmodern: New Essays in Continental Philosophy of Religion* (Newcastle upon Tyne: Cambridge Scholars, 2010); Claire Colebrook, *Death of the Posthuman: Essays on Extinction*, vol. 1 (Ann Arbor: Open Humanities, 2014); Armen Avanessian and Robin Mackay, eds., *#Accelerate: The Acclerationist Reader* (Falmouth: Urbanomic, 2014).

6 See, for example, Alaimo and Hekman in their introduction to *Material Feminisms* 1–19. Another story often told is of the ascendancy of historicism, social constructivism and cultural relativism in university humanities departments and their public equivalents leading to a position of impotence and anguished passivity where any real political and material advocacy or resistance might be required. See Slavoj Žižek, *First as Tragedy, Then as Farce* (London: Verso, 2009). A more recent extrapolation extended to the art world and its relation to neoliberalism may be found in Marc James Léger, *The Neoliberal Undead: Essays on Contemporary Art and Politics* (Winchester: Zero, 2013). A more positive side of this story, however, is examined by Howard Caygill in *On Resistance: A Philosophy of Defiance* (London: Bloomsbury, 2014).

7 Karl Marx and Friedrich Engels, *The Communist Manifesto* (London: Pluto, 2008) 38.

8 Jean Baudrillard, *The Ecstasy of Communication* (New York: Semiotext(e), 1988).

9 John Mullarkey (John Ó Maoilearca), *Post-Continental Philosophy: An Outline* (London and New York: Continuum, 2006) 7.

10 Gilles Deleuze wrote about the plane of immanence throughout his mid- to later work, but see note 2 above for a succinct paraphrase of one version of this conceptual array.

11 Benjamin Noys, *The Persistence of the Negative: A Critique of Contemporary Continental Theory* (Edinburgh: Edinburgh UP, 2010) 1.

12 Ibid.

13 Alberto Toscano, "Against Speculation, or, A Critique of the Critique of Critique: A Remark on Quentin Meillassoux's *After Finitude* (After Colletti)" in *The Speculative Turn: Continental Materialism and Realism*, eds. Levi Bryant, Nick Srnicek,

and Graham Harman (Melbourne: re.press, 2011) 84–91.

14 Ray Brassier, *Nihil Unbound: Enlightenment and Extinction* (London: Palgrave, 2007).

15 <http://simeon-nelson.com>.

list of works by simeon nelson

In order of appearance in this issue:

Cover image: *Desiring Machine* detail, 2009, laser-cut 16–24 mm galvanized steel plate, sections welded and bolted together, 38 × 10 × 10 m (http://simeon-nelson.com/index.php/desiring-machine).

Page 1: *Relicário*, modular sculptural system, 2011–12, laser-cut melamine-coated MDF, dimensions variable depending on site (http://simeon-nelson.com/index.php/relicario/).

Page 13: top and bottom – *Solid-State*, CAD drawings, 2010.

Page 31: *Plenum*, 2010–12, computer-generated high-definition projection, dimensions variable depending on site (http://simeon-nelson.com/index.php/plenum/).

Page 47: top – *Paratekton Tower*, 2010–11, furniture-grade plywood, wood dye, shellac (http://simeon-nelson.com/index.php/paratekton/); bottom – *Desiring Machine* detail, 2008, laser-cut 16–24 mm galvanized steel plate, sections welded and bolted together, 38 × 10 × 10 metres.

Page 63: *Relicário*, modular sculptural system.

Page 83: top and bottom – *Solid-State*, CAD drawings, 2010.

Page 99: *Paratekton*, modular sculptural system, 2010–11, furniture-grade plywood, wood dye, shellac (http://simeon-nelson.com/index.php/paratekton/).

Page 113: *Cryptosphere*, 2008–10, laser-cut plywood, steel sheet, dimensions variable depending on site (http://simeon-nelson.com/index.php/cryptosphere/).

Page 129: top – *Desiring Machine* detail; bottom – *Paratekton Tower*.

Page 151: *Relicário*, modular sculptural system.

Page 171: *Cryptosphere*, 2008–10, laser-cut plywood, steel sheet, dimensions variable depending on site.

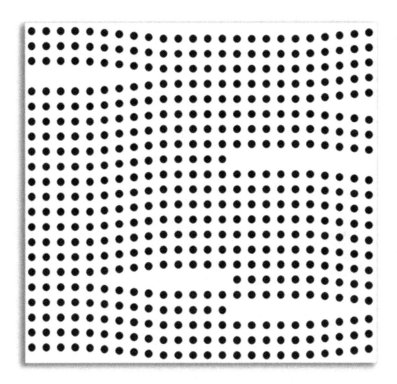
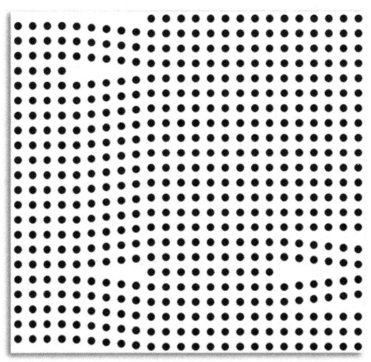

The duty of philosophy should be to intervene here actively, to examine the living without any reservation as to practical utility [...] Its own special object is to speculate, that is to say, to see.[1]

introducing the new materialisms: looking back again[2]

As soon as you believe social aggregates can hold their own being propped up by "social forces," then objects vanish from view and the magical and tautological force of society is enough to hold every thing with, literally, no thing. It's hard to imagine a more striking foreground/background reversal, a more radical paradigm shift.[3]

This essay will make an attempt to review a wide range of ideas stemming from recent work in Continental thought that espouse a turn to materialist and/or naturalist perspectives, be it through direct engagement with the natural or mathematical sciences, or more transcendental meta-theoretical approaches that either deduce or speculate upon (or both) certain findings. "Veracity," "validity," "coherence," "explanatory power," "truth-making" or any other epistemological value will not be explicitly invoked to assess these approaches. Rather, the attempt here is to gather them together in a value-neutral way and follow the hypothesis that these thoughts *of* materialism are materials themselves, consisting of both first-order macro-properties such as opticality, specularity, virtuality, (physical) consistency, circularity, clarity, darkness (or invisibility), and figures-grounds, as well as meta-level entities such as rigour, nihilism, consistency, logic, circularity, groundedness (foundations), and clarity. This

john ó maoilearca

SPIRIT IN THE MATERIALIST WORLD
on the structure of regard

gathering together is also a revisioning itself, a kind of "foreground/background reversal," that will involve a reverse orientation as regards the image of philosophical "orientations" as such, be they materialist (of a plain manila variety), mathematical-materialist, nihilist-materialist, or object-oriented.[4]

What is on offer here, then, is not an improved theory qua any putative correspondence with the facts of the matter – with what there is – but a more inclusive theorising whose only inimical moment is targeted solely at the exclusionary aspects of any one material theory qua theory; that is, we only reject those aspects of theories that mount unique and exclusive truth-claims for themselves. For there is also a parallelism between the thoughts of these materialists as regards their own thoughts (respecting their rigour, truth, logic, and even *what can count as thought and thinking*) and their views of what matter is, and with that also the value of life vs. death, the void, pure matter as abstract *matheme*, and so on. When such totalising claims are divorced from the theory, what remains are its *material* "correlations" with other theories *when held or reviewed together*. One can call this method a "non-philosophical" or "non-standard philosophical" approach if one wishes – it is certainly framed as such via the work of François Laruelle and Henri Bergson. The "non-" here is not *negation* but extension, an inclusive amplification of thought, an expanded approach to what counts as philosophy. So, it can also be understood as a kind of philosophy, or at least a kind of combined metaphilosophy and metaphysics (though Laruelle himself would abhor such terms). It can be *seen as* a philosophy that looks in a new way at the material metaphysics of metaphilosophy, of theories *as* theories, especially monistic ones.

And to do this we return, once again, to Bergson. As Jane Bennett writes when looking at the new materialisms in *Vibrant Matter*: in order to turn the "figures of 'life' and 'matter' around and around" such that a *"vital materiality* can start to take shape," one must awaken what Bergson described as "a latent belief in the spontaneity of nature."[5] But whether it be a "vital materiality" such as Bennett's, or a dark vitalism (as in Eugene Thacker's *After Life*), one question animating our research will be whether the dyad of life and matter can bring its two terms together without mutual asphyxiation.[6] Can the two persist in one; that is, does one need a minimal duality within every putative monism? Be it the unacknowledged signs of life in mathematicised matter (Meillassoux's mathemic valorisation of contingency), the avowed signs of death in cosmic thanatology (Brassier's nihilism), or the ubiquitous life of objects in Latour and Harman's ontology of *actants*/objects, the tensions brought out by such all-encompassing theories can themselves be reviewed as parts of a *real inherent* duality – one that is actually introduced by the Real (an introduction which some simply call error or illusion).

One recurring theme, then, will be the mind–body problem that Bergson put at the centre of *Matter and Memory*. It enters here, however, through the larger perspective of life and matter, and the interconnections between animate and inanimate objects, and even vitalism and anti-vitalism. We do this partly in order to look back again at the various purportedly mysterious, ghostly, "correlates" of the brain (often attacked simply as *qualia*, though sometimes also as an erroneous sense of self by the followers of Thomas Metzinger's work).[7] Far from wishing to explain such correlates away or eliminate them in the name of a new matter, we review them in order to raise their status as forms of haunting, background life. This will be an open exercise of "excessive anthropomorphism" on the one hand,[8] as well as an attempt to naturalise this ghostly life as *covarying* parts of the body, as affects that properly belong to me, to a brain that is also "my brain" (or "our brain" as Catherine Malabou puts it in *What Should We Do with Our Brain?*).[9] These "mysterious" correlates are explained both within "our" mind–body background and as *a* background to any viable (non-monistic) explanation. As such, they are rendered immanent equally as a physical, albeit disregarded, part of our material world and as a logical necessity when explaining the "hard problems" of the mind–body relation. The material medium *becomes* the spiritual medium.

The last time the question of materialism came to such prominence in French thought was in Bergson's era at the turn on the twentieth century, and his attempt to materialise spirit (including the practice of philosophical thinking) and spiritualise matter, via his conception of images, remains a powerful resource when looking at the resurgence of materialism and naturalism in contemporary Continental thought. For the notions of spirit, spectrality, ghosts, and animate matter (vitalism) are closely connected to many ideas operating within the new materialism, be it in the concept of inter-theoretical reduction, the mind–brain problem, contingency, conceptual rigour and consistency, as well as the ontology of objects.

mathematical-materialism: the thought of absolute contingency

> We are at ease only in the discontinuous, in the immobile, in the dead. The intellect is characterized by a natural inability to comprehend life.[10]

Outside of Marxist theories of production, it is probably the materialism born from contingency, from the *clinamen*,[11] the swerve, that has been the element colouring the materialism of Continental thought more than any other. This is the very French materialism of material-indeterminacy (rather than the Anglo-Saxon determinist materialism of Newtonian mechanics, which prevailed at least up until the rise of theories of quantum indeterminancy such as Roger Penrose's). Alain Badiou, with his theory of the event, is one inheritor of this line of thought, turning the cast of dice into an emblem of the event "because this gesture symbolizes the event in general; that is, that which is purely hazardous, and which cannot be inferred from the situation [...]" As pure randomness, hazard, or chance, the event is this "supplementation of being."[12] Deleuze, too, builds a philosophy out of the "pure chance" of the dice-throw (via Mallarmé as well, but now also cross-bred with Nietzschean forces and Bergsonian vitalism). Louis Althusser, of course, combined this contingency with Marxist economic materialism:

> That is the first point which [...] I would like to bring out: *the existence of an almost completely unknown materialist tradition in the history of philosophy: the "materialism"* (we shall have to have some word to distinguish it as a tendency) *of the rain, the swerve, the encounter, the take [prise] [...] Let us say, for now, a materialism of the encounter, and therefore of the aleatory and of contingency.*[13]

This aleatory materialism has been brought to an interesting limit in terms of the Badiouian philosopher Quentin Meillassoux, in his postulation of the necessity of contingency – an "absolute contingency – for which we shall henceforth reserve the term 'contingency' – designates a *pure possibility*; one which may never be realized."[14] Its suggestion must, he claims, be taken as a speculative rationalist one that is "fundamentally distinct from the concept of *chance*," the latter being merely a metaphysical or empirical proposition (that is, a *calculative* one that "presupposes the notion of numerical totality," something "we now know" is untenable on mathematical grounds).[15] And the legitimation for this distinction is noteworthy. Philosophy's task – at least as Meillassoux sees it – consists in "re-absolutizing the scope of mathematics."[16] Mathematical reason takes over from the sufficient reasons of metaphysics or empiricism (as though there were nothing in between, other forms of metaphysics and empiricism).

Yet this necessity, unifying the force of contingency for metaphysical ends, has an equally interesting heritage as well as some surprising consequences. The "new" philosophy of contingency forwarded in *After Finitude* actually reinvents, albeit incongruously, the French Spiritualist philosophy of Emile Boutroux, whose *De la contingence des lois de la nature* (1874) argues for a similar contingency *of law* in nature as Meillassoux's, only in the interests of spiritualism (here meaning anti-reductionism), rather than materialism (Meillassoux's subsequent linkage between contingency and "divine inexistence" is essentially non-spiritualist in our sense).[17] This makes Meillassoux's valorisation of the contingency of nature in the name of materialism all the more ironic. The contingent is a sign of life, not mathematised matter, for Boutroux. Indeed, there is a complex relationship between chance and necessity (fabulating randomness and rigour of the dice throw) that Bergson (who can also be numbered amongst the French Spiritualists, in part) links to spirits in an even stronger sense than only vitalism. Contingency is a sign of the *attribution* of life, of "an intention emptied of its content," but still living. However, whether the contingent is understood as a material aleatory encounter or a sign of freedom and the spiritual, in Bergson's account they both stem from a fabulation, a constructive representation born out of horror at the threat of contingent violence and death, at the unruliness of death (where there are "no set rules that you can live by"). It is noteworthy in this regard how Aristotle, in the *Poetics*, links narrative *causality* with the wondrous, or perhaps even the horrific, through the story of the statue of Mitys, which fell on Mitys' murderer as he stopped to look at it. Despite the contingency of the event, it does not seem random – the body of the statue, taking its revenge, inspires horror and wonder. So narrative causality is characterised by a strange form of horrific inevitability.[18] Such a fall, a *clinamen*, seemingly blind but *simultaneously* intentional (necessary chance), can only be explained through an attribution of mind, an anthropomorphism of the event – fabulation:

> A huge tile, wrenched off by the wind, falls and kills a passer-by. We say it was by chance. Should we say the same if the tile had merely crashed onto the ground? Perhaps, but it would then be because we were vaguely thinking of a man who might have been there, or because, for some reason or other, that particular spot on the pavement was of special interest to us, so that the tile seemed to have specially selected it to fall upon. In both cases chance intervenes only because some human interest is at stake, and because things happened as though man had been taken into account, either with a view of doing him a service, or more likely with the intention of doing him an injury. Think only of the wind wrenching off the tile, of the tile falling on the pavement, of the tile crashing on the ground: you see nothing but mechanism, the element of chance vanishes. For it to intervene it is indispensable that, the effect having a human significance, this significance should react upon the cause and colour it, so to speak, with humanity. Chance is then mechanism behaving as though possessing an intention […] But underlying it is a spontaneous semi-conscious thought, which superimposes on the mechanical sequence of cause and effect something totally different, not indeed to account for the falling of the tile, but to explain why its falling should coincide with the passing beneath it of a man, why it should have chosen just that very moment to fall […] Chance is therefore an intention emptied of its content.[19]

If "contingentism" is a hallmark of one kind of materialism, there remains something subjective in the very notion of chance or contingency that renders it spiritual. *Absolute contingency*, too, is a fabulation, a construction. Words like "chance," "luck," and "accident" are names that already indicate an anthropomorphisation of events reflecting both our interests ("lucky for me that the tile missed my head"), and a possible influence on the future ("I'd better keep my eyes open from now on").[20] And animism – the attribution of subjectivity to objects and objective events – is a powerful axiom, intimately connected with our psycho-cultural understanding of capricious events, as Stephen Asma writes:

> Animism, contrary to most Western portrayals, has its own empirical foundation, one that may be every bit as rational as ours. Animism can be defined as the belief that there are many kinds of persons in this world, only some of whom are humans. For an animist it is crucial to placate and honor these other spirit-persons. But it's important to remember that the daily lives of people in the developing world are not filled with the kinds of independence, predictability, and freedom that we in the developed world enjoy. Frequently, you do not choose your spouse, your work, your number of children; in fact, you don't choose much of anything when you are very poor and tied to the survival of your family. In that world, where life really is capricious and out of your control, animism seems empirically corroborated.[21]

Moreover, there is a link in Meillassoux's thought between absolute contingency, the impassability of mathematical reason and death. It is marked by Meillassoux most profoundly here: "[…] we will give life and existence to a *logos* of contingency, which is to say, a reason emancipated from the principle of reason – a *speculative form of the rational* that would no longer be a *metaphysical reason*."[22] And this "speculative philosopher," according to Meillassoux, will further maintain that we can *think* ourselves as no longer being; in other words, by maintaining that our mortality, our annihilation, and our becoming-wholly-other in God, are all effectively thinkable. But how are these states conceivable as possibilities? On account of the fact that we are able to think – by dint of the absence of any reason for our being – a capacity-to-be-other capable of abolishing us, or of radically transforming us. But if so, then *this capacity-to-be-other cannot be conceived as a correlate of our thinking, precisely because it harbours the possibility of our own non-being.*[23]

But to explain this link any further we must turn to another of the thanatophiles, Ray Brassier, who claims that "thinking has interests that do not coincide with those of living; indeed, they can and have been pitted against the latter."[24]

extinction beckons: rigor mortis, nihilism, and the omega point[25]

Alvy (Looking up at the doctor):
Well, the universe is everything, and if it's expanding, someday it will break apart and that would be the end of everything!

Disgusted, his mother looks at him.
Mother (shouting): What is that your business?
(She turns back to the doctor): *He stopped doing his homework.*
    Woody Allen, *Annie Hall*, 1976[26]

Don DeLillo's *Point Omega* makes explicit reference in its title and story to Teilhard De Chardin's concept of the "noosphere": this is the final destination for biological evolution, a plane of pure thought that life aims at through escaping its various earthly incarnations. And yet this flight of thought is also a flight from life and into death and the void. But it is death that is also material, albeit that of a pure matter untainted by subjective experience:

Isn't this the burden of consciousness? We're all played out. Matter wants to lose its self-consciousness. We're the mind and heart that matter has become. Time to close it all down. This is what drives us now [...] We want to be the dead matter we used to be. We're the last billionth of a second in the evolution of matter [...] Father Teilhard knew this, the omega point. A leap out of our biology. Ask yourself this question: Do we have to be human forever? Consciousness is exhausted. Back now to inorganic matter. This is what we want. We want to be stones in a field.[27]

In this new, secular End Time, Heidegger's anthropological *Sein-zum-Tode* collapses into the heat death of the universe in a cosmic thanatophilia. With this fascination with death, leading consequently to a love of the void, nothing of life can be spared: along with a love of matter, of anti-matter, dark matter, or dark fluid, comes a horror of life (both interior and exterior): anti-life (or anti-vitalism), after-life (or "dark vitalism").

Now this death conjoined with matter, as both become anti-life, can be founded on political argument (vitalism under critique from Foucauldian biopolitics, Giorgio Agamben's anthropological machine of bare life, or even Roberto Esposito's theory of auto-immunisation). Even simpler, however (in virtue of its consistency at least), comes the argument *from argument itself*, from pure thought understood as consistency, rationality, logic – rigor. The rigor, though, is a rigor mortis – the stiffness of the dead body launched against the living (a famous Roman torture) – a consistent body of thought, populated with "rigid" designators and robust logic. Here, various analytic names – Wilfred Sellars, Saul Kripke, Robert Brandom (the great arguers, philosophy becoming-argument, agonistics) – can be invoked as talismans of argumentative precision and conceptual scrupulousness, the "coruscating potency of reason."[28] Such reason acts against and even "destroys" the "Manifest Image" of apparent life – what is alive is actually already dead. Against what Brassier describes as the Deleuzian "vitalist sublation of physical death" (in which Bergson is his greatest mentor):

it is necessary to insist on the indivisibility of space and time and the ineradicability of physical annihilation. These provide the speculative markers for an objectification of thought that can be identified with a figure of death which is not the cancellation of difference but rather the non-dialectical identity of difference and indifference, of negentropy and entropy. We begin to broach the latter through questions such as: How does thought think a world without thought? Or more urgently: How does thought think the death of thinking?[29]

The death of thinking operates following Lyotard's most inhuman thought – that of the "solar catastrophe" whereby the earth is doomed to nothingness in an omega point of death: "[E]verything's dead already if this infinite reserve from which you now draw energy to defer answers, if in short thought as quest, dies out with the sun."[30] So Brassier concludes: "*everything is dead already.*" But what then do we make of the manifest image that distinguishes between the quick and the dead? If "the solar catastrophe needs to be grasped as something that *has already happened*,"[31] is *everyone alike* already dead, or are we who only appear alive actually ghosts of some sort? When Brassier calls vitalism a "spiritualist declaration," he might actually be speaking as much about his own thought as any thing else.[32]

This is also a monistic pronouncement of the type "everything is ... *x*." But instead of everything being matter, or even everything being thinkable, now everything is dead. Being alive but "already dead" is both a denial of time (which is at least consistent) and a denial of a necessary (and inescapable) duality of what we'll later call "this and that," of a meta-level duality necessary to explain anything, even illusions. For even the manifest image to be destroyed *is at least something*, if only an error. Phenomenologists, however broadly defined, hope to "save the appearances," but this need not entail the *survival* (after-life) of ghosts who remain alive *as the living are alive*, but simply the *appearance of life as something not yet dead*. No less than saying that everything is alive (or everything is matter), something must *not be alive or dead or material*, in order for this to *make sense*. But this *explanatory* principle is not merely epistemological in the representational sense of an unreal, totalised picturing of the real, but is itself *realised* as the way in which the Real resists any one *account* of it, any First Philosophy – materialism, nihilism, idealism. Its resistance is its reality (what the "spiritualist" Maine de Biran called *idée force*, a feeling of *conceptual* resistance). Ghosts resist their second death. Spirit is matter in another resistant direction (and so comprises a duality of two directions at least). When Canguilhem redubbed Bergsonism as a possible theory of the *élan matérielle*, what counted was the first term, the *élan*, movement, or direction.[33]

inanimate objects and background spirits: reverse orientations

Natalie: *Harry!*
Harry: *What?*
Natalie: *It's an inanimate fucking object.*
Harry: *You're an inanimate fucking object!*
Harry: *I'm sorry for calling you an inanimate object. I was upset.*
Martin McDonagh, *In Bruges*, 2008

In *Aping Mankind: Neuromania, Darwinitis, and the Misrepresentation of Humanity*, Raymond Tallis, having given short shrift to both reductive and non-reductive (or *emergentist*) positions in psychology or biology that assert a continuity between humans and other animals, entertains some of the more exotic possibilities that might explain how mind and matter might be connected (animals being on the side of matter here). One view that doesn't fall foul of the usual problems of reduction, emergence, or interaction (or indeed Meillassoux's "correlationism") is, as we saw, panpsychism. Going back at least as far as Spinoza and coming to us in modern forms through Fechner, Bergson, Whitehead, and Deleuze, its contemporary Analytical version can be seen in the work of Galen Strawson.[34] Alas, though, according to Tallis, this too harbours the same crucial explanatory gaps as all the others: "Unfortunately, [Galen] Strawson's vision, like Spinoza's, doesn't explain most key facts about consciousness: notably that some things (like you and me) *seem* to have it and others (such as pebbles) don't."[35] Stones again. In *Difference and Repetition*, Deleuze writes that "[...] everything is contemplation, even rocks and wood, animals and men."[36] But, *pace* Tallis, it is one thing to attempt to de-animalise the human in virtue of some purported exceptionality – the arguments for and against continuity are moot – it is another to base that discontinuity on a certain set of properties (or lack thereof) pertaining to rocks, stones, or pebbles (the *weltlos* par excellence, according to Heidegger). For that is a double-edged argument. As Don DeLillo writes again: "Think of it. We passed completely out of being. Stones. Unless stones have being. Unless there's some profoundly mystical shift that places being in a stone."[37] How things *seem* to "you and me" is fraught with both positive and negative anthropomorphism (that is, both attributing and stripping away properties or qualities of which we are either way ignorant). Starting with the Cartesian question, "how can I know?," always leaves us in doubt, always leaves us needing to give the benefit of the doubt, not just to stones, but to other animals, and other humans too; anyone but me (who, I rest assured, really is alive). There is always a need for a principle of charity, a leap of faith. But the affects of perspectival chauvinism may well be instructive when an object-ive democracy does appear before us, when the parliament of things starts to speak back, when, in other words, objects manifest all the signs of life and even thought that would normally horrify us.

Bruno Latour's actor network theory is a true democracy of materials at one level: as he puts it in *We Have Never Been Modern*: "we are going to have to slow down, re-orient and regulate the proliferation of monsters by representing their existence officially. Will a different democracy become necessary? A democracy extended to things?"[38] Harman glosses this as the view that "all entities are on exactly the same ontological footing" and that "Latour's guiding maxim is to grant dignity even to the least grain of reality" such that "Latour insists on an absolute democracy of objects: a mosquito is just as real as Napoleon, and plastic in a garbage dump is no less an actant than a nuclear warhead."[39]

Some have decried this democracy as one only of meaning, and so powerless in any effective way.[40] Moreover, this democracy is also its own *reductio ad absurdum* in as far as it exposes a limit to what can be thought (even in passing) and what can be lived: after all, in the parliament of things, *not everyone can nor even wants to vote*. We will soon see the Bergsonian twist to such inequality in as much as how, all things being equal,[41] there is nevertheless the necessity of a perspectival chauvinism (just on account of being located, or being a view from somewhere rather than nowhere) – which makes some things (like you and me) *seem* to have consciousness and others (pebbles) not, even when that appearance, that objective phenomenology, only emerges through horrific acts of violence on those stony things, a disenfranchisement wrought by the politics of life to create non-life, the undead or bare matter (the connection between Deleuze's "bare material repetition" in *Difference and Repetition* and Agamben's "bare life" is conspicuous or manifest: they all involve the reduction of matter to what is called "matter," namely, the unproductive, the static, and the lifeless respectively).

Which brings us to Thomas Nagel's objective phenomenology. Seemingly well rebuked at this stage of the game by a host of Wittgensteinian, deconstructive, and eliminativist arguments against not only the possibility of any privileged access to subjective states but even the existence of those states themselves (in a subject), it remains the case that there is a weakness in the anti-privacy critiques of Nagel: to wit, their conflation of the question of perspectivism as presented in Nagel's *The View from Nowhere* with the arguments for subjective *knowledge* in his earlier essay "What is it Like to be a Bat?" The barrage of criticisms that followed the 1974 essay concentrated on the question of whether or not *qualia* could be categorised as *facts*.[42] Yet there is a defence that does not see Nagel's position, at least in *The View from Nowhere*, as one concerning facts at all, but the ontological status of perspective.[43] It is no longer a matter (if it ever was) of whether what is known to the subjective view is true or false (that is, of whether it is real knowledge), but on *the very existence* of this perspective, right or wrong. The real issue would not be the absolute truth of subjective *content* so much as the fact that there are points of view at all. It is an ontological question, and, indeed, one pertaining to an objective phenomenology, the appearance of appearances in the objective world, in and as objects. Subjective experiences (or *qualia*) are not pure, direct, unrepresented, uninterpreted, or free of all citation; and yet, even being only *apparently* real holds for something – illusion exists *as* illusion, *error* exists *as* error (the so-called "error problem" for naturalism: how to account for epistemic norms when norms, the "as" of seeing aspects, imply a subjectivity within the objective). Our privacy may be haunted by others (as Wittgenstein and Derrida equally showed), but who would argue that ghosts are *no* different from flesh and blood people? They exist in space and time (even as they may float above the floor or pass through walls), which is a very "weird," embodied, and object-like thing for a spectre to do. It is a true "spectral dilemma" (which has less to do with an "essential mourning" of the victims of "terrible" deaths by inscribing their *memory* into our living existence, than the dead *physically* haunting us for killing them).[44]

The allusion here to Meillassoux is not without consequence for any further discussion of ghosts when discussing subjective experience: Gilbert Ryle's famous "ghost in the machine" (that Sellars also invokes),[45] and Hume's scepticism regarding causality (and spiritual substance – the subject) are key elements of Meillassoux's argument, the second being for some the "simplest way" to introduce his ideas to newcomers.[46] But scepticism can cut both ways. Let us imagine that ghosts, for example, were real – or in other words, that there were apparitions to the living, seemingly as evidence of the former's survival (though these two thoughts will remain separate here). Ghostly appearances suddenly become everyday and ordinary, that is, at time *t*, we begin to perceive apparitions on a constant and mundane level. Would ghosts still be mysterious, or, with this coherent and constant repetition, would they not, as our new familiars, eventually find a place within our other daily lives and activities, even while they remain resistant to explanation within the current naturalistic paradigm? Kantians, of course, might argue that to be an object of experience at all, the appearance of ghosts *must* be given a causal explanation that would also *eventually* render them accountable in principle within normal science (they are not wholly disembodied, after all, being made of light at least). Obviously, our laws of psychology, biology, and physics might have to be altered somewhat to accommodate them, but, in as much as these ghost-appearances *became* everyday, they would be testable occurrences, and so our laws would not alter to the extent of leaving the rest of the world that science currently does explain wholly incompatible and mysterious (at worst, the laws might simply defer judgement on these strange sights). Ghosts would become naturalised beings, legal aliens, blending into the background.[47]

If this account – of how the extraordinary becomes ordinary through seemingly ordinary means – itself sounds quite extraordinary and bizarre, think only of the contents of the mind, *qualia*, the ghosts in the machine, which are banal, everyday, and yet only *tenuously* linked to the laws of natural science (that is, by *correlation*): the mind's apparent immateriality should be enough for those who thirst for mystery (and even if its immateriality *is* only apparent, that dissimilitude is itself a mystery). Yet it is often not enough. Likewise, are not dreams also just such an example of a naturalised, non-scientific, apparition of ghosts? Of course, dream-experiences are correlated to the brain, but not in any functional manner currently known (that is, one that is not miraculous to science, even as it circumvents the "hard problem" by passing it off as temporary or trivial – part of the background). What the eliminativists want to "disappear" – namely *qualia*, people, life – re-appear as spirits in the material world, both literal and figurative.

This "background" can be tricky too. Berkeley had to resort to God to explain how and why things got on with their lives constantly and coherently behind our backs (when we are not looking at them). In *Matter and Memory*, Bergson likens the unconscious with an unperceived space (behind us):

> when a memory reappears in consciousness, it produces on us the effect of a ghost whose mysterious apparition must be explained by special causes. In truth, the adherence of this memory to our present condition is exactly comparable to the adherence of unperceived objects to those objects which we perceive [...] We have not, in regard to objects unperceived in space and unconscious memories in time, to do with two radically different forms of existence.[48]

The "Background" is the crucial semantic network that makes intentionality possible for John Searle; it is the ambiguous perceptual field that allows discrete objects or figures appear for Merleau-Ponty. But when that background figures itself, forwards itself as a set of objects, the glimpse, the blink of an eye (*Augenblick, clin d'œil*), can be realised in a form of *optical* horror. So, when Meillassoux critiques everything that even looks like panpsychism, "from Diderot's hylozoism, to Hans Jonas' neo-finalism," on account of "the same argumentative strategies [...] [being] reproduced time and time again in philosophical polemics on the possibility of life emerging from inanimate matter,"[49] the retort offered here is to think of this "life *emerging* from inanimate matter" no longer as a physical or descriptive, or even speculative metaphysical thesis, but as a revisionary one – which is to say, nothing like a "thesis" at all so much as an *aisthesis* of horror out of which all theses, beyond being either "right" or "wrong," ultimately arise.

Thinking objects, like contemplating stones, are horrific. Philosophical thought doesn't begin *in us alone* through our wonder at various perceptual paradoxes: it arises in horror as the perceived objects think *for themselves in us*, forcing a painful reversal of thought (that Bergson would call "intuition"). Objects think for themselves; indeed in this view they are alive and think. And this ubiquity of life is truly horrifying (indeed, the true philosophical horror is not that we are not (yet) thinking, but that thinking has already started without us, and everywhere). Philosophy, thought, and life start to ooze, to spread everywhere. Deleuze's shock to thought is also a horrific encounter with the philosophical monster – the object that *shows* us that it too is alive and thinks. To define thought according to one criterion, as rigour, clarity, simplicity (parsimony), is to forget that this requires the death of other possible thinkings and livings, other possible forms of clarity (perspicuity, for example, is not the same as deductive or definitional simplicity). It also induces a vertigo of falling onto, or regress into, the background: the meaning and value (or, if you prefer, "exact" definition) of terms such as "argument," "clarity," "rigour," "consistency," "coherence," "precision," "exactness," "evidence," "explanatory scope," "validity," "justification," and (most of all) "thinking" are all contentious, and cannot be invoked as determinants between philosophies in a non-circular way (and even this term, "non-circular," is multiple). Not only do they denote the death of other thinkings (and others' thinking): in their *rigor mortis* they are forms of death, or at least life that has become anti-life.

conclusion: against monism – "gotta be this or that"

> Let us call "speculative" every type of thinking that claims to be able to access some form of absolute, and let us call "metaphysics" every type of thinking that claims to be able to access some form of absolute being, or access the absolute through the principle of sufficient reason. If all metaphysics is "speculative" by definition, our problem consists in demonstrating, conversely, that not all speculation is metaphysical, and not every absolute is dogmatic – it is possible to envisage an absolutizing thought that would not be absolutist.[50]

Wilfred Sellars, a key thinker for Ray Brassier, opens his lecture "Philosophy and the Scientific Image of Man" thus:

The term "image" is usefully ambiguous. On the one hand [...] an image is as much an existent as the object imaged, though, of course, it has a dependent status. In the other sense, an "image" is something imagined, and that which is imagined may well not exist, although the imagining of it does – in which case we can speak of the image as *merely* imaginary or unreal. But the imagined *can* exist [...] One of these projections I will call the manifest image, the other the scientific image. These images exist and are as much a part and parcel of the world as this platform or the Constitution of the United States. But in addition to being confronted by these images as existents, he is confronted by them as images in the sense of "things imagined" – or, as I had better say at once, *conceived*; for I am using "image" in this sense as a metaphor for conception, and it is a familiar fact that not everything that can be conceived can, in the ordinary sense, be imagined. The philosopher, then, is confronted by two conceptions, equally public, equally non-arbitrary, of man-in-the-world and he cannot shirk the attempt to see how they fall together in one stereoscopic view.[51]

Despite this apparent ecumenism of the scientific and the manifest, however, wherever the two types of image do enter into conflict, Sellars will prefer the former over the latter. He advocates the primacy of the scientific image within any synoptic view of the two (as against the primacy of the perceptual image argued for by phenomenologists like Merleau-Ponty). Indeed, in a similar fashion, Bergson famously opens *Matter and Memory* with a discussion of images and image neutrality (images that are *between* the real and representations of the real). But the images here are not pictures of reality so much as parts of the whole: they indicate a mereological relationship rather than a representational one (complex and stealthy though Sellars' representationalism may be).[52] Hence, we're given the reality of the image rather than the image of reality, so long as the former is not taken to count for the whole; the reality of the image is only a part of the real, not its totality. By holding on to the ambiguity of the image as not merely metaphorical in nature but actually ontological, Bergson circumvents privileging any one image (such as of the brain). As he was to write later:

> to say that an image of the surrounding world issues from this image of a dance of atoms, or that the image of the one expresses the image of the other [...] is self-contradictory, since these two images – the external world and the intra-cerebral movement – have been assumed to be of like nature.[53]

And yet there is still the image of privilege, or perspectival chauvinism, the image of "*my* body" (as in Malabou's "our brain"), discovered through dissociative movements and affects (that is only rediscovered through a *reversal* of this process in the horror *of* perspective, of background objects returning to life, to claim us back – "one of us" – amongst the democratic neutrality of material image-objects). Such chauvinism is part and parcel of being alive – we make the world relative to us, we centre it on our point of view, make it our background. Not only must some things look inert, or become what we call bare matter, but also some thoughts *must not look like thoughts*, like proper (my) thinking (rigour, clarity, consistency proper to me), they must be non-philosophical (in the non-Laruellean sense of "non-").

In a world of plural perspectives, each must be located: there is no view from nowhere in objective phenomenology, but only a myriad of somewheres. But those somewheres act *as if* they alone are nowhere (or everywhere) and all others are somewhere.[54] There is discrimination, dualism, a *structure* of regard. And necessarily so, if we are to explain appearances. If everything is *really x*, then this "really *x*" is meaningless as an explanation. Meaning and explanation need discrimination. Even though Bergson was a process philosopher, he knew that postulating that "everything changes" (a monism) explains nothing:

> one can, then, and even should continue to speak of physical determinism even while postulating, with the most recent physics, the indeterminism of elementary events

which make up the physical fact. For this physical fact is perceived by us *as* submitted to an inflexible determinism.[55]

We make things static, inert, thoughtless. It is not that monism equals pluralism or even reduces to it: Deleuze and Guattari's "magic" formula is only magical in as much as it breaks the laws of *asubjective* objectivity – the objectivity that cannot account for illusion, appearance, subjectivity amongst (and "in") objects.

As the Benny Goodman song goes, it's "Gotta Be This Or That": bivalency, dialectic, either/or, dichotomy – such dyads are needed to explain anything, even when what they explain is uniform, a monism, the One, the Real (dualism as Deleuze's necessary enemy). Bergsonism is a "dynamic monism": a philosophy that is *both* "dualist and unitary" – dualising tendencies over dualistic states.[56] The "both" here resides in the seeing *as*, the levels, the situatedness of perspective that cannot always (when it is pluralist) practise what it preaches. Hence, too, the need for dialectic without also positing its priority: the circular *becoming* of the dialectic, of "yes" and "no," whose own circularity (the circle of becoming) leads to vertiginous regress, to falling back to the ground.[57] Which is why Bergson *has* to write this about all monisms, materialist or idealist, that say anything about *every* thing:

> to place will everywhere is the same as leaving it nowhere […] It makes little difference to me if one says "everything is mechanism" or "Everything is will": in either case everything is identical. In both cases, "mechanism" and "will" become synonyms of each other. Therein lies the initial vice of philosophical systems. They think they are telling us something about the absolute *by giving it a name* […] But the more you increase the extension of the term, the more you diminish comprehension of it. If you include matter within its extension, you empty its comprehension of the positive characteristics by which spontaneity stands out against mechanism and liberty against necessity. When finally the word arrives at the point where it designates everything that exists, it means no more than existence. What advantage is there then in saying that the world is will, instead of simply saying that it is?[58]

Matter is this, spirit is that – a minimal dyad or conjunction (be it of substance, property or process – all that matters is that they be mutually "irreducible") to explain why reality doesn't appear as just one thing, even if *only in virtue of the illusion* of at least two things (because then we have the illusion and non-illusion – two things): "spirit" and "matter," "manifest" and "scientific," "living" and "dead," "us" and "pebbles," or just "illusion" and "reality" – the names are unimportant, but the de-*monstrability* is (showing "this" and "that" by giving it a name): "You need to know the difference between this and *this*. And *that* is an elephant."[59]

Yet a "this *or* that" requires a "this" *and* a "that." Conversely, then, bivalency comes in different forms, not all of it a totalising logic of identity (everything is *x*, all images are this image, even when the *x* is difference or process itself). There are other, different, recursive logics of expression, logics based on objects which are not taken simply as mutually exclusive solids (they can be this *and* that, at *times* – but not at *all* times). There is a need for different logics that are for *and from* different things. Laruelle's and Bergson's democratic non-philosophies, their revisionary "metaphysics" (though Laruelle would not use the latter term), are attempts to *practise* this thought of such things – neutral and democratic, where everything lives, everything thinks, even *as these things think that they alone do*.[60]

notes

1 Bergson, *Creative Evolution* 206–07.

2 This heading is an allusion to Coole and Frost.

3 Latour, *Reassembling the Social* 71.

4 See Ahmed.

5 Bennett vii–viii.

6 See Thacker.

7 See Metzinger.

8 In this sense, Kant was not anthropocentric and anthropomorphic enough in his philosophy: if he had been *even* more anthropomorphic, objectively anthropomorphic rather than simply subjectively so (basing his critique on a transcendental knowing *human* subject), then a new centre, a new absolute knowledge, would have emerged through an immanent (non-Platonist, non-transcendent) metaphysics. It would not come through subtracting the world from, or relativising it to, the categories of human knowledge, but rendering them immanent within a "pluri-knowing" through the multiplication and expansion of categories, the monstrosity of cross-categorised and mis-categorised entities: non-human knowings and (non-)animate objects, a new set of multiple centres, a new kind of *moving* absolute found through relativising relativity – panpsychism over the human *psyché*.

9 See Malabou.

10 Bergson, *Creative Evolution* 182.

11 Meillassoux, *After Finitude* 99.

12 Badiou, *Being and Event* 193; idem, *On Beckett* 21.

13 Althusser 167–68.

14 Meillassoux, *After Finitude* 62.

15 Ibid. 100, 103, 108. For a critique of this duality, see Johnston 104–05.

16 Meillassoux, *After Finitude* 126.

17 See Meillassoux, "Spectral."

18 Aristotle 1452a.

19 Bergson, *Two Sources* 148–49.

20 Ibid. 141, 167, 176.

21 Asma 287 n. 22.

22 Meillassoux, *After Finitude* 77.

23 Ibid. 56–57.

24 Brassier, *Nihil* xi.

25 See Nelson.

26 From *Annie Hall* (1977, Woody Allen and Marshall Brickman).

27 DeLillo 50, 52–53.

28 Brassier, *Nihil* xi.

29 Ibid. 222–23.

30 Lyotard cited in ibid. 223.

31 Brassier, *Nihil* 223.

32 Ibid. 228.

33 Canguilhem.

34 See Strawson, "Realistic Monism."

35 Tallis, *Aping* 358; my emphasis.

36 Deleuze 75.

37 DeLillo 73.

38 Latour, *We Have Never Been Modern* 12.

39 Harman 14, 15, 34.

40 Brassier, "Concepts" 52: "In dismissing the epistemological obligation to explain what meaning is and how it relates to things that are not meanings, Latour, like all postmodernists – his own protestations to the contrary notwithstanding – reduces everything to meaning […]"

41 Indeed, for Bergson, matter, as seen from the human perspective, just is this *pure* equality, "where everything balances and compensates and neutralizes everything else" (Bergson, *Creative Evolution* 219).

42 See, for example, Churchland 199; Nemirow; and Lewis 516–17.

43 See Tallis, *Explicit* 149–55; Searle 116–18.

44 Meillassoux defines a "spectral dilemma" in terms of "the aporetic alternative of atheism and religion when confronted with the mourning of essential spectres" – it is essentially a theo-anthropological problem of evil (Meillassoux, "Spectral" 265).

45 See Brassier, *Nihil* xi: "According to Sellars, '[Thought] episodes are "in" language-using animals as molecular impacts are "in" gases, not as "ghosts" are in "machines"' (from Sellars' 'Empiricism and the Philosophy of Mind' 104)."

46 The "simplest way to introduce Meillassoux's general project is as a reformulation and radicalisation of what he on several occasions describes as 'Hume's problem'" (Hallward 131).

47 Note how Bergson argues that magical causality leaves the scene of explanation as soon as the phenomenon becomes habitual enough to be prone to simpler, mechanical causes (Bergson is here talking about crocodile attacks – see Bergson, *Two Sources* 149–50).

48 Bergson, *Matter* 145, 146.

49 Meillassoux, "Potentiality" 235.

50 Meillassoux, *After Finitude* 34.

51 Sellars 5.

52 Bergson, *Matter* 71: "between this perception of matter and matter itself there is but a difference of degree and not of kind [...] the relation of the part to the whole [...]"

53 Bergson, *Mind-Energy* 238.

54 See Bergson, *Duration*, on how we centre the universe around our own point of view (frame of reference).

55 Bergson, *Creative Mind* 303 n. 6 (hardback ed.); my emphasis.

56 Čapek, *Bergson* 193; idem, "Bergson's Theory" 132; Mourélos 90.

57 Hence, "*yes* and *no* are [still] sterile in philosophy. What is interesting [...] is *in what measure?*" (Bergson, *Mélanges* 477).

58 Bergson, *Creative Mind* 48–49; my emphasis.

59 See Read 81.

60 See Laruelle, *Philosophie*; Mullarkey, *Post-Continental* 125–56; idem, "Life"; Ó Maoilearca.

bibliography

Ahmed, Sara. "Orientations Matter." *New Materialisms: Ontology, Agency, and Politics*. Ed. Diana Coole and Samantha Frost. Durham, NC: Duke UP, 2010. 234–57. Print.

Althusser, Louis. "The Underground Current of the Materialism of the Encounter." *Philosophy of the Encounter: Later Writings, 1978–1987*. Ed. F. Matheron and O. Corpet. Trans. G.M. Goshgarian. London: Verso, 2006. 163–207. Print.

Aristotle. *The Rhetoric and the Poetics of Aristotle*. Trans. W. Rhys Roberts and Ingram Bywater. New York: Modern Library, 1984. Print.

Asma, Stephen T. *On Monsters: An Unnatural History of Our Worst Fears*. Oxford and New York: Oxford UP, 2009. Print.

Badiou, Alain. *Being and Event*. Trans. Oliver Feltham. London and New York: Continuum, 2005. Print.

Badiou, Alain. *Logics of Worlds*. Trans. Alberto Toscano. London and New York: Continuum, 2009. Print.

Badiou, Alain. *On Beckett*. Ed. and trans. Alberto Toscano and Nina Power. Manchester: Clinamen, 2003. Print.

Bennett, Jane. *Vibrant Matter: A Political Ecology of Things*. Durham, NC: Duke UP, 2010. Print.

Bergson, Henri. *Creative Evolution*. Trans. Arthur Mitchell. Basingstoke: Macmillan, 1911. Print.

Bergson, Henri. *The Creative Mind: An Introduction to Metaphysics*. Trans. Mabelle L. Andison. New York: Philosophical Library, 1946. Print.

Bergson, Henri. *Duration and Simultaneity, with Reference to Einstein's Theory*. Trans. Leon Jacobsen. Indianapolis: Bobbs-Merrill, 1965. Print.

Bergson, Henri. *Matter and Memory*. Trans. Nancy Margaret Paul and W. Scott Palmer. New York: Zone, 1988. Print.

Bergson, Henri. *Mélanges*. Ed. André Robinet. Paris: PUF, 1972. Print.

Bergson, Henri. *Mind-Energy: Lectures and Essays*. Trans. H. Wildon Carr. Westport, CT: Greenwood, 1975. Print.

Bergson, Henri. *The Two Sources of Morality and Religion*. Trans. R. Ashley Audra and Cloudesley Brereton, with the assistance of W. Horsfall Carter. Notre Dame, IN: U of Notre Dame P, 1977. Print.

Brassier, Ray. "Concepts and Objects." Bryant, Srnicek, and Harman 46–65. Print.

Brassier, Ray. *Nihil Unbound: Enlightenment and Extinction*. London: Palgrave-Macmillan, 2007. Print.

Bryant, Levi, Nick Srnicek, and Graham Harman, eds. *The Speculative Turn: Continental Materialism and Realism*. Melbourne: re.press, 2011. Print.

Canguilhem, Georges. "Commentaire au troisième chapitre de *L'Evolution créatrice*." *Bulletin de la faculté des lettres de Strasbourg* XXI.5–6 (1943): 126–43 and XXI.8 (1943): 199–214. Print.

Čapek, Milič. *Bergson and Modern Physics: A Reinterpretation and Re-evaluation*. Dordrecht: Reidel, 1971. Print.

Čapek, Milič. "Bergson's Theory of the Mind–Brain Relation." *Bergson and Modern Thought: Towards a Unified Science*. Ed. A.C. Papanicolaou and P.A.Y. Gunter. New York: Harwood, 1987. 129–48. Print.

Churchland, Paul. *The Engine of Reason, the Seat of the Soul: Philosophical Journey into the Brain*. Cambridge, MA: MIT P, 1995. Print.

Coole, Diana, and Samantha Frost. "Introducing the New Materialisms." *New Materialisms: Ontology, Agency, and Politics*. Ed. Diana Coole and Samantha Frost. Durham, NC: Duke UP, 2010. 1–43. Print.

Deleuze, Gilles. *Difference and Repetition*. Trans. Paul Patton. London: Athlone, 1994. Print.

DeLillo, Don. *Point Omega*. London: Picador, 2010. Print.

Hallward, Peter. "Anything is Possible: A Reading of Quentin Meillassoux's *After Finitude*." Bryant, Srnicek, and Harman 130–41. Print.

Harman, Graham. *Prince of Networks: Bruno Latour and Metaphysics*. Melbourne: re.press, 2009. Print.

Johnston, Adrian. "Hume's Revenge: À Dieu, Meillassoux?" Bryant, Srnicek, and Harman 92–113. Print.

Laruelle, François. *Philosophie non-standard. Générique, quantique, philo-fiction*. Paris: Kimé, 2010. Print.

Latour, Bruno. *Reassembling the Social: An Introduction to Actor-Network-Theory*. Oxford and New York: Oxford UP, 2007. Print.

Latour, Bruno. *We Have Never Been Modern*. Trans. Catherine Porter. Cambridge, MA: Harvard UP, 1993. Print.

Lewis, David. "What Experience Teaches." Lycan 499–519. Print.

Lycan, William, ed. *Mind and Cognition: A Reader*. Malden, MA and Oxford: Blackwell, 1990. Print.

Malabou, Catherine. *What Should We Do with Our Brain?* Trans. Sebastian Rand. New York: Fordham UP, 2008. Print.

Meillassoux, Quentin. *After Finitude: An Essay on the Necessity of Contingency*. London: Continuum, 2008. Print.

Meillassoux, Quentin. "Potentiality and Virtuality." Trans. Robin McKay. Bryant, Srnicek, and Harman 224–36. Print.

Meillassoux, Quentin. "Spectral Dilemma." *Collapse* IV (2008): 261–75. Print.

Metzinger, Thomas. *Being No One: The Self-Model Theory of Subjectivity*. Cambridge, MA: MIT P, 2003. Print.

Mourélos, Georges. *Bergson et les niveaux de réalité*. Paris: PUF, 1964. Print.

Mullarkey, John. "Life, Movement and the Fabulation of the Event." *Theory, Culture and Society* 24 (2007): 53–70. Print.

Mullarkey, John. *Philosophy and the Moving Image: Refractions of Reality*. Basingstoke: Palgrave-Macmillan, 2010. Print.

Mullarkey, John. *Post-Continental Philosophy: An Outline*. London and New York: Continuum, 2006. Print.

Mullarkey, John. "The Very Life of Things: Reversing Thought and Thinking Objects in Bergsonian Metaphysics." Introduction to *Henri Bergson: An Introduction to Metaphysics*. Trans. T.E. Hulme. Basingstoke: Palgrave-Macmillan, 2007. x–xxxii. Print.

Nelson, Mike. *Extinction Beckons*. London: Matts Gallery, 2000. Print.

Nemirow, Lawrence. "Physicalism and the Cognitive Role of Acquaintance." Lycan 490–99. Print.

Ó Maoilearca, John. *Postural Mutations: Laruelle and Non-human Philosophy*. Forthcoming 2014. Print.

Read, Alan. *Theatre, Intimacy and Engagement: The Last Human Venue*. Basingstoke: Palgrave-Macmillan, 2009. Print.

Searle, John. *The Rediscovery of the Mind*. Cambridge, MA: MIT P, 1992. Print.

Sellars, Wilfrid. "Philosophy and the Scientific Image of Man." *Empiricism and the Philosophy of Mind*. Ed. Wilfred Sellars. London: Routledge, 1963. 1–40. Print.

Strawson, Galen. "Realistic Monism: Why Physicalism Entails Panpsychism." *Consciousness and its Place in Nature: Does Physicalism Entail Panpsychism?* Ed. Galen Strawson et al. Exeter and Charlottesville, VA: Imprint Academic, 2006. 3–31. Print.

Tallis, Raymond. *Aping Mankind: Neuromania, Darwinitis, and the Misrepresentation of Humanity.* Durham: Acumen, 2011. Print.

Tallis, Raymond. *The Explicit Animal: A Defence of Human Consciousness.* Basingstoke: Macmillan, 1991. Print.

Thacker, Eugene. *After Life.* Chicago: U of Chicago P, 2010. Print.

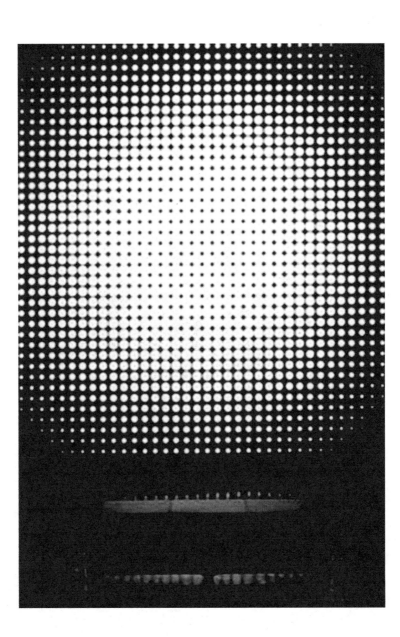

The instincts connected with the need of nutrition have furnished all animals with some virtual knowledge of space and force, and make them applied physicists. The instincts connected with sexual reproduction have furnished all animals at all like ourselves with some virtual comprehension of the mind of other animals of their kind, so that they are applied psychists. Now not only our accomplished science, but even our scientific questions have been pretty exclusively limited to the development of those two branches of natural knowledge. There may for aught we know be a thousand other kinds of relationship which have as much to do with connecting phenomena and leading from one to another, as dynamical and social relationships have. Astrology, magic, ghosts, prophecies, serve as suggestions of what such relationships might be.[1]

joshua ramey

CONTINGENCY WITHOUT UNREASON
speculation after meillassoux

Is there a reason, independent of human cognition, for why the world is as it is, or for why there is a world, at all? Many in modernity, from Montaigne to Wittgenstein, have dismissed the question as nonsensical. But in *After Finitude: An Essay on the Necessity of Contingency*, Quentin Meillassoux revives the issue of the ultimate sense of the world, and the question of why there is something rather than nothing.[2] His answer to the question is both unusual and counterintuitive. It is an answer grounded on a principle Meillassoux takes as axiomatic. He calls this the "principle of unreason." The principle is posited in order to account for contingency in the world. According to Meillassoux, in order that there be genuine contingency, there must be no reason for anything to be or to remain the way that it is: "everything must be able, without reason, to be other than it is;

everything must, without reason, be able not to be and/or be able to be other than it is" (AF 60).[3] That is to say, if there is to be genuine contingency, there can be no ultimate reason for contingency, since such a reason would presumably entail the existence of some necessity, some necessary cause of contingency, as such. This would constitute a contradiction: if there were a reason for contingency itself, then there would be no genuine contingency in the world. But if for things to possibly be otherwise, or not to be at all, is for them to be contingent, then this world must exist for no reason. Given that this world is a world of contingency, the answer to the question "Why is there something rather than nothing?" can only be answered "for no reason at all."

In what follows I will attempt to outline a position on contingency that contrasts with the one for which Meillassoux argues. In *After Finitude*, Meillassoux defines contingent being as that which can possibly be or not be. That is to say, contingent being is possible being. But based on considerations from Avicenna (Ibn Sina) and Charles Sanders Peirce, I will argue that contingency should not be understood in terms of possibility alone but must be conceived, in some sense, in relation to actuality.

As a corollary to my argument, I will explore in closing how the relation of the actual and the contingent is exemplified in divination. Ultimately what I want to explore, in a somewhat cursory and tentative way here, is how the logic of divination corroborates the irreducibility of the actual for contingency. In conclusion, rather than link contingency as Meillassoux does to unreason, I will argue that contingency can only be fully appreciated by understanding it in terms of a highly peculiar form of reason, the sort of reasoning that takes place in practices of divination, even if divination as a practice remains obscure.

contingency as unreason

Although I have begun with its baldly metaphysical précis, Meillassoux's *After Finitude* is in fact a complex intervention into the two-hundred-year legacy of Kantian transcendental philosophy. Kant famously argued that there is no knowledge of ultimate being, of the noumenon, apart from a peculiar mind–world conjunction. We have no access to reality itself, according to Kant, apart from the categories of the understanding. Meillassoux calls this view, and others like it, "correlationism." Various post-Kantian traditions, he argues, can be distinguished by diverse accounts of the "correlation" they posit between thought and being. Yet all such traditions, he argues, agree that there is no intelligible being apart from the constraints on knowledge germane to some "correlation" between thought and being, however the correlation is construed (AF 5–8).[4]

In *After Finitude*, Meillassoux does not attempt so much to refute correlationism as to push the tradition to an unexpected speculative conclusion. Meillassoux begins by noting that various post-Kantian traditions all converge upon what Heidegger called the "facticity" of the mind–world relation. That is to say, from within the correlationist "circle," there is no way of knowing why a particular mind–world relation holds. We are, as Heidegger put it, thrown into the world, meaning that we do not know why or on what basis a particular mind–world conjunction might obtain. But Meillassoux observes that, as such, facticity is open to two very different interpretations: facticity can mean that the contingency of the correlation conditions all knowledge of being, or facticity can imply that being itself is "factical" – that is to say, that absolute reality is contingent, in itself. In any case, it seems the correlationist is faced with a choice: either the factical character of the mind–world nexus does not bear on the character of the absolute, or it does (AF 42).

According to Meillassoux, Kant takes the first position. For Kant, facticity is a condition of all knowledge of being, but not necessarily a condition of being itself. Consequently, Kant holds that, while the in-itself is unknowable, it is nevertheless thinkable as independent from the conditions of knowledge. Although we cannot know that it is so, for Kant we can think the noumenon, the in-itself, as existing and non-contradictory (AF 35). Meillassoux calls this the "weak" interpretation of facticity. Here, the factical character of our knowledge is unrelated to the character of the absolute, the noumenon. By contrast, a thinker Meillassoux calls a "strong" correlationist – such as Heidegger or Foucault – asserts that facticity entails contingency in both knowledge and being. The strong correlationist asserts that it is not our situated, finite experience as observers that denies us knowledge of the absolute, we are rather denied such knowledge because we cannot exclude the possibility, from within the correlationist circle, that the in-itself is contingently whatever it is. Against Kant, we cannot suppose that the in-itself is not self-contradictory, or even that it exists, without supposing some reason for the world being thus and not otherwise, a reason that should be inaccessible to us from within the correlationist circle. And so, the strong correlationist asserts, if to be known is to have a reason, and there is no discernible reason why the world is such and not otherwise, then the ultimate nature of reality itself is subject to the same kind of contingency as is all knowledge of being, and thus the absolute is itself subject to facticity. The strong correlationist cannot claim securely even to think the in-itself as necessarily existent or as non-self-contradictory.[5]

If one accepts the strong correlationist's decision that contingency pertains to the absolute itself, Meillassoux thinks that it is possible to take two further speculative steps. In the first place, he thinks, we can posit that the in-itself is contingency. And based on this legitimate supposition, he thinks that we are entitled to know that the in-itself is not self-contradictory. The argument for the first claim is simply a restatement of strong correlationism in conjunction with the principle of unreason. According to the principle, it must be an absolute possibility that all things may be other than they are, and that they might cease to be entirely. But to think a world in which the principle was not true would be to think a world that denied facticity. This would, in Meillassoux's terms, be tantamount to a denial that there was no reason for the correlation. If one accepts strong correlationism, one is bound to accept the view that contingency is necessary, a character of the absolute, in-itself.

The second claim is that one can not only think, but can actually know that the in-itself is non-contradictory. Meillassoux reasons for this radical claim as follows: since a contradictory entity is always already everything it is not, it would have already become everything it can be. Thus, if it exists, a self-contradictory being would be a necessary being. But if contingency is absolute, there must be a possibility for change. Thus things in themselves cannot be self-contradictory; otherwise, everything would necessarily be and remain what it is, and all contingency would evaporate. As Meillassoux puts it:

> [...] we know by the principle of unreason why non-contradiction is an absolute ontological truth: because it is necessary that what is be determined in such a way as to be capable of becoming, and of being subsequently determined in some other way. It is necessary that this be this and not that, or anything else whatsoever, precisely in order to ensure that this can become that or anything else whatsoever. Accordingly, it becomes apparent that the ontological meaning of the principle of non-contradiction, far from designating any sort of fixed essence, is that of the necessity of contingency, or in other words, the omnipotence of chaos. (AF 71)

This demonstration that the in-itself must be non-contradictory in order to be contingent also indicates why it is necessary that there be a contingent entity (i.e., that that absolute must be contingency, as such). We cannot think becoming without something that becomes. Since pure nothingness is inconceivable, we must conceive an entity that exists, and exists contingently, in order to conceive contingency, at all. This ultimate entity, this absolute in-itself, Meillassoux calls the "omnipotence of chaos." Here is how Meillassoux describes such "hyper-chaos." He writes:

> If we look through the aperture which we have opened up onto the absolute, what we see there is a rather menacing power – something insensible, and capable of destroying both things and worlds, of bringing forth monstrous absurdities, yet also of never doing anything, of realizing every dream, but also every nightmare, of engendering random and frenetic transformations, or conversely of producing a universe that remains motionless down to its ultimate recesses, like a cloud bearing the fiercest storms, then the eeriest bright spells, if only for an interval of disquieting calm. We see an omnipotence equal to that of the Cartesian God, and capable of anything, even the inconceivable; but an omnipotence that has become autonomous, without norms, blind, devoid of the other divine perfections, a power with neither goodness nor wisdom, ill-disposed to reassure thought about the veracity of its distinct ideas. We see something akin to Time but a Time that is inconceivable for

physics, since it is capable of destroying, without cause or reason, every physical law, just as it is inconceivable for metaphysics, since it is capable of destroying every determinate entity, even a god, even God. This is not a Heraclitean time, since it is not the eternal law of becoming, but rather the eternal and lawless possible becoming of every law. It is a Time capable of destroying even becoming itself by bringing forth, perhaps forever, fixity, stasis, and death. (AF 64)

The most significant idea to be culled from this description of the absolute is that the absolute is not the possibility of absolute becoming but the absolute becoming of all possibility: hyperchaos may be the end (or the beginning) of either change or stasis, either creation or destruction. In fact, the laws of nature themselves may change or be destroyed, since they but express the character of one particular possibility. For the possibilities that are, have been, or will be realized, it is not incumbent upon us to laud or honor the Principle of Ultimate Reality. There is something rather than nothing, this world rather than another, for no reason at all.

Before I begin to outline my own, contrasting position, one more observation on Meillassoux's view is in order. Meillassoux notes that "strong" correlationism, from Heidegger and Wittgenstein through Levinas and Derrida, has validated a form of mystical openness to what the ultimate character of reality might turn out to be. This is, he argues, because the possibility of some Ultimate Purpose behind the world cannot rationally be denied without presupposing what facticity cannot – namely, that there is access to the ultimate ground of reality (AF 42). Meillassoux observes that on this basis a plethora of "postmodern mysticisms" have been validated by correlationism, according to which Ultimate Reality, while inaccessible to reason, may yet reveal itself by some other means. On Meillassoux's view, such "religio-poetic" openness to ultimate (if ultimately enigmatic) meaning is misguided. He writes:

> If the strong model of correlationism legitimates religious discourse in general, this is because it has failed to de-legitimate the possibility that there might be a hidden reason, an unfathomable purpose underlying the origin of our world. This reason has become unthinkable, but it has been preserved as unthinkable; sufficiently so to justify the value of its eventual unveiling in a transcendent revelation. This belief in an ultimate Reason reveals the true nature of strong correlationism – far from relinquishing the principle of reason to the point where this relinquishment is converted into a principle, which alone allows us to grasp the fact that there is absolutely no ultimate Reason, whether thinkable or unthinkable. There is nothing beneath or beyond the manifest gratuitousness of the given – nothing but the limitless and lawless power of its destruction, emergence, or persistence. (AF 63)

Meillassoux here adopts what he takes to be a more stringent and consistent attitude toward the potential mystery of the absolute than that found in strong correlationism. He strives, in *After Finitude*, to ground a new kind of positive philosophical project, one that he calls a non-metaphysical speculation on the in-itself. Meillassoux's manifesto is that "we must show why thought, far from experiencing its intrinsic limits through facticity, experiences rather its knowledge of the absolute through facticity" (AF 52). Fully grasping the nettle of strong correlationism, for Meillassoux, means embracing not just the possibility but the necessary truth that the absolute is itself contingent, and that the first item of "positive knowledge" revealed to us about the absolute is that there is no reason for the way the world is such as it is. There is on this view no basis for the "finitist piety" that leaves room for an unknowing apprehension of the absolute, since knowledge of contingency exhausts the absolute, as such. While Meillassoux's argument may be a devastating blow to postmodern mysticism, I will argue in my own conclusion here that another view of the absolute character of contingency both supports and is ramified in a more archaic religiosity, that embodied in the practice of divination. But to demonstrate that claim, I must first outline an alternative view of contingency.

contingency as actuality

While there is something in Meillassoux's thought that I find profoundly intriguing and compelling, it is nevertheless both possible and necessary to object to Meillassoux's basic vision of contingency as entailing unreason. We can do that by posing the following modal question: why does this world, or any actual world, have the particular consistency that it has? This possible world may have that consistency (however minimally or maximally construed) contingently, but the contingency of an actual world is not simply a matter of its abstract possibility to be or not to be, its possibility to have been otherwise. Meillassoux seems to be anxiously aware of this problem, as he fails to specify how one passes from a hyper-chaos of pure possibility to the consistency of an actual world. Other commentators besides me have noticed that *After Finitude* is radically inconclusive on this point.[6]

To restate the problem slightly, we might accept that the ultimate nature of reality is marked by a possibility to be otherwise, or to not have been at all, but it is not clear what such an "existent rather than inexistent" status contributes to the ontological structure of a given world. That is to say, we could grant that the realm of whatever is logically possible is a realm defined only by contingency and non-contradiction, but the bearing of the possible upon any actual world would still be left entirely unspecified. Surely contingency is not simply a matter of whether an abstract possibility is realized but is also a matter of the specificity of relations in a given configuration. The contingency of the world must ultimately refer not simply to its possibility to be or not to be, but also to the actual fact of the existence of relations of some entities with other entities, or even at its radical minimum, the relation of an event to itself. Can contingency really be thought without thinking relations, even if only a minimal relation of the actual to itself?

If one accepts a real modal distinction between the possible and the actual (and Meillassoux, if pressed, may not accept the distinction as real), Meillassoux's position cannot eliminate the fact that, in addition to hyper-chaos, there is something else other than sheer chaos from which to legitimately speculate: another absolute, or another dimension of the absolute bears down on thinking with equal force: namely the actual, singular character of a given world. That is to say, there is arguably something "absolute" about contingency not merely in terms of possibility but also in terms of the actual relations that obtain in a given world. Even if "it is the contingency of the entity that is necessary, not the entity" (AF 65), Meillassoux is still obliged to determine the absolute nature of contingency both as a set of possibilities "hovering" over any series of actual events and entities, and as a determination of the singular character of any given actual world that exists. Yet his position does not really address this second, equally important sense of contingency.

In the eleventh century, Avicenna had already argued that contingent being is, logically speaking, more than the mere possibility to be or not to be.[7] For a being to be contingent, he argued, is also for it to exist in and through another. Avicenna identified three modalities of being: impossibility, contingency, and necessity. Necessary being is clearly distinct from both impossible and contingent being. It is that which cannot be thought not to exist without contradiction. Avicenna's position here is not remarkable – it is effectively that of Anselm or any other major medieval thinker. But on the distinction between contingent and impossible being, Avicenna is uniquely insightful. While impossible being is that whose existence cannot be thought without contradiction, contingent being is that whose existence or inexistence can be thought without contradiction. While impossible being is sheer nothingness (since a contradictory being cannot exist), contingent being is at least potentially something, a potential existence. That is to say, the contingent is distinct from the merely impossible because it can actually be something rather than nothing. But in order for such a "possibility of something" to be distinct from an empty possibility (or sheer nothingness), contingent being must actually exist. In other words, there is no contingent being that is not actually contingent. But in order for contingent being to be actual, it requires something else for it to be brought into existence: contingent being is by definition dependent upon, and inherently related to, some other being. It is that which exists in and through another. Thus for Avicenna there is no contingent being that is not actual being, and there is no actually contingent being that is not dependent upon and related to another being. Avicenna called the necessary being (the actual being necessary for contingency) "God," but his point about contingency holds, whether one accepts the existence of God, opts for hyper-chaos, or simply acknowledges the irreducible modal status of the actual.

This position on contingency has dramatic consequences for Meillassoux's argument, consequences that can be better illustrated by turning to another thinker for whom actuality was irreducible, namely Charles Sanders Peirce. Peirce's thought is notoriously challenging and multi-valent, and I fully admit that what follows may be, for those more deeply initiated than myself, a rather simplistic and one-dimensional reading of Peirce.[8] In several of his most famous essays, Peirce seems to suggest that, at the highest level of generality, there can be no actuality without relations.[9] Peirce's arguments (not unlike Meillassoux's) follow in the wake of Cantor's work on the infinite. Cantor had demonstrated that the class of non-totalizable sets, such as the whole numbers, cannot be counted. In "The Logic of Relatives," Peirce concludes that Cantor's work entails that within a non-totalizable class of entities, or a pure continuum, there are in fact no distinct individuals, but only pure potentials. In the "Logic of Relatives" he defines the continuum in the following way. He writes:

> A continuum is a collection of so vast a multitude [i.e., entities, events, etc.] that in the whole universe of possibility there is not room for them to retain their distinct identities, but they become welded into one another. Thus the continuum is all that is possible, in whatever dimension it be continuous.[10]

Note that this is not a denial that there are, ultimately, individuals, but rather a claim only that whatever can be generalized from an actual individual is not itself an individual (thus avoiding the famous "third man" problem in Plato, the problem of the medium or means by which the actual participates in its ideal Form). That is to say, if we are to speak coherently of the contingency of an individual event, entity, or possible world, we are not speaking atomically, but of types or kinds of things, where such types are potentials of a given continuum. In order for there to be distinct individuals, such a continuum must be logically presupposed, and Peirce claims that it is to the continuum that any perfectly "general" or universal term refers. Thus, in another essay, he writes that

> [...] the potential aggregate is with the strictest exactitude greater in multitude than any possible multitude of individuals. But being a potential aggregate only, it does not contain any individuals at all. It only contains general conditions which permit the determination of individuals.[11]

In other words, if we ultimately cannot discern distinct individuals within the largest possible (i.e., transfinite) aggregate, it must be the case that individuals become distinct only through relations to one another.[12] Thus, in "The Logic of Continuity" Peirce concludes that

> a potential collection more multitudinous than any collection of distinct individuals can be[,] cannot be entirely vague. For the potentiality supposes that the individuals are determinable in every multitude. That is, they are determinable as distinct. But there cannot be [a] distinctive quality for each individual; for these qualities would form a collection too multitudinous for them to remain distinct. It must therefore be by means of relations that the individuals are distinguishable from one another.[13]

From Peirce's perspective, it is a valid inference to claim that actual relations distinguish possible worlds from one another, such that "possible worlds" are not conceivable as distinct without also being actual. Within a pure continuum, a pure potentiality, there are no distinct individuals until there is at least one relation. Relations make individuals distinct. Such a thought is highly significant, here, because it runs contrary to Meillassoux's supposition that the absolute, as hyper-chaos, is characterized by isolated, randomly interactive possibilities. If hyper-chaos is itself an abnumerable set of possible entities or events, which Meillassoux himself claims it is (AF 105), and Peirce is correct that within any abnumerable aggregate there are no distinct individuals, then there are in fact no distinct individual possibilities within hyper-chaos. For any of the possibilities within hyper-chaos to be distinct they would have to be actually determined by some minimal relation. Otherwise, each possibility is inherently indistinct, indeterminate. Determination, for Peirce, entails relation, such that within the ideal continuum of general characteristics, for possibilities to be actual they must be conceived as, at minimum, at least related to themselves. But if Meillassoux were to accept this conclusion it would alter his entire vision, since it would entail that at least one relation within an actual world is essential to that possible world, and thus that there is something absolute about actuality, and not merely about possibility.[14]

The upshot here is that, if hyper-chaos is a realm indifferent to actuality, where it is radically unclear what is possible and what is not, then the hyper-chaotic cannot be said to be the domain of contingency but rather simply of inchoate nothingness. And from the point of view of Avicenna, what we have in Meillassoux's vision is not the necessity of real contingency, which always has to do with relations of dependency (in and through) some actuality. What we have, rather, is the simple thought of abstract possibility masking itself as the necessity of contingency. But given that there is something rather than nothing (which Meillassoux admits there is), it is radically unclear what bearing Meillassoux's thought of abstract possibility has to do, in the end, with contingency, because it is unclear what connection this thought has to the reality, and of real contingency, which always involves reference to some minimal actuality. Perhaps that is Meillassoux's ultimate gambit, that there really is nothing essential (from the point of view of the absolute) about this particular world. But this is a claim Meillassoux has yet to make explicit, or to defend.

In other writings, Meillassoux expresses hope, grounded in the fecundity of absolute chaos, for another world to arise, one in which a God of justice and beauty finally appears to conquer the injustice and ugliness of this world, and to bring about the resurrection of our otherwise unmournable deaths.[15] But the basic structure of Meillassoux's thought makes it ambiguous as to how such a God would arise from this world, since there is nothing in particular about this present actuality upon which such an unthinkable alternative would depend. That, of course, may be the appeal of Meillassoux's perspective, in that it insists upon the necessity of unreason, a defiance of all calculation, in order to found alternative possible worlds to this present one, filled as it is with the endlessly cruel spectacle of unrecoverable loss. But there is another form of speculative reason that can approach contingency differently and also claim to speak from the absolute.

contingency without unreason

To conclude, I would suggest that Meillassoux's despair of finding in the contours of the actual some connection to the possible world we desire might be unwarranted.[16] With Peirce and Avicenna, we can argue that it is incoherent not to aver that the particular relations that have been actually realized in this world are necessary to its contingency. Both of these thinkers seem to suggest that for a contingent reality to be distinctly individuated (and thus to exist) it must in some sense be actual. Following Peirce, we can suppose that it is not merely the unbounded realm of possibility but particular *relations* that make contingent existences distinct. If Peirce is correct, part of the contingency of this world are the peculiar forms of relation germane to it.[17] And this is simply another way of saying, with Avicenna, that to be contingent is to exist in and through another, rather than merely to possibly be or not be. Thus there is really no such thing as wholly arbitrary contingency, unless contingency is erroneously conflated with arbitrary possibility – with that chaos that for Peirce was equivocal with nothingness, or for Avicenna was equivocal with impossibility.

But the appearance of a kind of nihilism here is not accidental. Shifting from a metaphysical to a religious register, Meillassoux's rejection of any reason beneath or "beyond the manifest gratuity of the given" is part of his argument against the fideism of a "finitist piety" that restricts knowledge of the absolute in order to leave room for mystery at the level of the absolute as such. This is the dimension of contingency that is accessed through abject submission to some vague mystical "outside" of reason, such as that signified by the "Other" in Levinas, the "outside" in Blanchot, or the *Ereignis* in Heidegger. On this view, "scientific" knowledge is given complete dominance of the interior realm of the finite, while the givenness of finitude itself is abandoned to an exteriority that can only be the subject of sublime ecstatic abandonment. Meillassoux rightly rejects the nihilism inherent in finitist piety, but offers a yet-more-accelerated nihilism to take its place, one that invites us into a deeper abandonment to an even more inchoate hope.

But there is a different religiosity supported by the view of contingency I would propose, as an alternative to Meillassoux. *This* religiosity, I would suggest, is embodied in the archaic and universal arts of divination – arts that are, at least formally speaking, precisely designed to address the problem of a world that is replete with contingency, yet whose contingency is linked to actuality in ways that recur in patterns that are uncannily significant. For an initial description of divinatory logic, we can begin with E.E. Evans-Pritchard's classic study of witchcraft among the Azande:

> As a natural philosophy it [witchcraft] reveals a theory of causation. Misfortune is due to witchcraft co-operating with natural forces. If a buffalo gores a man, or the supports of a granary are undermined by termites so that it falls on his head, or he is infected with cerebro-spinal meningitis, Azande say that the buffalo, the granary, and the disease, are causes which combine with witchcraft to kill a man. Witchcraft does not create the buffalo and the granary and the disease, for these exist in their own right, but it is responsible for the particular situation in which they were brought into lethal relations with a particular man. This granary would have fallen in any case, but since there was witchcraft present it fell at the particular moment when a certain man was resting beneath it. Of these causes the only one which permits intervention is witchcraft, for witchcraft emanates from a person. The buffalo and the granary do not allow of intervention and are, therefore, whilst recognized as causes, not considered the socially relevant ones.[18]

If we follow Evans-Pritchard, here, witchcraft (here figured as divining the cause of an accident) involves a theory of causation that is anything but primitive. Far from denying the power of efficient and material causes, divinatory reason fully recognizes their rights and privileges. We might say that witchcraft recognizes all four Aristotelian causes, but adds a fifth cause, the "divining cause," as it were. The divining cause is in some sense the *cause of the occasion*, equivalent to the contingent or chance element, itself.[19] The divining cause is linked, as it were, to the singularity of an event. But unlike Meillassoux's sense of the absolutely aleatory (hyper-chaos) as unreason, the divining cause represents, paradoxically, the aleatory nature of intelligibility, as such. That is to say, it demonstrates a reasoning that is by nature occasional, not so much subject to chance as taking chance as its subject.

Witchcraft is, of course, the art of enchantment, and the cause in question here is ineluctably *charmed*, personal, and enigmatic in the way that persons also are. To divine why an event took place when and where it did, by witchcraft, is a matter of determining *who* caused the event, by witchcraft. Thus Evans-Pritchard says that witchcraft creates the "particular situation" of an event, "permits intervention" and "emanates from a person." But to make this determination is to search for the sense or the reason for contingency as such. It is to search for an irreducibly situational and personal cause that, unlike efficient and material causes, *could always have been otherwise*.

Despite a modern prejudice that might dismiss divination as mere wish-fulfillment, or the projection of unconscious fantasies upon a truly indifferent cosmic medium, anthropologists, scholars of religion, and practitioners of divination have long insisted that the power to divine is not a personal, subjective, or otherwise capricious affair. I cannot undertake to defend this claim at length here, but it is worth noting that the cultures most concerned about charlatans are, in fact, the cultures which tend to take divination most seriously.[20] It surely cannot be said that divination practices *eliminate* human caprice, in principle; it would, however, be possible to show that divination *resists* such caprice, in practice. For my purposes here, what is significant about divination is that, for the practitioner, knowledge of contingency is taken to emanate, through a divining practice, from actuality itself. The "divining cause," as I have dubbed the power of divination to determine the sense of the event, thus provides a kind of immanent reason for contingency.[21] That is to say, divination in practice discovers a contingency without unreason, in principle.

Such a "seeing," if and when valid, is not subjective but involves an objectively uncanny dimension of the real. Divination is able to somehow exploit, or rather *evoke*, a kind of irreducible enigma within actuality: the fact that actuality is never quite itself, always shot through with a contingency that opens the actual onto the very dimension that divination explores. This is why divination practices involve subjecting certain actual determinants in the present (yarrow stalks, arcana, bones, seeds, runes, etc.), to *explicitly* aleatory methods (throws, spreads, casts), as if chance were not the ultimate horizon of events but some strange connecting thread between past and present actualities.[22] Chance on this view is activated not abstractly but concretely, through an actual event of casting. And this event is inherently relational: the sense of what occurs (in a divining chance) is *more* than brute necessity, more than mere material or efficient cause, precisely to the extent that chance is activated, engaged. Divination does not see the abstract future, but takes up elements in the present – cards, yarrow stalks, or the entrails of a beast – in order to see through a chance into its concrete, contingent potencies. In some sense divination exploits the fact that contingency itself is not the derivation of the actual from an arbitrary set of possibilities but an effect of a dynamic tension within the actual itself.[23] In this way contingency, paradoxically, has everything to do with the continuous rather than with the discrete – with a continuity, however fleeting and enigmatic, rather than an absolute discontinuity in the real. Such is the speculative insight of divination: in order for there to be contingency, the chance particular relations of any given world must be taken as an absolute feature of that world.[24]

speculation on the actual

What I am trying to suggest is that if one is serious about thinking contingent being, contingency should be thought not in relation to an abstract set of inherently unrelated possibilities, not thought in terms of nothingness, but in terms of an enigmatic *something*: a continuum within which actual entities are specifiable in terms of relations. This perspective that grounds a mode of speculation was, for Peirce, the meaning of life itself. Peirce writes:

> Even in this transitory life, the only value of all the arbitrary arrangements which mark actuality, whether they were introduced once and for all "at the end of the sixth day of creation" or whether as I believe they spring out on every hand all the time, as the act of creation goes on, their only value is to be shaped into a continuous delineation under the creative hand, and at any rate their

only use for us is to hold us down to learning one lesson at a time, so that we may make the generalizations of intellect and the more important generalizations of sentiment which make the value of this world. Whether when we pass away, we shall be lost at once in the boundless universe of possibilities, or whether we shall only pass into a world of which the one is the superfices and which itself is discontinuity of higher dimensions, we must wait and see. Only if we make no rational working hypothesis about it we shall neglect a department of logical activity proper for both intellect and sentiment.[25]

If it is simply Meillassoux's "working hypothesis" that we are part of a discontinuity of higher dimensions, and thus that the existence itself should be seen as an ultimately discontinuous affair, that might be an interesting and provocative axiom. But if it is an axiom, it can only be judged by its consequences. And it is a consequence of Meillassoux's axiomatic recusal of contingency to hyper-chaotic possibility that contingency is ultimately meaningless. The axiom I have pursued here, following Peirce and Avicenna, is that contingency is given sense by its relation to actuality. A consequence of this axiom is that practical approaches to the absolute, such as divination, constitute genuine speculation: informal yet rigorous explorations of contingency taken as the enigma (and not the nothingness) of actuality. The fact that divination is often carried out in ad hoc and improvised ways might be a testament to the devotion of "sensitives" to contingency itself. Such devotion represents speculation from the actual, and not the merely possible world.

As Gilles Deleuze once realized, there is an ethical dimension at stake in divination.[26] In the *Logic of Sense* he was quite explicit in his belief that we can live the continuity of change only insofar as we become adequate to it through divination. "Divination grounds ethics," Deleuze wrote bluntly.[27] As a book on ethics, *Logic of Sense* attempts to address the problem of ethics as first conceived by the Stoics. In Deleuze's own words, that problem is "how could the event be grasped and willed without its being referred to the corporeal cause from which it results, and through this cause, to the unity of causes as *Physics*?"[28] In other words, how is freedom to be conceived in relation to the determining power of events? The answer, Deleuze contends, is divination. He writes:

> [...] divination grounds ethics. In fact, the divinatory interpretation consists of the relation between the pure event (not yet actualized) and the depth of bodies, the corporeal action and passions whence it results. We can state precisely how this interpretation proceeds: it is always a question of cutting into the thickness, of carving out surfaces, of orienting them, of increasing and multiplying them in order to follow out the tracing of lines and incisions inscribed on them. Thus, the sky is divided into sections and a bird's line of flight is distributed according to them; we follow on the ground the letter traced by a pig's snout; the liver is drawn up to the surface where its lines and fissures are observed. Divination is, in the most general sense, the art of surfaces, lines and singular points appearing at the surface. This is why two fortune-tellers cannot regard one another without laughing, a laughter which is humorous.[29]

Not only is divination figured as the key to the problem of ethics but it is conjoined to two other concepts not generally thought of as ethically central: humor. And the third term between divination and humor, for Deleuze, is health. If our health is paradigmatically subject to the forces of chance, humor paradigmatically plays with chance, or redoubles chance in the mode of a creative engagement that has the potential to increase our potential capacity for health. Divination produces the link between health and humor: the vicissitudes of the body and the infinite labyrinths of the mind. Making the mind (potentially) adequate to the contingency proper to events, divination exploits the sense and nonsense they portend, becoming the science of contingency and the religion of chance. Indeed, as Giambattista Vico speculated and subsequent anthropology has confirmed, divination is the oldest, the most archaic form of religion, or the binding (*religio*) of heaven to earth.[30] The potentially humorous enigma is not that of hyper-chaos but of actuality itself, contingent but without unreason: redolent with as-yet-unexplored relations.[31]

notes

1 C.S. Peirce, "The First Rule of Logic" in *Reasoning and the Logic of Things*, eds. Kenneth Laine Ketner and Hilary Putnam (Cambridge, MA: Harvard UP, 1992) 173.

2 All references to *After Finitude* will be indicated by AF. All such references are to Quentin Meillassoux's *After Finitude: An Essay on the Necessity of Contingency* (London: Continuum, 2008).

3 What is the basis for this principle? Meillassoux calls it "anhypothetical," in the Aristotelian sense that anhypothetical is any principle that, while it cannot be deduced from other propositions, can be proven to be true by showing that anyone who assumes the principle is false falls into inconsistency (AF 61). Aristotle's famous example of an anhypothetical principle is the principle of non-contradiction, which can only be denied by assuming that it is true. Meillassoux asserts that one cannot deny the principle of unreason without denying the reality of contingency in the universe.

4 In Kant, that correlation is structured by the transcendental deduction of space, time and the categories of the understanding; in Hegel by the historical dialectic of Spirit; in Husserl by the intentional arc of the noesis–noema dyad; in Heidegger by the *ekstasis* of Dasein's temporality as care. These are simply the three most well-known variants in the Continental tradition; Wittgenstein's thesis that there is no access to being apart from language would be the analytical variant.

5 As Hegel had already argued, Kant had given us no account of how it is that the mind is in a position to discern the difference between the phenomenal and the noumenal, since the categories of the understanding are fully in and of the phenomenal. In this sense, the "correlation" for Hegel is already itself the Absolute. Each finite, contingent act of knowing is simply the absolute self-reflection of Spirit coming to recognize itself. But, Meillassoux argues, to deny the contingency of the in-itself, as Hegel ultimately does, is tantamount to a denial of facticity. To be strict or "strong" correlationists we must entertain every possibility, including the possibility that facticity is not simply for-us but a dimension of reality, in-itself. We must acknowledge the absolute necessity of contingency.

6 See Brassier, *Nihil Unbound: Enlightenment and Extinction* (New York: Palgrave-Macmillan, 2008); and also Martin Hägglund, "Radical Atheist Materialism: A Critique of Meillassoux" in *The Speculative Turn: Continental Realism and Materialism*, eds. Graham Harman, Levi Bryan, and Nick Srnicek (Melbourne: re.press, 2011) 114–29.

7 Nader El-Bizri, "Avicenna and Essentialism," *Review of Metaphysics* 54 (June 2001): 753–78.

8 For a much more comprehensive view of Peirce on the continuum, see Fernando Zalamea, *Peirce's Continuum: A Methodological and Mathematical Approach*, available <http://acervopeirceano.org/wp-content/uploads/2011/09/Zalamea-Peirces-Continuum.pdf>.

9 For my part, I would like to call the necessary logical interdependency between contingency and actual being the "enigma of the actual." It seems to me that Meillassoux, and others working under the aegis of speculative realism, are much more fascinated by the enigma of the possible, the problem of what may be, rather than the problem of what is. I am not prepared to fully defend this claim yet, but I think that the withdrawn nature of the object, in Graham Harman, is not an actual object but a possible object. Likewise, it seems to me that the "inexistence" that Brassier is fascinated by is not the actual unraveling of the world or a world but a purely logical possibility. Likewise, I think Meillassoux's hyper-chaos is an abstraction, and actually has to do only with abstract possibility, and not with real contingency. I am fully prepared to have to nuance these claims in the future, and I'm less interested in these negative claims than in trying to work out a positive project of thinking the enigma of the actual, one that I can only lay out here in outline. I hope to further articulate this project at length in work tentatively entitled *Contingency and Actuality: Metaphysics, Divination, Speculation*.

10 C.S. Peirce, "The Logic of Relatives" in *Reasoning and the Logic of Things* 162.

11 Idem, "The Logic of Continuity" in *Reasoning and the Logic of Things* 247.

12 This is the point at which Meillassoux's thinking falters. Meillassoux treats the contingency of the absolute as if, even though he describes it as a non-totalizable class of possibilities, it nevertheless contains distinct individual possibilities, as such. As if every possible event, entity, or world, every possible being, were determinate, quite apart from becoming actual. But Peirce, along with Avicenna before him and Deleuze after him, would point out that this position is suspect.

13 Peirce, "The Logic of Continuity" 248.

14 Meillassoux could, of course, dismiss Avicenna's teaching on contingency, and simply insist that by contingency he means only the possibility to be or not be. But this would make Meillassoux's an idealism of the possible rather than a speculative realism of the actual. And perhaps, in the end, that is precisely what it is.

15 See Meillassoux's "Immanence of the World Beyond" in *The Grandeur of Reason*, eds. Conor Cunningham and Peter M. Chandler (London: SCM, 2010) 444–78.

16 On one surprising level, however, Peirce and Meillassoux are in fundamental agreement: Peirce would actually agree with Meillassoux on the issue of the contingent status of the laws of nature. Like Meillassoux, Peirce sees the stability of natural laws and the possibility of science as nested within a universe ultimately defined by contingent emergence within an indefinite continuum of possible worlds with possibly different sets of physical laws. This world, this actuality, with its laws, is contingent. As Meillassoux demonstrates, those who hold that the laws of nature are necessary across possible worlds depend on a "frequentialist" inference, one that assumes that a universe in which the laws of nature were not necessary would be one in which the laws would frequently change. But as Meillassoux shows, such a thinker (like Kant, for instance), assumes that the possible can be totalized and thus that it would be highly unlikely that the same possible world with these natural laws would continue to prevail (AF 103). But because the possible cannot be totalized, one does not need to presuppose the necessity of natural laws for there to be a stable actual world.

17 As Putnam explains:

> the Peircean picture is that the multitude of possibilities is so great that as soon as we have a possible world in which some of these possibilities are realized – say, a possible world in which some abnumerable multitude of the divisions are made – then we immediately see that there is a possible world in which still *more* divisions can be made, and hence there is no possible world in which all these *non-exclusive* possibilities are *all* actualized. We might summarize this by saying that the metaphysical picture is that possibility intrinsically outruns actuality, not just because of the finiteness of human powers, or the limitations imposed by physical laws. ("Peirce's Continuum" in *Peirce and Contemporary Thought: Philosophical Inquiries*, ed. Kenneth Laine Ketner (New York: Fordham UP, 1995) 19)

18 E.E. Evans-Pritchard, "Witchcraft," *Africa* 8.4 (1955) 418–19.

19 C.G. Jung suggests, of course that the logic of the occasion is not causal at all but rather the manifestation of an "acausal connecting principle" that he famously named "synchronicity." See C.G. Jung, *Synchronicity: An Acausal Connecting Principle* (Princeton: Princeton UP, 2010).

20 Theodor Adorno famously criticized belief in astrology and other occult forms of divination within the fully-administered society of capitalism, but I have argued elsewhere that Adorno's critique has more to do with a critique of facile reactions to the total dominance of disenchantment within the dialectic of Enlightenment than it does to do with a critique of authentic magic, about which Adorno is much more ambivalent (see my "Lost Magic: The Hidden Radiance of Negative Dialectics," *Radical Philosophy Review* 12.1 (2009): 315–37). Exemplary studies of how divination is legitimized, authenticated, and mutated within a broader range of cultures are by Marcel Mauss, *A General Theory of Magic* (London: Routledge, 2001); Henry Corbin, *Temple and Contemplation* (London: Routledge, 1986); and Mircea Eliade, *Shamanism: Archaic Techniques of Ecstasy* (Princeton: Princeton UP, 2004).

21 Although I cannot defend this conception here, I would like to claim, in fact, that the divining cause *gives* contingency to the actual, it is the source of

contingency, as such. The other causes are in some sense pre-determined to behave as they do. They express what is predictable and more or less probable in nature. But divination is not the discernment of necessity, or even of probability, but rather of contingency.

22 In future studies I hope to deal directly with Meillassoux's own view of chance as outlined in his *Le Nombre et la sirène. Un déchiffrage du Coup de dés de Mallarmé* (Paris: Fayard, 2011).

23 This irreducible status of the continuum is arguably the precise reality that Deleuze ascribes to the virtual. The virtual is fully of this world: it is the unbounded yet finite set of relations that make a given world distinct, at the levels of both thought and being. See Deleuze, "The Actual and the Virtual" in *Dialogues II*, trans. Eliot Ross Albert (New York: Columbia UP, 2002) 148–52.

24 On Peirce's avowedly extreme form of realism, *all* continuities are real, whether these be physical or psychical, sensory or rational. That is to say, everything in our experience, for Peirce, points to the conclusion that everything that we think has a referent somewhere in the world. Even the *fact* that there is a world (something rather than nothing) is itself a function of *this world as it actually is*. As he puts it:

> Whatever unanalyzable element *sui generis* seems to be in nature, although it be not really where it seems to be, yet must really be in nature somewhere, since nothing else could have produced even the false appearance of such an element *sui generis*. For example, I may be in a dream at this moment, and while I think I am talking and you are trying to listen, I may all the time be snugly tucked up in bed and sound asleep. Yes, that may be; but still the very semblance of my feeling a reaction against my will and against my senses, suffices to prove that there really is, though not in this dream, yet somewhere, a reaction between the inward and the outward worlds of my life. (Peirce, "The Logic of Relatives" 162)

For Peirce it is incoherent to presuppose that logic, causation, and even dreams do not refer to *something* in the real, because there is no other source of reality or of knowledge than this actual world as it unfolds. Yet Peirce is no "correlationist": for him there is no problem of how access is possible because the category of possibility is itself an abstraction from actuality, and in actuality itself – although steeped in complexity and the dense fabric of continua – there is in some sense nothing *but* knowledge. (I am grateful for conversations with Rocco Gangle for the development of these formulations.)

It is not incidental that Peirce, like Deleuze, had no qualms about the legitimacy of esoteric modes of mind such as divination. On Peirce's view, science and magic, laboratory life and divinatory chances, are allied in exploration of relations. In fact, Peirce's theory of hypothesis formation in science, the theory of abduction, ultimately links the very possibility of science to something like divination. Peirce calls abduction the process by which hypotheses are formed that can be subsequently tested. In some sense an abduction is a guess, as in the guess that it might have rained last night (hypothesis), because the ground is wet (observation). How does one pass from the in-principle infinite set of possible hypotheses to the one worth testing? Although no hypothesis can be logically eliminated, for Peirce there is nevertheless an intuitive, quasi-instinctual process by means of which unlikely hypotheses are eliminated. The existence of this rigorous yet informal process, Peirce sometimes speculates, is evidence of our ever-increasing sense of the coincidence of mind and the potencies of the universe, as such. (See "A Neglected Argument for the Reality of God," available <http://en.wikisource.org/wiki/A_Neglected_Argument_for_the_Reality_of_God>.)
In a certain way, Peirce is advocating for intellectual intuition, developed over time, at the level of scientific practice itself. Not scientific representation, but scientific practice at the level of abduction somehow rigorously yet informally "sees" directly into things in themselves. Scientific practice, because it is ultimately divinatory practice, is a mode of "speculative realism."

25 Peirce, "The Logic of Relatives" 163.

26 Part of why divination is crucial for Deleuze is that he arguably maintains a conception of contingency as linked to the necessity of the continuous (virtual), and in this way agrees with Avicenna and Peirce that there can be no concept of contingency that does not entail minimal continuity, and no concept of continuity that does not entail minimal relationality.

27 Deleuze, *The Logic of Sense*, trans. Mark Lester with Charles Stivale (New York: Columbia UP, 1990) 163.

28 Ibid.

29 Ibid.

30 Giambattista Vico, *The New Science*, trans. David Marsh (New York: Penguin, 2001) 7. In his "Foreword" to the Wilhelm translation of *The I Ching*, Jung notes that this derivation of *religio* from *religare*, "to bind," originated with the Church Fathers, but that the older, classical derivation is of *religio* from *relegere*, "a careful observation and taking account of the numinous." C.G. Jung, "Foreword" to *The I Ching, or Book of Changes*, trans. Richard Wilhelm and Cary F. Baynes, 3rd ed. (Princeton: Bollingen, 1967) xxviii.

31 And this, finally, is where health and humor might take on the status of "absolute" conditions for existence. Divination is neither merely ludic nor simply perverse, unless playful polymorphous perversity defines existence as such. And if it does, then the humorous dimension of existence has no real contrast. The ethics of the *Logic of Sense* could then be read no longer as a logic of perversion but as a survival mandate: occupy, and practice divination.

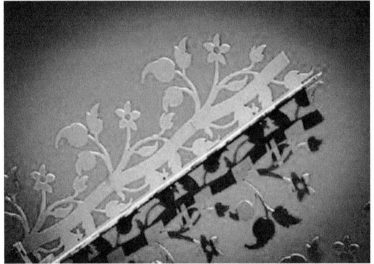

> In a certain respect, philosophy amounts to an astonishment that God does not exist.
> Quentin Meillassoux, The Divine Inexistence 177

How is an immanent religion, a religion *of* immanence itself, to be positively conceived? Following the critical destruction of all transcendent religions entailed by the acknowledgement of the ontological primacy of immanence – and the return to it, as their source, of all aspirations to the transcendent – the task of articulating the religious self-expression of immanence itself becomes ever more apparent. This amounts to nothing less than the identification, within immanence, of the *essence* of religion, the concealed – intrinsically religious – sources appropriated without acknowledgement by the religions of the transcendent. Once the various forms of human pathology and ideological struggle (as identified by Marx, Nietzsche, Freud and others) – the merely anthropological sources – are sifted out then the indigenous religion of immanence itself, barely discernible in the history of human religion, can be avowed in its own terms – arguably for the first time as such.[1]

The urgency of the task of elaborating the indigenous religion of immanence is underlined by the prevalence of those forces – anti-religious per se – which seek to perpetuate the erroneous identification of religion, *in toto*, with the transcendent as if the only sources of religion in immanence were inherently non-religious (e.g., human psychology, sociological conflict, etc.). Such viewpoints seek to halt the progress of critique and valorise, as its culmination, the desultory and reactionary vistas of rational humanism and scientific atheism, as if these represented the consummation of the critical dynamic of

jim urpeth

RELIGIOUS IMMANENCE
a critique of meillassoux's "virtual" god

the "Enlightenment." For such "false friends" of immanence the collapse in credibility of the transcendent seems to entail only one possible approach to religion – reductive explanation and dissolution. It thereby forecloses an arguably unique historical possibility, namely, the human recognition and affirmation of the religious life of natural immanence itself. Furthermore, should it be the case that the human species is, in religious terms, "chosen" by natural immanence as the vehicle for its religious self-expression then non-religious misappropriations of the advent of the primacy of immanence have even more significant, negative consequences. For not only is the legitimacy of a contemporary (non-transcendent) religious sensibility threatened but, more importantly, the very religious self-expression of immanence itself – its joyous self-affirmation beyond all functional definition – is stymied (at least as regards its relationship to the human species).

The question such a thought raises as to whether or not such a post-theistic religious realism refers, necessarily, to either the reality of a *relation* (that between the inherently religious aspects of immanence and the human species as, apparently, the only animal that "has" religion) or to an immanence that remains religious independently of the human species will not be pursued in depth in this piece. Suffice to say that it is a core claim of religious immanence that, even if its relation to the human species is regarded as essential, the relation is weighted heavily in favour of immanence in that religion is a phenomenon that far surpasses the capacities of the species caught up in its expression. The religion of immanence may well be inherently relational without constitutive reference to any species at all and, in any case, even if such a relation to something "outside" itself is thought to be necessary all such relata are themselves products of immanence without remainder. Of course, should religion disappear with the human species, it does not follow that it was therefore a "manmade" phenomenon. This would be to regard as sufficient what at best may be a merely necessary condition of religion. For the religion of immanence there is an irreducible poverty within the human (or any other) species regarding the sources of religion even if it is a prerequisite that one of its products is constitutive for it. The basic error of the modern critique of religion (apart from its tendency to identify religion exclusively and ineliminably with the transcendent) is the assumption of the sufficiency of the human regarding it. The non-negotiable insights of Feuerbach into the anthropological origin and nature of religions of the *transcendent* are thereby mistakenly generalised, erroneously assumed to be applicable to religion per se. From the perspective of religious immanence the unmasking of the transcendent personal God as a human "projection" merely demonstrates the deficiencies of its species-dominant type, an impoverishment on such a scale as to be more a symptom of the denial of religion than a variety of it.

It is this wider project – the clarification and articulation of the religion of immanence (as distinct from the attempt made by progressive strands of transcendent religions to become ever more immanent) – that provides the context for this critical consideration of some recent texts by Quentin Meillassoux. In "Spectral Dilemma" (hereafter SD) and the extracts available from *The Divine Inexistence* (*L'Inexistence divine*, hereafter DI), Meillassoux has made an important and striking contribution to contemporary philosophy of religion. These texts offer a positive conception of a "philosophical divine" (DI 227, 237) which is, according to Meillassoux, consistent with, indeed the highest expression of, immanence and the ontology of radical contingency which it, in his view, entails. The critical question pursued here is the extent to which Meillassoux's articulation of the religion of the "speculative materialism" he promotes remains faithful to immanence, remains, that is to say, positively disposed to *its* religious self-expression.[2] It shall be argued that, although impressive in many respects, Meillassoux's articulation of the religious dimension of his radical ontology of contingency fails to sustain immanence in so far as it seeks to retain key aspects of the ethical and evaluative agenda of transcendent religion.

I

There is no doubt that in "Spectral Dilemma" Meillassoux identifies and articulates very evocatively an indisputably significant existential-emotional experience and life-challenge, namely, how to complete successfully the mourning of those who have suffered, "[…] terrible deaths: premature deaths, odious deaths […] deaths which cannot be come to terms with" (SD 262). Such "essential spectres" require, Meillassoux claims, an "essential mourning" and it is his conception and account of the conditions that make its realisation possible that are our concern here. Is Meillassoux's sense of the religious response required to the real existential problematic he addresses an immanent one? Does he identify correctly and articulate accurately the immanent realm's religious interpretation of, and response to, such phenomena? Before attempting an answer to these questions a sense of Meillassoux's account of the conditions for "essential mourning" is required.

For Meillassoux, the resources offered by the traditional alternative between religion and atheism to resolve the problem of "essential mourning" are inadequate. Neither the "religious" perspective (i.e., a transcendent omnipotent, benevolent God exists) nor the "atheistic" (i.e., God does not exist) provide the means to make "essential mourning" possible. After, in effect, reformulating the "problem of evil" that lies at the heart of the exchange between the traditional alternatives, the key "dilemma" is formulated thus: "either to despair of another life for the dead or to despair of a God who has let such deaths take place" (SD 265). Hence, all the traditional alternative can offer to the problem of being haunted by an "essential spectre" is "despair."[3] In response to the deficiencies of both parties Meillassoux sketches a possible means of resolving their "aporetic alternative" (SD 265), a response which would be "neither religious nor atheistic" (SD 266). This response must be sketched briefly.

Meillassoux's solution to the "spectral dilemma" argues for the legitimacy and credibility of an alternative to both the "religious" and "atheistic" approaches which retains the key insights of both, from religion – "hope" in resurrection, from atheism – the "inexistence of God" (SD 268). In order to combine this avowal of hope with God's non-existence Meillassoux introduces the key notion of "*divine inexistence*" (ibid.), a deliberately equivocal notion that acknowledges both the inexistence of the transcendent God whilst retaining the "possibility of a God still to come" (ibid.), a God capable of rectifying the injustice of the deaths suffered by the "essential spectres." Hope is still constitutively linked to God in this approach as it is accepted that such a redemptive deity neither does nor ever has existed.

At this point in his argument Meillassoux changes philosophical gear for, in order to make any further progress, it is necessary to "shift the battle to the terrain of modalities" (ibid.). That is to say that – rehearsing the impressive discussion in *After Finitude* of early modern conceptions of the necessity/contingency opposition – the shared commitment of both religion and atheism to necessity regarding God's existence (i.e., God either exists necessarily or necessarily does not exist) must be challenged and overcome. This is not a simple retreat to agnosticism as it is a crucial component of Meillassoux's ontology that the necessarily existent God of transcendent religion cannot, in principle, exist. On this point, atheism is confirmed. On the basis of his celebrated interpretation of Hume's critique of metaphysical necessity, Meillassoux promotes an alternative beyond the religious/atheistic opposition, namely, "that *God is possible*" (SD 269) in the sense of a "virtual" God that *could* exist. A contingent God that, as logically possible, becomes conceivable on the basis of the collapse of metaphysical necessity.[4]

The critical question Meillassoux's avowal of a "virtual" God raises is whether or not such a contingent God gives adequate expression to a religion of immanence, to the God *of* ontological contingency itself. The central critical claim of this piece is that it is a necessary condition for the articulation of the religion of immanence that, without relapsing into the variety of necessity espoused by atheism, Meillassoux's "virtual" God is excluded in principle. For immanent religion, God – in any sense other than as an explicit signifier of impersonal processes – necessarily cannot exist. Hence, even if logically possible, Meillassoux's "virtual" God is, from the point of view of religious immanence, an ontological impossibility, indeed, no less so than the necessarily existent God posited by transcendent religion. The historical advent of the primacy of immanence and its indigenous religiosity just simply *is* the insight into the derivative status of *all* Gods within an order of being the self-sufficiency of which precludes the need for them as anything other than cultural symbols. This requires a questioning of the ontological status Meillassoux seemingly accords to logical modality which would seem to license the possible existence of anything whose concept is non-contradictory. From such a perspective only what is contradictory can be prohibited from possible existence. Whilst the religious immanentist might endeavour to establish the logical impossibility of Meillassoux's "virtual" God this would not be its only or strongest critical riposte. Ontologically, religious immanence both affirms a reality irreducible to the law of contradiction and precludes the possibility of various entities consistent with it. In line with the spirit of realism, religious immanence, in any case, is not unduly impressed with logical possibilities. There are other, more rigorous, gatekeepers of being than either logic or empirical verification (on the level of atomised facts).

The broad claim of the conception of religious immanence from which Meillassoux is here interrogated is that the encounter with it (taken as possible in principle) reveals the redundancy of any concept of God – not merely the onto-theological "God of metaphysics" (that Meillassoux also refutes). That is to say that a religion of immanence excludes in principle (indeed as irreligious) the very pursuit of what Meillassoux terms "divinology" (SD 275), the attempted articulation of a non-metaphysical God. To amend a famous slogan, for the religion of immanence, "God – *in any conceivable sense* – is dead." Only thus can religious *realism* – the view that impersonal immanent processes have an intrinsic religious self-expression – come into view.

In "Spectral Dilemma," having licensed the continuation of the philosophical discussion of the nature of "God," Meillassoux focuses on the temporal conditions required for the possible future manifestation of his contingent God and the critical revisions of various modal norms – particularly those entrenched commitments concerning the alleged "*necessity of the laws of nature*" (SD 272) – that are a further prerequisite. A trademark distinction is made between a "speculative" rather than "metaphysical" thinking, with the former defined as "*a reason emancipated from the Principle of Sufficient Reason*" (SD 273). For such speculative thought reason's native powers of a priori intuition are radicalised, giving it access to a reality liberated from metaphysical necessity such that the "laws of nature" are more modestly conceived in terms of contingent stabilities.[5] These themes – a groundwork essential to the credibility of the notion of the "god to come" in Meillassoux's sense – form the basis of an important acknowledgement of the entirely *derivative* ontological status of God thus conceived. As Meillassoux states: "God must be thought as *the contingent, but eternally possible, effect of a Chaos unsubordinated to any law*" (SD 274).

Whilst it is hard to imagine a more radical ontological demotion of God than Meillassoux here undertakes, the critical charge is that, if the religion of immanence is to be attained, even this contingent God must face critical elimination. Meillassoux closes "Spectral Dilemma" with some intriguing questions to indicate the sorts of issues to be explored in a future "divinology" (SD 275) or specification of the nature of the "future and immanent god" (ibid.) whose possibility has, he believes, been established. A promising affiliation is evoked in this respect: "what will be the most singular possible divinity, the most interesting, the most 'noble' in a sense (paradoxically) close to Nietzsche's?" (ibid.). In the following sketch of some critical questions to "Spectral Dilemma" aspects of Nietzsche's conception of critique – especially his "genealogy" of the affective sources of philosophical questioning – will be evoked on the assumption that such a critical project would have rendered redundant at the outset the problem to which Meillassoux seeks a solution.

II

In many respects "Spectral Dilemma" can be identified as a further venerable example of a text in which exemplary theoretical and ontological radicality is combined with a singular absence of a comparably rigorous critique of the existential-evaluative issues in which it originated and which sustain it. This is particularly pertinent in relation to the evaluation of constitutive features of reality. In Meillassoux's case formidable speculative gifts are, seemingly uncritically, put at the service of the pursuit and consequential re-enforcement of values incompatible with an affirmation of immanence. A sensibility in which a capacity for the self-critical evaluation of founding values and affective responses to key aspects of reality would have a different stance towards the existential-emotional challenge to which "Spectral Dilemma" is a response – the encounter with "essential spectres." Rather than seek a resolution to the existential challenges raised by unjust death, the initiating problem could have been so interrogated at source as to be *dissolved* – put aside as clearly indicative, in being framed at all, of a dubious evaluative stance towards existence, an outlook sourced in transcendent religion. Meillassoux is hence seen to be calling upon the resources of immanence to address a problem derived from the transcendent mind-set, a "category mistake" that significantly compromises immanence.

For all its radicality it is hard not to identify "Spectral Dilemma" as a text offering a reformulation, in strikingly contemporary terms, of the "problem of evil" and, furthermore, attempting to offer a solution to it, thereby *endorsing the credibility of the "problem"* as such. In short, Meillassoux engages in *theodicy* – albeit in a post-metaphysical form – in which an unexamined desire for justice and redemption, recognisable to a medieval theologian, is pursued in the direction of the possible advent of a God "innocent of the disasters of the world" (SD 268). It is as if the order of immanence stood in need not only of justification (because of certain negative aspects) but also of a particular type of redemption in which the problematic negative features are denied. There can be no doubt that, for Meillassoux, "terrible deaths" are an aspect of reality that call it into question per se and thereby trigger the search for justification. The endeavour to establish at least the possibility of an "essential mourning" is nothing less than an attempt to justify existence itself – to *make* it affirmable – as if, without such a prospect, its value and meaning are questionable. The key philosophical (and religious) issue here is the evaluation of existence inherent in the sort of response to its most horrendous and negative features found in "Spectral Dilemma." The suggestion of this paper is that the founding evaluative stance of Meillassoux's argument towards the negative aspects of reality in question is a perspective, a sensibility, entirely alien to a religion of immanence.

It is worth recalling at this point Nietzsche's crucial lesson as regards the critical work that needs to done on the affective-evaluative roots of philosophical problems as a condition of their validation as problems for which a solution is required. In the following celebrated passage Nietzsche gives a more accurate expression to the sensibility of religious immanence than that which prevails in "Spectral Dilemma":

> One will see that the problem is that of the meaning of suffering: whether a Christian meaning or a tragic meaning. In the former case it is supposed to be a path to a holy existence; in the latter case, being is counted as holy enough to justify even a monstrous amount of suffering.[6]

The question thus arises as to which of the religious sensibilities outlined in this passage prevails in Meillassoux's text. Whilst the radical ontology of immanence found in "Spectral Dilemma" is unequivocally incompatible with any notion of transcendent being, its implicit evaluation of existence – which, given the phenomenon of the "essential spectre," allegedly stands in need of a justificatory redemption – remains mired in the inherited affective and evaluative economy of transcendent religion. Throughout "Spectral Dilemma" its initiating existential-evaluative problem is implicitly universalised. At no point is any critical evaluation of the initiating problem undertaken or doubt entertained concerning the trajectory of the alleged solution. As Meillassoux states of the relation to "essential spectres," "whoever commits the imprudence of lending an ear to their call risks passing the rest of his life hearing their complaint" (SD 262). Whilst the glib response – "don't lend an ear therefore" – is not endorsed here, the universalising assumption made by Meillassoux that such an encounter induces a crisis of meaning that demands redemption of the sort he explores is identified as contentious.

This critical concern also bears upon the model of redemption (derived from the sensibility of transcendent religion) pursued should the evaluations of existence that are a necessary condition of being haunted in the way described be in place. Surely the following questions need to be asked as a condition of pursuing – rather than putting aside – such a "problem": who exactly is confronted by such "spectres," phenomena whose very appearance as such presupposes a specific evaluation of them? Why are we obliged to share in the proposed negative evaluation of such encounters? Why is it assumed that immanence does not have its own – immanent – means of redeeming such "spectres" that does so without the negation and denial of the phenomenon ("injustice") as such; a redemption without redemption as it were? Is this not what is meant by the expression "time heals?" Meillassoux's transcendent model of redemption – which he merely gives an immanent articulation – assumes the identity of redemption with an ultimately qualified affirmation of reality. This continues to fall short of an unqualified affirmation of immanence because it denies the possibility of a fully self-sufficient process of redemption that addresses and resolves phenomena such as "essential spectres" without defeating "injustice" or positing its ultimate deference to justice. Immanent redemption both interrupts the appearance of "essential spectres" as such – the "problem" as Meillassoux outlines it is a pseudo-problem born of a questionable evaluation of life – and, in any case, redeems on the basis of a *complete* rather than partial self-affirmation, without ultimately passing a negative judgement on any constitutive aspect of reality, without "improving" it. Faith in the redemptive powers of immanence itself entails the rejection of "hope" in the "religious" sense that Meillassoux seeks to retain and removes the requirement to contrive a way of thinking the possibility of God whilst accepting atheism.

It is clear that Meillassoux has little faith in the inherent religious capacities of immanence itself to complete the justificatory task he credits to a possible emergent "God." From the perspective of religious immanence life achieves a self-justification which retains, indeed affirms, senseless death. Its challenge to the human animal is to live with – indeed unconditionally affirm – all constitutive features of reality. Given that Meillassoux does not, of course, evoke a transcendent omnipotent and benevolent deity the shortfall in his affirmation of immanence in the text under consideration is subtle. It consists in both the very pursuit of a resolution to the "problem" of the "essential spectre" – that refuses to affirm, without qualification, a life so characterised and the ultimate referencing of the powers of immanence to one of its potential products – the "virtual" God.

This appeal to a product of immanence rather than to it per se points to a disparity in "Spectral Dilemma" between, on the one hand, an unambiguous endorsement of the ontological primacy of impersonal immanence (or "Chaos") – in relation to which any emergent, contingent God is an "effect" and, on the other, the ceding to the "virtual" God, if and when they exist, of the redemptive powers required to solve the problem that threatens immanence with meaninglessness. In a sense the critical concerns this raises are simply those familiar from notions such as "projection" (Feuerbach) and "spiritualization" (Nietzsche) which remind us that all "Gods" are simply reifications and personifications of the ideals and values sanctified by a historical culture. The (impersonal) forces that generate and venerate the values and affects thus personified are more ontologically fundamental than the "Gods" thereby produced (and mistakenly presented as the origin and ideal exemplar of the values in question). Yet this familiar problem of inverted ontological priority does not seem to impinge on Meillassoux's argument.

Throughout "Spectral Dilemma" a radical ontology is elaborated the religious nature and orientation of which is ignored at the expense of the pursuit of an incompatible existential problematic fundamentally reminiscent of its sources in an alien transcendent religious perspective. Meillassoux characterises reality or immanence as "a purely intelligible Chaos capable of destroying and of producing, without reason, things and the laws which they obey" (SD 274). Surely the question arises here as to why this sublime force of immanent Chaos is not to be the object of our religious yearnings? Why is the inherent impersonal divinity of Chaos itself not recognised and celebrated? How can the capacity of immanence to destroy *without reason* – which Meillassoux clearly endorses – be reconciled with the staging of the existential problem he demands it answers? A fully realised and affirmed religion of immanence sanctifies a reality that destroys senselessly, that is to say, that generates unjust death, death "without reason." For the immanentist all phenomena – including untimely death – carry their justification in themselves as their condition of becoming real. Justification is never deferred or pending. It is an internal, constitutive feature of immanent being, not a matter of external reference (even within an exclusively immanent field). In short, immanence knows no "essential spectres" – these are figments produced by a failure to affirm it. Not everyone who has suffered such loses is "haunted." There are alternative, more immanent, religious responses to such negativities than that articulated in "Spectral Dilemma." For this reason, the true immanentist would not honour or recognise the divinity of Meillassoux's "virtual God" were it to appear – such recognition presumably being a condition of divinity? Schooled in the lessons of Nietzsche's *Genealogy* these future immanentists would be very wary of any suggestion that unjust deaths call existence into question and that the only way to establish a harmonious relationship to such "spectres" is by the form of the overcoming of injustice in question. We shall now consider whether these broad reservations concerning the extent to which Meillassoux attains a fully realised religion of immanence are also applicable to his other main "religious" text thus far, extracts from *The Divine Inexistence*.

III

It is clear that Meillassoux *believes* in his "inexistent" or "virtual" God, the prospect of which he promotes with an unashamed "fervour" (DI 195) in a, frankly "messianic," pursuit of universal justice. There can be no doubting the sincerity of Meillassoux's ethical concerns or the unambiguous nature of his claim that their solution requires the existence, for the first time, of "God." Furthermore, both "atheism" and what Meillassoux terms "promethean humanism" (DI 213) are subjected to a sustained and rigorous critique clearly more intense than his, nonetheless unequivocal, dismissal of the "priest" and "religion." Indeed, in a clear indication that a "religious" sensibility is ultimately fuelling Meillassoux's ontologico-ethical project, he condemns belief in a transcendent God as "blasphemy and idolatry" (DI 235).

These features of Meillassoux's thought indicate the significant common ground between the realist religion of immanence implicit in the critical stance of the claims made in this paper and the evaluation of religion offered by Meillassoux in the texts under consideration. Indeed, for the religious immanence endorsed here, religion is *the* primary process of the real itself, that through which reality realises and celebrates itself most fundamentally. For the religious immanentist, the real is, first and foremost, religious in nature. From such a perspective the task of philosophy is to develop, independently of theology and science, a religious ontology (rather than an ontology of religion) in which this primacy is acknowledged and underlined. Such a stance is unambiguously *impersonalist* – it is the a-subjective essential processes of the real that are sanctified in such an approach. In this sense, the religion of immanence is uncompromisingly atheistic. Meillassoux, it is argued, fails to attain to the "religious atheism" demanded by the thought of unconditional immanence.

Meillassoux's endorsement of the value of "universal justice," particularly as articulated in relation to the alleged problem of the justification of an existence which contains "absurd" (DI 191) death, remains problematic. As argued above, the very articulation and pursuit of this "problem" reveals an unexamined sympathy with the constitutive values and affectivity of transcendent religion. A kinship only reinforced by the exploration of a "moral" variety of redemption by way of response. Meillassoux thereby simply uncritically grants ontological status to the values of a specific religious tradition. This pre-given sympathy for a particular religious sensibility ("Jewish Messianism," DI 228f.) threatens to condition, and thereby compromise fatally, Meillassoux's ontology of becoming and contingency and impede his access to *its* religious essence.

It is striking that for Meillassoux "religion" is synonymous with "transcendence" (in turn identified with the "transcendent") and the personal God of monotheism.[7] Whilst Meillassoux's sense that the complete discrediting of religion in this sense is a basic requirement for any philosophy of immanence, it is noteworthy that this seems to preclude the rehabilitation of the term "religion" per se and its redeployment – outside of the articulation of an ethics – in the elaboration of a primary ontology. For Meillassoux, "religion" seems to have an *exclusively* pejorative resonance. This blindness to the religious possibilities of reality itself is particularly striking in Meillassoux's texts, particularly as there are some occasions when he seems to glimpse the possibility of a genuinely *impersonal* religious viewpoint.

On the basis of his restricted, exclusively transcendent, conception of "religion" Meillassoux inevitably conceives his radical temporal ontology of contingency and becoming as an "irreligious notion of the origin of pure novelty" (DI 179), a "radically irreligious ontology" (DI 188). Making a powerful case for "advent *ex nihilo*" (DI 175ff.), in which time is identified as the creative and sustaining source of a "becoming-without-law" (DI 177), Meillassoux does not "deify" this impersonal creative becoming per se. He is, it seems, unable to appreciate the "auto-deification" that immanence achieves in simply opening and maintaining futurity, possibility and "promise" as such in the (finite) priority these have over whatever specific contingencies, in fact, arise.

Of course, Meillassoux does establish an important critical context, pursued throughout the texts under consideration, within which a religious conception of the nature of the real marks a surrender of the possibility of a "rational" account of it, thereby admitting its ultimate incomprehensibility with (irrational) "faith" the only alternative. To question the continuity of the real and the rational is, for Meillassoux, to unavoidably evoke a "hidden," "mysterious," source or origin of the world and thereby refer immanence to transcendence. Meillassoux's strategy here is as perilous as it is uncompromising. Metaphysical reason – or the endorsement of the "principle of sufficient reason" – is unseated in the name of a reason of immanence that is insisted upon in order "to neutralise in advance any religious exploitation of the 'miracle of life'" (DI 184). Whilst such a hyper-critical sensitivity to the undoubted opportunism and residual appeal of transcendent religion is laudable it, in effect, sacrifices the very possibility of accessing the religious essence of the real; that is to say, it strangles at birth the religious possibilities opened by the "death of God." Suffice to say that the more that Meillassoux's remarkable avowal of contingency sinks in, the stranger his conception of a non-metaphysical "reason" – charged with limning the course of the creative becoming of an essentially a-rational reality – seems. This is certainly not "rationalism" in any traditional, reductive or "algebraic" sense and it appears to include factors that seem to stretch its exclusively rational self-image to the limit. For example, Meillassoux writes approvingly of a "non-reflective intuitive perception of the world in its ultimate truth" (DI 197) and of an "amorous knowledge of the promise of the world" (DI 233).

To summarise, Meillassoux refuses to conceive the "staggering power of novelty of *our own* world" (DI 177) in religious terms. Although he offers a number of formulations to encapsulate his vision of a radically contingent immanence that have a decidedly religious resonance – "the simple blind power of becoming" (DI 212); the "innocent barbarism of pure contingency" (DI 213); the "amoral manifestations of the chaotic power of the world" (ibid.); the "limitless power of a time delivered to itself" (DI 220) – for reasons that become clear upon reading the ethical dimension of his project, none of these features of reality can be revered *in themselves* or taken, without further qualification, as religiously self-sufficient.

There are occasional hints that Meillassoux appreciates the possibility of religious immanence. As he states, "to believe in the existence of God is not to believe in God but to believe in existence" (DI 235). However, this breakthrough to a religion of the impersonal is not sustained. On another occasion Meillassoux seems to detect the possibility of the deification of the process of creative becoming or contingency per se. He acknowledges that it is possible to have a "fascination with the productive power of being" (DI 222) and to attain thereby what he terms, astutely, "a divinized Real" (ibid.). However, this aberrant possibility is dismissed as a "desiring the inhuman" (ibid.) which "amounts once more to a religious subordination" (ibid.) that can only induce "despair" (ibid.). In an evocative passage in *After Finitude* Meillassoux articulates his sense of the (immanent) "absolute" in terms which have a decidedly atheistic religious resonance. He writes of "an omnipotence equal to that of the Cartesian God [...] that has become autonomous, without norms, blind, devoid of the other divine perfections [...] capable of destroying without cause or reason [...] capable of destroying every determinate entity, even a God, even God."[8] That such a reality has, supposedly, to subsequently atone for its a-rational destructive force in relation to, for example, unjust death in order to justify its existence – the ethical dimension of Meillassoux's thought – seems particularly inexplicable – why not (simply) religiously affirm the creative ground of necessary contingency (or "time") so effectively evoked in its ontological pre-eminence?

Meillassoux's avowal of justice and the "hope" associated with its pursuit indicates that his "inexistent God" draws heavily upon a specific religious tradition. Whilst the attributes of Meillassoux's "God" are not fully elaborated in the texts in question it is clear that the notion is central to his thought. As he states, "God does not exist, and it is necessary to believe in God" (DI 233) and, in a similarly striking vein, the "philosophical divine [...] faces two catastrophic and constitutive illusions of contemporary history: *the first being that God exists, the second being that one can do without Him*" (DI 237). Meillassoux's audacious inventory of possible contemporary religious stances all concern the possible permutations of belief in, and existence of, God (however conceived).[9] His endorsement of a hitherto unforeseen and undefended possibility, "*believing in God because he does not exist*" (DI 238) cannot disguise his residual attachment to a notion – God – that, however radically conceived, remains – from the perspective of the atheism inherent to a religion of immanence – neither a sufficient nor even a necessary condition for religion. "God" always was, and always will be, a manifestation of a more primary phenomenon – religious desire. Perhaps it is the case that human beings, for instrumental reasons, have to "personify" impersonal processes of desire and are inclined, or even required, to "forget" having done so. If by "virtual God" Meillassoux were similarly giving expression to the values and desires that he endorses then the critical discussion could shift to a deeper level – the evaluation of the competing claim to ontological primacy of different economies of value and desire. Once it is accepted that the referent of the concept God is not a personal being then debate can commence regarding the values, desires, processes, etc., that are being sanctified towards the goal of identifying those deifications that are most native to immanence itself rather than being merely of anthropological origin. We might, for instance, hold that a thorough genealogical critique of value indicates that the impersonal forces celebrated in the pantheon of the ancient Greeks is more ontologically fundamental than those valorised in the God of Christianity. Unfortunately this discussion, in relation to Meillassoux's thought, is stalled due to his insistence on foregrounding as meaningful the concept of "God" rather than explicitly confirming that this is a shorthand for the desires and values he takes to be demonstrably ontologically primary. This remains strange as it is clear that Meillassoux, correctly, posits that reality is essentially an *impersonal* process (of life and time). For the immanentist – amongst whom we can presumably number Meillassoux, natural life is intrinsically a religious phenomenon. It is the task of human religions to align themselves with this reality in so far as they are able to do so, this being ultimately a physiological-psychological issue.

IV

Meillassoux offers a vision of justice and its alleged requirement for individual immortality or the "rebirth of bodies" (DI 189) and the advent of a currently inexistent God that is highly ingenious. His insistence that ethical values have an ontological foundation, and that the project of elaborating an "immanent ethics" (DI 187) is both coherent and urgent, are features of his thought that are to be endorsed enthusiastically. The critical issue does not concern the pursuit of an ontological ethics but rather its proposed content – which values exactly are identified as fundamental, as expressive of a self-affirmation of immanence.

For Meillassoux an "immanent ethics" concerns a "desire for life" itself presupposing a notion of "immortality." This is, ostensibly, an immortality of life itself, a non-transcendent eternity. It is noteworthy that Meillassoux acknowledges both Spinoza and Nietzsche as key precursors of the thought of immanent immortality. However, in a remarkably contentious formulation of significant import, Meillassoux describes both thinkers as the two pre-eminent "masters of irreligiosity" (DI 188)! Again, this seems strangely to grant the "moral" religions, i.e., those premised on the notion of the transcendent, a monopoly over religion per se (rather than simply acknowledge their historical success in misappropriating the naturalistic sources of religion). Such an alignment undermines the prospects for an atheistic religion of immanence – developed in different ways by both Spinoza and Nietzsche – as it fails to distinguish between such an ontologically grounded sense of religion and its pejorative alternative.

Meillassoux's conception of a non-transcendent immortality reflects aspects of his use of the term "God." In both cases the implication is that Meillassoux seemingly grants a primary ontological status to individuation. It's clear that Meillassoux has in mind the immortality of *individuals* (particular those who suffered an unjust death).[10] Religious immanence, in contrast, emphasises what it takes to be more real – non-individuated or trans-personal life itself, it is a religion of *impersonalism*. Indeed, *in extremis*, it is religiously affronted and ethically troubled by such an emphasis on the fate and possible redemption of any erroneously isolated, individuated life. For the immanentist, life is irreducible to its products whilst nonetheless being nothing without them. Death – however unjust – is not an occasion for the living being to gain finally an ontological independence unattainable whilst alive. It is, rather, the process whereby individuated beings' derivation from life itself is ultimately reaffirmed as they return to it. For the immanentist, death marks the terminal return to non-individuated life not its diminution or an escape from it.

Meillassoux works very hard to divest "hope" and the "messianic" of their transcendent lineage and to articulate their profounder, immanent, meaning. However, this seems to compromise the very contingency and becoming they are presented as confirming. To make this point crudely, any discussion of contingent becoming that goes beyond its affirmation per se, that is to say, any expression of preference or aim as to its trajectory or direction, all "aspiration" regarding becoming beyond its promotion as such, unavoidably conditions and thereby qualifies immanence. The challenge of religious immanence is, among other things, the requirement to affirm the intrinsic divinity of contingency regardless of what it produces. Furthermore, it is taken that such an affirmation of bare contingency per se is, in any case, much more likely to yield beneficial effects for the species than any attempted moral loading of it.

The notion of "hope" and its concern for the future course of contingency cannot be inscribed within a genuine philosophy of immanence without compromising it. The task, rather, is to articulate a non-pessimistic eradication of hope as this concept is irretrievably linked to the view that there is something wanting or lacking in temporal passage as such when it is affirmed for its own sake. Hope is the enemy of novelty. The future, as the very process of temporal becoming, does not depend on such human investment in it. For the religious immanentist the affirmation of futurity without hope is sufficient for joy.

A fundamental evaluative assumption underpins Meillassoux's entire pursuit of justice and, furthermore, in relation to a paradigmatic aspect of existence – death. For all his avowal of immanence Meillassoux seems to hold to the negative evaluation of an existence for which death is a constitutive feature. The phenomenon of unjust death raises for Meillassoux a quasi-theodicical problematic no less pressing, he suggests, for a philosophy of immanence as for its transcendent predecessors. To respond adequately to such a shortcoming in reality itself requires, Meillassoux argues, that we posit the possible advent of universal justice involving the redemptive resurrection of those who suffered such a death and the emergence of a hitherto non-existent God immune to – as not present at the scene of the crime – the "problem of evil" which so bedevilled his (in any case non-existent) putatively transcendent predecessor. For Meillassoux, as we have seen, it is the future possibility of such an "innocent" God that provides the allegedly required alternative to what, he argues, is the only other option – the despair of atheism.

In *The Divine Inexistence* we find the following statement:

> of all the injustices the most extreme is still death: absurd death, early death, death inflicted by those unconcerned with equality [...] those who exercise their humanity [...] *can only hope for the recommencement of our lives in such a way that justice would surpass the factual death that has struck down our fellow human beings.* (DI 191–92)

It is harder to imagine an expression of value further removed from those at the heart of a religion of immanence for which life is to be affirmed on the basis of its constitutive features (which include, ineliminably, death). To suggest in any way that there are aspects of its basic nature that generate a problem as regards its justification is – however subtly elaborated – to display one's pre-critical attachment to the constitutive *values* of transcendent religion. Leaving aside the details of their respective ontologies (in any case the least consequential issue) there would seem to be a total agreement here between Meillassoux and the "priest" he claims to despise in relation to this shared negative evaluation of life given the existence of unjust death, perhaps even death per se. Here we see how Meillassoux's conception of a philosophy of radical contingency can – in so far as it can only exclude from being phenomena that violate the law of contradiction – not preclude in principle being co-opted by the reactive desires of those incapable of affirming "this world" without qualification.

Of course, the religious realism advocated here will also balk at any apparent sourcing of religion per se in the ethical-existential dilemmas of a specific animal, however significant it seems to be. Ultimately, the issue might revolve around the "location" of religion within Meillassoux's thought. It appears that religion only enters his positive philosophy in the context of the realm of value (the "Good"). It is thus excluded from his theoretical account of the nature of the real, enabling this to be articulated in exclusively mathematical terms. For Meillassoux, it would appear, religion has no place in "first philosophy" itself. This precludes, without argument, the possibility that religion might be a constitutive feature of the ontology of the real itself prior to its ethical elaboration.

It is noteworthy that when Meillassoux discusses the philosopher from whom, in many respects, he has most to learn, namely Nietzsche, he endeavours to avoid a serious engagement through the construction of a "straw man." For Meillassoux, in a surprising endorsement of a received reading, Nietzsche supposedly promotes the "derealization of all value" (DI 205) rather than, and more accurately, being acknowledged as a fellow ontologist of value who argues convincingly for the primacy of an alternative economy of value and desire. More disturbing is Meillassoux's overt universalism – "everyone can desire the possible advent of a World of justice" (DI 228) because, presumably, "everyone" ought to experience despair at the thought of an existence which contains unredeemed unjust and untimely death. A normativity of sinister lineage operates in such passages supporting the exclusive appropriation of "justice" by a specific perspective.

For Meillassoux it is a question of retaining the "desirable content from the religious" (DI 230). Whilst his vision of an autonomous philosophical elaboration of religion is laudable, the identification of the "desirable content" of religion is, from the perspective of a religious immanence, problematic. Meillassoux's choice is clear – "the hope of justice supplied by the promise of Jewish time" (DI 229) which, as he notes approvingly, "breaks with the cyclical time of the pagans (a time that is inegalitarian since it is devoid of promise)" (DI 228). However, the "pagan" alternative, as described, would seem to be more rooted ontologically, more expressive of the nature of immanence itself.

In sketching an inventory of all the possible "links" between human beings and God, Meillassoux claims (probably correctly) that he is the first to elaborate and defend the possibility of "*believing in God because he does not exist*" (DI 238). The suggestion pursued here has been that this inventory needs to be extended to include *being religious because God will never exist*. Whilst, perhaps, "God" is not a logically contradictory concept, this, in itself, is not sufficient for possibility. The formulation of a religion of immanence precludes the possibility of God despite the logical legitimacy of the concept. Critical reflection on the notion of immanence establishes the impossibility not only of a necessarily existing being (the transcendent God) – a prohibition Meillassoux also insists upon[11] – but also, beyond Meillassoux, the advent of any logically possible (immanent) entity charged with the task of resolving alleged deficiencies in being itself and credited with the powers so to do. Yet how can the possible existence of a logically possible being be excluded a priori? The answer proposed from the perspective of a religion of immanence is that such an exclusion of possible existence is the product of ontological and genealogical critique founded upon an *affective intuition* of the nature of reality, a power formally akin to Meillassoux's reconfiguration of "intellectual intuition" which granted itself the right of a priori access to the nature of Chaos.[12] Just as Meillassoux's rational intuition knows that ultimate reality is contingent Chaos, so the religious immanentist's affective intuition confirms that the real is both intrinsically religious and atheistic.

Focused solely on impersonal processes, the religion of immanence would not, in any case, recognise such a "God" beyond a valorisation of any such figure as a particularly significant manifestation of impersonal life. In its religious self-expression immanence eschews not only its origination in God but any prospect of providing the conditions for the emergence of a contingent variant. For the religion of immanence to emerge two inherited appropriations and alignments need to be overthrown. Religion must be wrested back from God and nature from science. On the basis of these two dissociations the religion of natural immanence can be articulated. Meillassoux's doubtless impressive "religious" texts ultimately resist the advance of such a religious realism as they deny both its impersonalism and a-moralism.

notes

1 The positive task of articulating the religion of natural immanence rather than its deployment in the critique of transcendent religion obviously has a number of important historical exemplars including, among others, Spinoza, Nietzsche, Bergson and Bataille. The contentious issue of the significance of *historicality* to this discussion, particularly in relation to the "death of God" as an alleged necessary condition for the pursuit of the task in its most radical form, will not be addressed

explicitly in this paper. Such a consideration would require extensive discussion as it raises the incendiary topic of "pre-" vs. "post-"critical thought and the interpretation of the significance and orientation of Kant's project of critique, i.e., how "post-Kantian" thought is to be characterised. This context of historical interpretation and affiliation is, of course, particularly pertinent in relation to any discussion of the thought of Quentin Meillassoux who, in *After Finitude: An Essay on the Necessity of Contingency* (hereafter AF), has, in a brilliant fashion, refocused attention on the stakes involved.

2 I have benefited from the discussions of Meillassoux's work in texts by Ray Brassier and Graham Harman respectively.

3 For Meillassoux's account of the resources provided by the "religious"/"atheistic" dichotomy for addressing the "spectral dilemma" see SD 263–66.

4 For Meillassoux's reading of Hume's critique of necessity see AF 82–111; SD 270–75. Throughout we refer to the notion of the "virtual" God on the basis of Meillassoux's clear implicit alignment of his conception of the "virtual" and "inexistent God" respectively. For an example of this see SD 269.

5 This is a brief summary of SD 270–75.

6 Nietzsche §1052. Clearly Nietzsche's sustained focus, early and late, on the "problem of the meaning of suffering" in relation to the question of the justification of life (and in pursuit of life's immanent self-affirmation in this respect) is highly pertinent here.

7 DI 175f., 187f., 212f., 221, 223, 225ff.

8 AF 64.

9 See DI 237f.

10 See DI 188f.

11 This rejection of the possibility of necessary being is entailed by Meillassoux's ontology of necessary contingency. See AF 65.

12 See SD 273 for a brief account of how Meillassoux reworks the classical notion of "intellectual intuition."

bibliography

Ansell-Pearson, K., and J. Urpeth. "Bergson and Nietzsche on Religion: Critique, Immanence, and Affirmation." *Bergson, Politics, and Religion*. Ed. A. Lefebvre and M. White. Durham, NC: Duke UP, 2012. 246–64. Print.

Brassier, R. *Nihil Unbound: Enlightenment and Extinction*. Basingstoke: Palgrave, 2007. Print.

Burns, M. O'Neill. "The Hope of Speculative Materialism." *After the Postsecular and the Postmodern: New Essays in Continental Philosophy of Religion*. Ed. A.P. Smith and D. Whistler. Newcastle upon Tyne: Cambridge Scholars, 2010. 316–34. Print.

Harman, G. *Quentin Meillassoux: Philosophy in the Making*. Edinburgh: Edinburgh UP, 2011. Print.

Meillassoux, Q. *After Finitude: An Essay on the Contingency of Necessity*. Trans. Ray Brassier. London and New York: Continuum, 2008. Print.

Meillassoux, Q. "Excerpts from *L'Inexistence divine*." Trans. Graham Harman. *Quentin Meillassoux: Philosophy in the Making*. By Graham Harman. Edinburgh: Edinburgh UP, 2011. 175–238. Print.

Meillassoux, Q. "Spectral Dilemma." *Collapse* IV (May 2008): 261–75. Ed. R. Mackay. Print.

Nietzsche, F. *The Will to Power*. Trans. W. Kaufmann and R.J. Hollingdale. New York: Vintage, 1968. Print.

Urpeth, J. "'Health' and 'Sickness' in Religious Affectivity: Nietzsche, Otto, Bataille." *Nietzsche and the Divine*. Ed. J. Lippitt and J. Urpeth. Manchester: Clinamen, 2000. 226–51. Print.

Urpeth, J. "Reviving 'Natural Religion': Nietzsche and Bergson on Religious Life." *Nietzsche and Phenomenology*. Ed. A. Rehberg. Newcastle upon Tyne: Cambridge Scholars, 2011. 185–205. Print.

introduction

In the last few years, the work of Italian philosopher and cultural theorist Giorgio Agamben has begun to arouse great interest, not only among those immersed in philosophical and political theory but also among those in literary circles, critical-legal studies, theology, feminism, post-colonial thought and history.[1] Despite the critical-constructive work being done with regard to his writings, however, it has almost escaped notice that there has been little account given for Agamben's overtly *theological* claims by the discipline of academic theology proper.[2] This is a lamentable fact in many respects, most notably because his rereading of the theological tradition – as well as the centrality it plays in his work – contains significant consequences for the way theology is both perceived and performed on the whole. His work in fact often focuses on redefining traditional theological terms as philosophical ones, a process which appears in many ways to threaten the integrity of theological study as it has generally (historically) been conceived. This would include the complete revision (or, better, *profanation*) of concepts such as: revelation, redemption, original sin, profanation, the messianic, sovereignty, the sacred (especially through the figure of the *homo sacer*), glory, the "name of God" and creation, among others. Demonstrating his close proximity to theology time and again, these terms are continuously explored in his work in direct relation to the history of theology as well as theology's attempts to formulate its various doctrines and creeds, yet in relation to the history of Western thought. The disciplines of theology and of religious studies thus would be greatly amiss if they were to continue

colby dickinson

THE PROFANATION OF REVELATION
on language and immanence in the work of giorgio agamben

neglecting the radicality of his thought in producing their very self-definition.

It is with all of this in mind that I set out in this essay to articulate something of the many implications which Agamben's work holds for theological study specifically, its past, present and future. First, I intend to do so in relation to his (re)conceptualizations of language, something he formulates in light of particular historical glosses on the "name of God," and which ultimately leads him to a re-evaluation of the nature of the "mystical." In this fashion, I hope to show how Agamben's critique of mysticism can open theology to a new perspective on both its nature and its essence. Second, I will turn to the way in which Agamben lays out the political task of profanation, one of his most central concepts, in relation to the *logos* said to embody humanity's "religious" quest to find its Voice. By doing so, I am aiming to present Agamben's challenge to those standard (onto-theological) notions of transcendence which have been consistently aligned with various historical forms of sovereignty. And, finally, I will close with a section presenting revelation as being solely the unveiling of the "name of God" as the fact of our linguistic being, a movement therefore from the transcendent divine realm to the merely human world before us. By proceeding in this manner, I am trying to close in on one of the largest theological implications contained within Agamben's work: the establishment of an ontology that could only be described as a form of "absolute" immanence, an espousal of some form of pantheism (or perhaps pan*en*theism) yet to be more fully pronounced within his writings.[3]

language beyond the "mystical"

From the outset, Agamben's pursuit of the origins of language does not deviate too greatly from the heritage which seemingly bequeathed it to him. From more remote mystical traditions to the most "authoritative" theologians, Agamben draws from a rich history of theology in order to move, in effect, to a place that seems to be entirely beyond its contours. Even when he engages with philosophy directly, and this throughout several of his works (see, for example, his *Kingdom*; *Sacrament*; *Nudities*), it is from a quasi-theological-mystical interest that he analyzes its most fundamental propositions, thus giving rise to those comments which would see his work as being somewhat overtly theological (cf. the conclusions made in Durantaye; Dickinson, *Agamben*). For example, and as an introduction into these theological-philosophical juxtapositions in his writing, it is within the context of his depiction of the "coming community" that Agamben carefully situates his discourse in between two of the twentieth century's greatest philosophical minds, two thinkers who arguably also happened to achieve a remarkable proximity to the mystical: Martin Heidegger and Ludwig Wittgenstein. If their works appear at moments to be isolating the borders of the mystical rather than giving way to it (as Wittgenstein's famous comments on the "mystical" in his *Tractatus* appear to do, the only text of his to which Agamben refers) then so much the better for Agamben, who finds an oscillation between both thinkers to be the approximate dynamic he needs to achieve a liquidation of the mystical in its near entirety (Agamben, *Coming Community* 90–106; Wittgenstein).[4]

His immediate references are language and its relation to our being-in-the-world, that which has directly occupied thought, he tells us, since the time of Plato (Agamben, "The Thing Itself," *Potentialities*). Situating himself within this historical trajectory, Agamben begins to formulate the precision of his thoughts on language and the mystical in relation to the singular act of naming, something which reaches its pinnacle expression in the various historical attempts on the part of theologians to formulate (or *pronounce*) the "name of God." For him, the act of naming, that is, our attempt to deal with our being-in-the-world as revealed in the existence of language itself, is what should be considered as the primary "content" of religious expression. It is a fact of our (linguistic) existence that we are unable to state *as such*, and this gives rise to its "mystical" aura, to mysticism itself in fact and to any accompanying religious impulse. This is indeed what enables him to say that

> What remains without name here is the being-named, the name itself (*nomen innominabile*); only being-in-language is subtracted from the authority of language. According to a Platonic tautology, which we are still far from understanding, the idea of a thing is the thing itself; *the name, insofar as it names a thing, is nothing but the thing insofar as it is named by the name*. (Agamben, *Coming Community* 76–77; emphasis in the original)

This name is far from being understood by us, not solely because it is an obscure (and obscuring) thought in itself but because the relationship between them, between name and thing (as between language and being-in-the-world), constitutes the essential problematic of a determinate existence: how are we to move from one to the other? In other words, it forms the problematic contours *of transcendence itself*.

In its basic structure, this problematic nestled within the event of language itself, its "taking-place" as it were, reveals the fundamental division that grounds much of Agamben's ontological reflections. The partition between language and our being-in-the-world is opened up for him by those philosophical figures who were fascinated by our dwelling in language, such as Aristotle, Heidegger and Wittgenstein, figures who were no less interested in "theological" claims, even if they do not always express it directly as such. As he unfolds this event's history,

> The scission of language into two irreducible planes permeates all of Western thought, from the Aristotelian opposition between the first *ousia* and the other categories […] up to the duality between *Sage* and *Sprache* in Heidegger or between *showing* and *telling* in Wittgenstein. The very structure of transcendence, which constitutes the decisive character of philosophical reflection on being, is grounded in this scission. (86)

The difficulty of conceptualizing this scission rivals only the comprehension of the difficulties embedded within the structure of transcendence itself, or that which indeed limits any understanding within the realm of ideas – or even the realm said to be inhabited by the divine (Agamben, "What Is a Paradigm?," *Signature*). It is, however, precisely this domain of thought that Agamben, despite declaring that we are still quite unable to comprehend it, hopes to explicate as something immanent to our existence, the very fact of the existence of language itself (Agamben, "The Idea of Language," *Potentialities*; see also his *Sacrament*). For, as he will put it in another, earlier context, though one that nonetheless sets the course for these later ruminations, it is "Only because the event of language always already transcends what is said in this event" that "something like a transcendence in the ontological sense" can be shown to take place (Agamben, *Language* 86). This is a "transcendence" that does not ultimately transcend the world but remains entirely immanent to its linguistic economy, not necessarily even a transcendence-in-immanence because it in fact blurs the line between them (Agamben, *Time* 25). Seeing reality thus would in fact seem to confirm the significance of Agamben's taking up of Heidegger and Wittgenstein at the conclusion of his political formulations in his work *The Coming Community*.

The oscillation between these two contemporary thinkers with an almost mystical trajectory is subsequently consulted in relation to medieval theologians for whom the problem of a transcendence-in-language appears to be *the* fundamental philosophical problem, according to Agamben's reading. It is a short step from here to inspecting this "event of language" as the fundamental structure of our "being-in-the-world," one conceived in relation to the grounds and origins of what constitutes the theological in the first place. In an earlier work, *Language and Death*, Agamben renders it as such:[5]

> The transcendence of being and of the world – which medieval logic grasped under the rubric of the *transcendentia* and which Heidegger identifies as the fundamental structure of being-in-the-world – is the transcendence of the event of language with respect to that which, in this event, is said and signified; and the shifters, which indicate the pure *instance* of discourse, constitute […] the originary linguistic structure of transcendence. (26)

As the ontological difference that Heidegger had always claimed constituted the "always forgotten ground of metaphysics," this transcendent structure of our linguistic being is what captured the medieval mindset as being constituted solely under the auspices of the divine. It was the difference which, likewise, gave rise to the originary line of signification drawn between human beings and God, or between human and animals, as also perhaps between such divisions as gender and race (Agamben, *The Open*; cf. Calarco). And it is *this* difference which continues to haunt Western thought (and theology) to this day.

As Agamben frames the issue, while simultaneously expanding upon it:

> The opening of the *ontological* dimension (being, the world) corresponds to the pure taking place of language as an originary event, while the *ontic* dimension (entities, things) corresponds to that which, in this opening, is said and signified. The transcendence of being with respect to the entity, of the world with respect to the thing, is above all, a transcendence of the event of *langue* [language] with respect to *parole* [speech]. (26)

These reflections on the event of language lead Agamben back to the medieval theological tradition which perhaps best exemplified this step beyond the mystical and toward the root of language itself, a state *beyond* all grammars. In *Language and Death*, for example, he notes how in the work of the medieval logician Albert Magnus, faith is defined as

> a particular dimension of meaning, a particular "grammar" of the demonstrative pronoun, whose ostensive realization no longer refers to the senses or the intellect, but to an experience that takes place solely in the instance of discourse as such (*fides ex auditu*). (28)

Something thus occurs in the *parole* (speech) concerning the nature of *langue* (language) itself and is therefore central to comprehending the grounds of faith, something which Agamben passionately seeks further to discern.

The division between being-in-the-world and language is thereby asserted once more as the fundamental scission within Western thought (Agamben, *Infancy* 11ff.). This takes Agamben inevitably, and as one might nearly guess, from the reception of Magnus' work to the thought of his most-prized student, Thomas Aquinas. For Aquinas, similarly, the name of God can only be illuminated as "that in which no determinate being is named," the beyond of language that is not, however, to be confused with the realm of the mystical – but rather seen as the origin of language itself, located in a realm beyond utterance. There is therefore an opening made to "the infinite and indeterminate sea of substance," which, according to Aquinas, is said to be "a certain shadowy realm said to be inhabited by God" (29). In this fashion, and now by Agamben's reckoning, the "dimension of meaning at stake here goes beyond the vagueness normally attributed to mystical theology (which is on the contrary, a particular but perfectly coherent grammar)" (29–30). Consequently, and with no resources to describe this state inherent within the theological tradition, as Agamben relates, Christian ontological musings turn to Hebrew conceptions of the *nomen tetragrammaton*, "the secret and unpronounceable name of God," as the source of linguistic signification, hence as the source of language itself.

Theology has dealt often with the erasure of the verb "to be," the verb of existence stated in relation to God (cf. Marion). It is this very tenuous relationship which is subsequently mirrored in the various historical acts of trying to define the difficult relationship between mystical experience and language (*apophatics*). Agamben is no stranger to this theological tradition, as we have seen. Indeed, he is quick to extend this discourse even further in order to encompass the entire realm of human existence and thereby to demonstrate what a true nature beyond even the mystical might be, a proposition which in itself may actually approach an apophatic thinking itself *beyond* apophatics. For example, in another context, Agamben has recourse to describe the effect of the revealing of the origins of language upon the (Western, philosophical) subject as such:

> We see that the *cogito*, like mystical synderesis [the capacity to intuit the universal principles of humanity], is what remains of the soul when, at the end of a "dark night", it is stripped of all its attributes and content. The heart of this transcendental experience of the I has been signally described by an Arab mystic, Al-Hallaj: "I am *I* and the attributes are no more; I am *I* and the qualifications are no more [...] I am the pure subject of the verb." (Agamben, *Infancy* 34)

The experience of what it means to be human (the fundamental proposition behind the *cogito*) is revealed in its relation to language, in the verb "to be," and is as such founded upon this "I" that is said to exist without being, that is, in a state of indeterminable essence, "stripped of its attributes and content." The subject, the Western political, philosophical and theological subject of so much historical focus and scrutiny, lies in between its being-in-the-world and language; *it is founded upon this scission*, and this is a fact seemingly only approachable through recourse to near-apophatic language. It is also, and not surprisingly, what is "revealed" by Agamben as comprising the essence of the various mystical traditions arising from the three traditional monotheistic faiths.

The linkage of medieval mystical traditions to the transcendental subject of modern philosophy becomes a central recurring point of the reference for Agamben throughout his work, as well as the most immediate reference point for grounding his theological musings on the nature of language (see Agamben, *Sacrament*; *Potentialities*). This connection is indeed what lends him the confidence to go a step further and re-articulate the place of the subject in relation to language altogether (Agamben, *Infancy* 53). Therefore, in the context of perusing the decline of experience in the contemporary world, and of humanity's increased isolation of itself, Agamben declares, in a typically aphoristic manner, that: "The transcendental cannot be the subjective; unless transcendental simply signifies: linguistic" (54). And there it is: transcendence appears to be nothing more than a veiled attempt (within all religious aspirations) to articulate the origin of language, one that in the end ultimately fails. And its failure, in turn, gives birth to the subject of Western rational thought.

The entire problematic of transcendence, as well as its accompanying transcendental subject, is rendered visible through this fundamental disclosure: truth itself, and the truth of language's existence foremost among them, cannot be spoken of *in* language, or even *by* language, but must only be revealed indirectly.

And this, more than anything else, is what has given rise over time to the fundamental impulses behind our most basic religious and apophatic aspirations. As Agamben will most directly formulate the intersection of truth and language in his work *Infancy and History*:

> Truth is not thereby something that can be defined within language, nor even outside it, as a given fact or as an "equation" between this and language: infancy, truth and language are limited and constituted respectively in a primary, historic-transcendental relation [...] (58)[6]

An essential juncture is consequently reached through the determination of these coordinating points, one that still bears down significantly upon our definitions of humanity. For it is at the moment where infancy, truth and language all meet up that the constitution of the transcendental subject is effected. The subject, the intrusion of the "I" into language at the point of infancy, must join up with what Agamben, following Mallarmé, will term "la voix sacrée de la terra ingénue" (the sacred voice of the unknowing earth), the language that animals need not conceive because they are already inside it, but which humanity must enter into, must assert itself within: "Man, instead, by having an infancy, by preceding speech, splits this single language and, in order to speak, has to constitute himself as the subject of language – he has to say *I*" (59).

As Agamben will make foundational to his elaborations on the (in)distinction between human and animal, it is with this understanding that humans must continuously re-constitute themselves against an undefined (undecidable) background of this vacuous sacred language, this empty space wherein the human being is nearly engulfed in the world of its own animality (Agamben, *Open*). Humanity, finding itself in this situation, tries to posit itself as an unambiguous existence, despite the fact that it exists in reality (as "humanity") because of its fractured dwelling in language.

Citing Aristotle, Agamben is able to extract the overall import of these reflections by considering how

> [...] if language is truly man's nature (and nature, on reflection, can only mean language without speech, *genesis synechés*, "continuous origin," by Aristotle's definition, and to be nature means being always-already inside language), then man's nature is split at its source, for infancy brings it discontinuity and the difference between language and discourse. (Agamben, *Infancy* 59)

Unlike the world of animality, human beings develop a sense (or "faculty") for history, one grounded precisely in this difference and discontinuity. As it develops,

> It is infancy, it is the transcendental experience of the difference between language and speech, which first opens the space of history. Thus Babel – that is, the exit from the Eden of pure language and the entry into the babble of infancy [...] – is the transcendental origin of history. (60)

As Agamben seeks to stress over and again, we (humans) live in a post-Babelian world, one that must recognize its unique situation among the ruins of paradise and become conscious of the transcendental subject at history's center. And it is the logical, and inevitable, conclusion which follows from these premises that if the singular sacred voice within which all creation lives is continuously brought about by a fractured state through which humanity attempts to elevate itself above the rest of creation, then the task unique to humanity, one that humanity will ultimately have to embrace if it is to cease engaging in such violent reductions of being, will be one of *profanation*, of ridding itself of its various notions of "the mystical" which still haunt our world and which testify only to the fracture within our being without really doing anything about it.

the profanation of our dwelling in language

It should come as no surprise, then, that his most direct expression of the task of profanation inscribes itself at the heart of our dwelling in language. There are perhaps a number of ways that we might envision the "task of profanation" which Agamben sets before humanity, framed as the daunting and yet necessary operation of the "coming community" beyond the confines of our ongoing political representations (Agamben, *Community*; *Profanations* 73–92). It is a "going beyond" representation that seeks what lies before language and in which humanity more primordially dwells. In other words, it is a profanation which must emerge from a deeper intake of what truly lies at the origins of language and religious thought, indeed from the silence which is said to give rise to both. It is thus entirely beyond the grammar of the mystical-transcendental.

Like Aquinas' "infinite and indeterminate sea of substance" that is God, the mythogeme of a silent voice becomes a subsequent point of departure for Agamben's reflections on the origin of language, as well as theology's repeated attempts to articulate it. As he describes it, this mythogeme is the ontological ground of language itself, one that likewise appears in the earliest Christian mystical texts (Agamben, *Language* 63). Again, the history of theology becomes imperative for Agamben as he performs his critical philosophical examination of its mystical traditions. But it is also necessary for him to examine this theme if he is to conceive of this exercise as one of being both a philosophy of theology and a theology of philosophy, hence situating his reflections within the wide berth of the history of philosophy and the "end of metaphysics" often suspected as lurking within its core (see Phillips and Ruhr). Within this context, the distance between mysticism and the Western philosophical legacy of nihilism is quickly closed, though it is also re-opened from another angle and explored anew. Any attempt to think the negative foundations of speech will be a return to metaphysics proper, even if it is a metaphysics of nihilism, or a metaphysics not immediately recognizable as such.

Here, as he puts it,

> the Abyss (*buthos*) – incomprehensible, unformed, and eternally pre-existent – contains within itself a thought (*Ennoia*) that is silent, *Sigé*. And this "silence" is the

primary, negative foundation of revelation and of *logos*, the "mother" of all that is formed from the Abyss. (63)

Echoing what were to be the seminal biblical texts on the origin of the *logos* (Proverbs 8.22ff. and John 1.1ff.), Agamben, without entering into the debate on Christ's nature (*homoousios*), is content to merely circumscribe the boundaries of a silent abyss that could be said to contain God's name, to give rise to the *logos* and to all revelation. This abyss, however, is no small characterization of a rich theological tradition; rather, it forms the basis of how God's self is possibly comprehended. In this sense, there is little difference between language and God, at least insofar as the silence in question "negatively unveils the arch-original dimension of the Abyss to sense and to signification," and as such becomes "the mystical foundation of every possible revelation and every language, the original language of God as Abyss (in Christian terms, the figure of the dwelling of *logos* in *archē*, the original place of language)" (63–64).

Ranging over a broad tradition of – and often not discriminating between – ancient Gnostic texts and apocryphal works, Agamben is contented to conclude these reflections with reference to a strain of mystical thought found in Augustine's *De Trinitate*, where the "silent Word" comes to dwell "as unspeakable in the intellect of the Father" (64). Or, as another perspective on the subject would have it, "In its silent 'spiritual prayer,' the Syrian mystical tradition will seize upon this experience, recounting how a praying man arrives at a place where the language is 'more internal than words' and 'more profound than lips,' a language of 'silence' and 'stupor'" (65). This portrayal of "silence as Abyss" is what allows him to conclude that the distinctions often made between orthodoxy and heresy, at least in this regard, do not hold as such; indeed "[...] there is no absolute opposition between the Gnostic *Sigé* and the Christian *logos*, which are never completely separated" (65). The common ground between them, their shared proximity as it were, is a silence existing as

[...] the negative foundation of *logos*, its taking place and its unknown dwelling (according to Johannine theology), in the *archē* that is the Father. This dwelling of *logos* in *archē* (like that of *Sigé* in *Buthos*) is an abysmal dwelling – that is, ungrounded – and Trinitarian theology never manages to fully emerge from this abysmalness. (65)

Though he provides no further comment here upon these Trinitarian claims, Agamben's presentation of the relation between *logos* and *archē* is fundamental for the structuring of Western thought as a whole, and it is what will enable him later once again to pick up this strand of Trinitarian thought, as we will see in a moment (see Agamben, *Kingdom*). Here, however, culture itself, in all its varied and multiple forms, rests upon this silent unpronounceable abyss of dwelling from which everything else proceeds, akin only to Aquinas' "infinite and indeterminate sea" that is God and from which all else (and not just the Trinity) proceeds. All creation is to be found here (see Agamben, "Creation and Salvation," *Nudities*). As he phrases it,

> It is important to observe here how the "conscience" of Western philosophy rests originally on a mute foundation (a Voice), and it will never be able to fully resolve this silence. By rigorously establishing the limits of that which can be known in what is said, logic takes up this silent Voice and transforms it into the negative foundation of all knowledge. On the other hand, ethics experiences it as that which must necessarily remain unsaid in what is said. In both cases, however, the final foundation remains rigorously informulable. (*Language* 91; cf. Agamben, *Remnants*)

More than a "veiled theology," it is important to note, Agamben's remarks here appear as a nod in the direction of the very grounds upon which theology is deemed possible, the point of its articulation within an all-too-human thought. It is a solid movement perhaps best situated within the Kantian search for religious structures of thought, yet with a linguistic twist, that which aims toward depicting the grounds of possibility for the existence of theology *tout court*.[7]

The stakes for understanding the significance of this import are great. Agamben proposes nothing less than a reformulation of Western thought, or that which was once heavily based upon its onto-theological foundations. In fact, "The mystical is nothing but the unspeakable foundation; that is, the negative foundation of onto-theology" (Agamben, *Language* 91). The task of profanation, one of the central recurring terms in Agamben's philosophical corpus, is here opened up by the erasure of what presents itself as the mystical: "Only a liquidation of the mystical can open up the field to a thought (or language) that thinks (speaks) beyond the Voice and its *sigetics*; that dwells, that is, not on an unspeakable foundation, but in the infancy (*in-fari*) of man" (91). The conclusion is stark: this side of our infancy, the mystical has no currency, no economy in which it could be said to function. It is only an opening to our "infantile dwelling" in language which characterizes this age in which we live, the result of an "extreme nihilistic furor" which has seen the liquidation of all onto-theological masks (92). In turn, and as a result of this context in which we are immersed, metaphysics must make an attempt to "think the unthinkable," to comprehend its own negative foundations, but not to solidify them into a dangerous ontic political form, one that operates with traditional representational limits, as Heidegger had once been tempted to do (see Žižek 7f.). This is a case of language expressing its own existence; in short, to think that which he will term "the Absolute."

Indeed, thinking "the Absolute" becomes, for Agamben, a thinking beyond conceptual oppositions, beyond the scissions and negativity that mark our dwelling in this world (our being-in-the-world) (Agamben, "Paradigm," *Signature*). It is that which returns to its own place and which he will equate directly with the appearance of the Voice, for "Only the Voice with its marvelous muteness shows its inaccessible place, and so the ultimate task of philosophy is necessarily to think the Voice" (Agamben, *Language* 92). This is an "ultimate task" indeed, one that comes in many ways to mirror the Hegelian quest for the "absolute spirit," which in this case *is* language. To think the "Absolute," then, beyond any signified conceptual oppositions, appears as the primary initiative embedded in the search for Voice. And the *Absolute*, as it traverses the history of philosophical thought, becomes a process of crossing over both "negativity and scission in order to return to its own place" (92). This is the unending journey that characterizes the potential of our existence, or its "pure potentiality" as it were (Agamben, "On Potentiality," *Potentialities*; see also Bartoloni).

Much like Aristotle before him, and as his later development of the concept of "potentiality" will only further cement, Agamben turns to the problematic latent within the basic principles of thought in order to delve further into the line between potentiality and actuality, to move closer toward the former in the form of the *Absolute* which remains *Absolute* only through avoiding its concretion in actuality. For Agamben, this will mean that

> To think the Absolute *signifies*, thus, to think that which, through a process of "absolution," has been led back to its ownmost property, to itself, to its own *solitude*, as to its own *custom*. For this reason, the Absolute always implies a voyage, an abandonment of the originary place, an alienation and a being-outside. (Agamben, *Language* 92)

This is an abandonment that is at the same time an "absolution," something which will later be developed in his work under the banner of "profanation" (see Agamben, *Profanations*). It is also what he considers, following the German poet Novalis, to be a form of "nostalgia," or the "desire to be at home everywhere" and thereby "to recognize oneself in being-other" (92). It is only because philosophy is not "at home with itself" that it must entertain the journey back to itself, and this is exactly the process of "absolution" we search after (and often unknowingly), another theological term re-appropriated for its profane and entirely immanent usage. Implying the full theological cycle that would see human existence through from its entrance into language and the original sin of signification, to its absolution (as a sort of "forgiveness" to this state of sin) upon return to its infancy, Agamben circulates a pseudo-theological grammar that could be said, in many ways, to hinge upon the experience of being "born again," or perhaps even "resurrected," here expressed as a continuous act of returning to our infancy (see Agamben, *Idea* 98; *Infancy*).

What we again seem to find here, as elsewhere in his work, is an immanently profaned *re-birth to the theological itself*, one where the terms are destabilized and inverted, providing a significant reflection on the shift in perceiving God as immanent rather than transcendent, or as a form of transcendence-in-immanence or immanence-in-transcendence perhaps (Agamben, *Time* 25). Rather than perceive philosophy as *ancilla theologiae* (the "handmaiden") to theology, as Aquinas among others was wont to do, this movement is one that would rather posit philosophy as that which points toward the realm of the divine and theology as a purely immanent exercise, yet with an absolute gulf still existing between them. Philosophy remains in the domain of the immanent and transcendence remains muted, a silent partner on the other side of the abyss. Theology is therefore historically perceivable as an attempt to formulate this chasm between the immanent and the transcendent, but not strictly established as a discourse *on* the transcendent as such. Rather, it exists today as a sort of ruin, a failed historical (and political) attempt to bridge an unbridgeable gap.

Thus, when referring to these processes of a purely immanent absolution, Agamben can determine that philosophy is capable of doing what theology cannot, of providing us with a "revelation" of its own:

> Philosophy is this voyage, the human word's *nostos* (return) from itself to itself, which, abandoning its own habitual dwelling place in the voice, opens itself to the terror of nothingness and, at the same time, to the marvel of being; and after becoming meaningful discourse, it returns in the end, as *absolute* wisdom, to the Voice. Only in this way can thought finally be at home and "absolved" of the scission that threatened it from there where it always already was. Only in the Absolute can the word, which experienced "homesickness" (*Heimweh*) and the "pain of return" (*nost-algia*), which experienced the negative always already reigning in it habitual dwelling place, now truly reach its own beginning in the Voice. (Agamben, *Language* 93)

The Voice can be found in our immanent dwelling, and only established thus as "Absolute." This is the *ethos* of humanity, that which, according to Heraclitus, and as Agamben tells us, lacerates and divides into a demonic (*daiomai*, *daimon*) scission that must be fought and resolved. Philosophy, in many ways functioning here as if a quasi-"theological" paradigm in its own right, becomes for Agamben that which guides and renders meaningful the search throughout life for this return to our origins, our infancy.

Philosophy is hence considered to be a dialogue between humanity and its Voice, to be an embodied search for this Voice, one that faces the certainty of death at the same time as it attempts to "assure language of its place" (95). It is only through the death of the Voice that something like the end of philosophy could be considered, and this would likewise be the only possible way to experience a language without negativity or death. What it could also be, however, is the starting point of a theology *that has yet to be written*. The possibility of such an experience – no matter how difficult it might seem to formulate – is what appears to fascinate and center Agamben's philosophical quest. His articulation of this goal is consequently rather sharp: "What is a language without Voice, a word that is not grounded in any meaning? This is something that we must still learn to think" (95). And if this goal is achievable, then "[...] with the disappearance of the Voice, that 'essential relation' between language and death that dominates the history of metaphysics must also disappear" (95). Only then can *something else* appear.[8]

In short, theology is re-born as a purely profane endeavor. And so, as the task of profanation, or living in a world marked by God's absence, will later encapsulate, this experience of a language severed from negativity and death is one wherein humanity must regain a connection with its primordial infancy. It must face the terror of remaining within the absence of Voice, face, in fact, its own silence: "To exist in language without being called there by any Voice, simply to die without being called by death, is, perhaps the most abysmal experience; but this is precisely, for man, also his most *habitual* experience, his *ethos*, his dwelling [...]" (96). As his reflections upon the history of theology have already illustrated quite well, this is a state that was "[...] always already presented in the history of metaphysics as demonically divided into the living and language, nature and culture, ethics and logic, and therefore only attainable in the negative articulation of a Voice" (96). Breaking free of the Voice would posit a humanity freed from God, from the Name-of-the-Father that calls us into a realm of signified things and which constitutes the "original sin" of human-being (see Agamben, *Infancy* 32; *Community* 80). Thus it is with the eclipse of the Voice that it becomes possible for humanity to experience a more radical poverty of world than hitherto known (Agamben, *Language* 96). We must share in the animal's poverty of world, enter the Open space between things and realize ourselves anew (Agamben, *Open* 49–56). But it is a poverty, no doubt, that is also humanity's most natural state of dwelling and to which we must and will return to over and again. This, and little else, is what actually serves to situate the various discourses of his "homo sacer" series (see Agamben, *Homo*; *State*; *Remnants*). It is likewise the basis for what Lorenzo Chiesa, among others, has referred to as Agamben's "Franciscan" (because "poor" or "weak") ontology (Chiesa 162). As Agamben will himself speculate, it is perhaps within this loss, within this poverty, that humanity can sever the "chain of tragic guilt" that seems to exist without resolve, and enter a land free from pain.

Utilizing a Greek term that was to become so fond to Derrida (Derrida, *Name*), Agamben foresees how

This *chora*, this country without pain where no voice is spoken at death, is perhaps that which, beyond the Voice, remains to be thought as the most human dimension, the only place where something like a *me phunai* is possible for man, a not having been born and not having nature. (Agamben, *Language* 96)

This is a utopian dream, a hope that human nature can get beyond cultural significations, beyond political representations and enter into an unforeseen world that can only be conceived as rightly theological inasmuch as it is (paradoxically) free of the theological. In what might be the simplest clarification on what paradise could in fact be: "[...] here language [...] returns to that which never was and to that which it never left, and thus it takes the simple form of a habit" (97). For Agamben, of course, this state seems only just out of reach, something nearly obtainable that should yet be here. It is an eschatological dimension within being itself that will bear a strong affinity with the writings of St Paul, though perhaps more strongly with the early Paul, the new apostle for whom the Kingdom of God was so near at hand that he advised the earliest churches not to invest too heavily in their worldly life (see, for example, his advice on marriage in 1 Corinthians 7).

This is to conceive of the end of philosophy as the beginning of a theology of sorts, an entirely immanent theology that is severed from all false notions of sacrality which have come to dominate our world through their imposition and alignment with worldly forces of sovereignty – onto-theological notions based solely on the interplay of the sovereign and the *homo sacer* as constitutive of the political domain in which they were conceived (see Agamben, *Homo*; *State*). This previous model involved a theology of sacrifice and its requisite blood, and which functioned solely on the principles of (political) representation and exclusion. The profanation of such models, on the other hand, and as Agamben continues to edge closer toward, provides a theology almost unrecognizable to the historical discipline of theology proper because it is not wedded to a sovereign-transcendent political paradigm. Though this may appear to some like a headlong plunge into a form of political (or even theological) nihilism,[9] in many ways what Agamben offers is a revelation for those who are able to see it, for those with ears to hear it, a dismantling of our most fundamental representational contents and yet a presentation (or *revelation*) of our true nature.

revelation, or the name of god as presupposition of the existence of language

Revelation, for Agamben, is not a theological matter of little worth today, in many ways shattered and left in pieces only to be discarded by the secularized world in which we live. To conceive of it as such is to grossly misrepresent the trajectory of his thought as it bends toward its ultimate goal of profanation, something drawn by him in stark contrast to secularization, as well as the (often theological) materials with which he works, so diligently preserving their historical and conceptual implications (Agamben, *Profanations* 77ff.). Indeed, as he will there succinctly put it, it is the structure of revelation that conditions "the very possibility of knowledge in general" (Agamben, *Potentialities* 39). Thus, again and again, Agamben will approach the bedrock of our linguistic being, the origin of language and its potential for exposition through the richness of the Western theological tradition, revealing it for what it is and with the full consequences of this revelation on display. In this regard, Agamben chooses to focus his remarks on the manner in which language coincides with religious pronouncements on the nature of revelation, finding no complete similarity between them and yet no great difference either: that is to say, revelation expresses nothing if not the existence of language itself (Agamben, *Sacrament*). For this reason,

> It is this radical difference of the plane of revelation that Christian theologians express by saying that the sole content of revelation is Christ himself, that is, the Word of God, and that Jewish theologians affirm in stating that God's revelation is his name. (Agamben, *Potentialities* 39)

Both traditions in fact participate in the same essential task, the return of all our discourses to the foundation of language. For Agamben, "That there is language is as certain as it is incomprehensible, and this incomprehensibility and this certainty constitute faith and revelation" (42).

In these foundational terms, he conceives of language as the "nullification and deferral of itself," hence rendering the signifier as "nothing other than the irreducible cipher" of the "ungroundedness" at the heart of religious thought (44). This is a destabilization of traditional religious frameworks indeed, but also perhaps their only hope of survival. In this sense, he is able to underscore the remarkableness of a recent shift in the borders separating philosophy and theology, for, though it was once thought that theology determined its content to be "incomprehensible" to reason, it now stands to reason that the "incomprehensible" object is the very foundation of all comprehension itself (44–45). Despite this being the general trend of recent thought, however, Agamben, seeks to go beyond this formulation and to reawaken the true philosophical impetus to free thought of all presuppositions, even from the incomprehensibility that nonetheless remains along the margins of our world, supporting the world as it were (Agamben, *Idea* 32ff.). In this manner, Agamben intends to be free of theology, or at least of that historical discourse which has, and would, continue to attempt to comprehend what is, in the end, incomprehensible.

The Wittgensteinian proposition "How things are in the world is a matter of complete indifference for what is higher. God does not reveal himself in the world" (Wittgenstein §6.432) thereby gives Agamben the chance to attach new meaning to the claim that "God is dead," or rather than "dead," unknown just outside our world, which in a practical sense amounts perhaps much to the same thing. Our world is to be profaned, on track toward its "absolute profanation," and it is as if God were really dead, and as if that may or may not be expressing reality as such (see Johnson). This equivocity on the existence of God is really a claim intertwined with what could be called "God's abandonment" of the world, something intriguingly close to Jesus' dying words on the cross ("My God, my God, why have you forsaken [or abandoned] me?"). As Agamben himself will substantiate the point, "If God was the name of language, 'God is dead' can only mean that there is no longer a name for language. The fulfilled revelation of language is a word completely abandoned by God" (Agamben, *Potentialities* 45). This is an attempt to reside in the sphere of the profane, of the world abandoned by God, but also the space where the revelation of language is fulfilled, something which more than casually reflects the claims of the *logos* to be a fulfillment of the revelation which preceded it and which was seemingly accomplished at a moment when God appeared to be absent (or "dead"). Hence, it would seem to be a fundamentally *Christian* theological presupposition that defines the structure of Agamben's thought here, inasmuch as it is also a theological presupposition, he might otherwise argue, which attempts to disclose the (more) fundamental fact (in that it is ontologically prior) of our linguistic existence prior to any onto-theological presuppositions themselves.

In what appears to mimic the phenomenon of glossolalia (or "speaking in tongues"), and perhaps then also the tongues which are spoken at the origins of the Church in the moments soon after the *logos* had been fulfilled and thus departed (Acts 2.1ff.), Agamben ponders how humanity is left on its own to search for a way to communicate meaningfully – that is, "[...] human beings are thrown into language without having a voice or a divine word to guarantee them a possibility of escape from the infinite play of meaningful propositions" (45). There is only a radical sense of alienation, coupled indissociably with a profound sense of mission and energy, the rising perhaps of the potentiality of our being which yet refuses to become a concrete form in actuality. For this reason, the overlap between the seminal, biblical moments after the death of Jesus (the "death of God") and its alignment with Agamben's work are not to be underestimated, despite his at times only vague references to it. For Agamben, this is the moment indeed when no decision (historically aligned with the rule of sovereignty) need be made, and the gamble to move toward our infancy must be realized:

> Thus we finally find ourselves alone with our words; for the first time we are truly alone with language, abandoned without any final foundation. This is the Copernican revolution that the thought of our time inherits from nihilism: we are the first human beings who have become completely conscious of language. For the first time, what preceding generations called God, Being, spirit, unconscious appear to us as what they are: names for language. (45–46)

Perhaps this is also why the apostle Paul will later on appeal so strongly to Agamben, for it is Paul who appears most forcefully to grind all representations to a halt through an entrance into what could only surface as a kind of cultural death (Agamben, *Time* 47ff.; Badiou). This is the apostle indeed who considered all representations to be as nothing, and who considered the ultimate act of fidelity to the *logos* to be an embraceable death in imitation of this loss (Galatians 3.28; Romans 7). This is, as much as it was, a welcoming of the abandonment of God in order to work beyond speech and rather through the activity of the Spirit (Romans 8).

If Agamben is correct, then what Paul was actually advancing was a genuine profundity for religious thought historically, beyond the bounds of any one particular tradition, an embracing of the "nihilistic" tendencies that would see all political representations ground to a halt, their dialectics brought to a standstill in time. Like the curtain in the Temple that tore in half only to reveal that the sacred dwelling place of God was empty (Matthew 27.51) – an act of profanation if ever there was one – the only thing to be shown is the emptiness within, the fact that nothing was there except the words we had formed around the absent center in order to demarcate a "sacred space" in the first place.

This would be, for Agamben, the birth of a "religious nihilism" in Paul that *should* only become more central to religious thought over time (see, among others, Vattimo). As he elsewhere stresses the importance of this fundamental shift,

> Nihilism experiences this very abandonment of the word by God. But it interprets the extreme revelation of language in the sense that there is nothing to reveal, that the truth of language is that it unveils the Nothing of all things. The absence of a meta-language thus appears as the negative form of the presupposition, and the Nothing as the final veil, the final name of language. (Agamben, *Potentialities*, 47)

This last act of the Gospels, one ultimately of blasphemy, sacrilege and indeed profanation, was the essential gesture of a religious tradition brought to its pinnacle expression through the full disclosure of the *logos* that yet remains *completely immanent* to our world. Under these conditions, we may greet the *logos* as if nothing were transcendent to this encounter, because, truly, there *is* nothing transcendent within it. The *logos* is all that matters, as many a Christian commentator has been at great pains to demonstrate. But this realization is also a self-conscious revelation that Agamben cannot simply contend is a subtle retooling of the theological tradition, allowing it thus to continue along *as if* this revelation counted for little or nothing. As he summarizes the stakes,

> This is why for us, any philosophy, any religion, or any knowledge that has not become conscious of this turn belongs irrevocably to the past. The veils that theology, ontology, and psychology cast over the human have now fallen away, and we can return them to their proper place in language. We now look without veils upon language, which, having breathed out all divinity and all unsayability, is now wholly revealed, absolutely in the beginning. (46)

This is an interesting return to the *logos* in *archē* within a Western context wherein the "religions" of the past are being jettisoned at a great pace. Here, for Agamben, there is only a return to our infancy, to our "being-without-God" that is the absolute profanation of the world, one that may yet harbor a silent transcendence along its borders, forever inaccessible yet grounding everything that is said, one that exists, if at all, *as if* it did not really matter at all. This is to behold a revision of theology that perhaps appears to some to amount to a practical form of atheism. *Perhaps*. Or, it might appear as an absolute kenotic self-emptying of God to the world, perhaps even *becoming* the world itself as it were. And these two positions are as radically similar as they are *dis*-similar.

In effect, what this situation testifies to is the fact that there are at least two theologies at work in Agamben's thought: the historical theology of the Church, with the veils it seeks to throw over the eyes of humanity due to its failure to accurately articulate the "other side" of our infancy, one in league with a certain historical legacy of onto-theology, *and* yet another "theology," the *possibility* for another theology, one that remains as obscure as it is informulable, and yet perhaps the only true path open to the possibility of a divine presence in our world.

In the end, Agamben seems to point most directly toward the "idea of language" as a "vision of language itself," *as such*, as an "immediate mediation" which is the only way to reach the infancy of an "unpresupposed principle," a "pure potentiality" within our being (47). We are returned, in no uncertain terms, to the thoughts of Aristotle, to Aristotle's thoughts on thought, to the thinking of thought itself and the principle of the "unmoved mover" behind it all, the original ground of a form of deism or theism upon which Agamben appears in many regards to leave open as a genuine possibility. As he formulates this "belief" in relation to the work of the early Wittgenstein, a reference point to which he returns again and again in contemplation of the linguistic immanence of our being: "The proposition that God is not revealed *in* the world could also be expressed by the following statement: What is properly divine is that the world does not reveal God. (Hence this is not the 'bitterest' proposition of the *Tractatus*)" (Agamben, *Community* 91). Not the "bitterest" proposition perhaps because it leaves open the chance that God still does exist, though there is no way of knowing whether or not any such conjecture is possible. This in fact remains the silence of that which would be transcendent (Agamben, *Time* 25). Thus also are the terms traditionally reserved for theological dogma displaced and inverted, illustrating again the proximity of Agamben's thought to theology, but also his absolute distance. As he himself will demonstrate it,

> Revelation does not mean revelation of the sacredness of the world, but only revelation of its irreparably profane character. (The name always and only names things.) Revelation consigns the world to profanation and thingness – and isn't this precisely what has happened? The possibility of salvation begins only at this point; it is the salvation of the profanity of the world, of its being-thus. (Agamben, *Community* 90)

And this remark is immediately followed by another parenthetical one: "This is why those who try to make the world and life sacred again are just as impious as those who despair about its profanation" (ibid.).[10]

There is a new theological horizon opened up by this disclosure, one that is not as "new" perhaps as it might seem: it is the only option left to this form of rationalism, one that Spinoza had detected many years ago and which is the only sufficient successor to the deistic model of Enlightenment thought (Spinoza). This option is an immanent materialism, an immanent theology, as Antonio Negri has noted concerning Agamben's position (Negri).[11] It is perhaps even a form of pantheism or panentheism, as difficult to discern in Agamben's work as it was in Spinoza's (see Dombrowski; Keller). Yet everything in Agamben's thought seems only to draw toward this conclusion: "The world – insofar as it is absolutely, irreparably profane – is God" (Agamben, *Community* 90). And, perhaps, this is the real revelation that Agamben has been working toward all along.

conclusion

As a theorist who works directly to end all forms of cultural and political representation, to bring about a pure presentation beyond representation as a philosophical task (see Ross), Agamben here comes closest to those theological frameworks (mainly feminist and post-colonial) which would likewise envision some model of pantheism or panentheism as preferable to the transcendent-male-sovereign ones that have already dominated centuries of theological discourse. Indeed, feminist theology, for its part, has consistently looked towards pan(en)theism as a way to open up humanity to the immanence of our gendered being (Daly; Jantzen; Welch), something which theology as a whole has been loathe to acknowledge, but for which Agamben's formulations might provide yet another avenue of expression. The problem of merging such a view with an historically revealed religion, however, remains a central problematic needing to be more fully resolved (Surin; Crockett). Yet it is a problematic that Agamben's work situates within the confines of traditional onto(theo)logical arguments, thus, in a sense, attempting to provide a more "solid" foundation outside these confinements than those critical discourses which would only seek to destabilize and not re-construct the traditions they dismantle (see Dickinson, *Canon*). For this reason, Agamben's theological profitability, I would conjecture, should only increase over time, offering a plausible ontological re-working for theological claims of representation, including those most dogmatic representations (i.e., of Christ's nature, of the Trinity, etc.) that seem perhaps otherwise forever unalterable.

notes

1 See the main monographs on his work to appear recently, including: Calarco and DeCaroli;

Dickinson, *Agamben*; Durantaye; Mills; Murray; Murray, Heron, and Clemens; Norris; Wall; Watkin; and Zartaloudis.

2 See the small but growing amount of writing which has attempted to deal with his more "theological" claims, though mainly in relation to his work on St Paul, including: Bertozzi; Bretherton; Boer; Colilli; Dickinson, "Canon"; Meyere; and Presutti. Despite these minor attempts, however, there has been little reflection yet made on the implications his work holds for theological study on the whole, as I am here otherwise attempting to investigate.

3 Agamben himself, of course, does not use either term to describe his writings, thus rendering any attempt to affix such a label to his work as extremely difficult. His overlap on just such a point is no doubt akin to those attempts to discern what form of divinity is at work in Spinoza's philosophy, the source from which many of Agamben's reflections flow. See Deveaux; Mason.

4 Quentin Meillassoux, however, argues that it is precisely Heidegger and Wittgenstein who have been responsible for the proliferation of "mystical" thought in a contemporary philosophical context. See his *After Finitude* 41–42.

5 Durantaye's choice to exclude *Language and Death* from his otherwise near comprehensive survey of Agamben's work means that he misses an opportunity to explain how this work in particular frames so much of Agamben's subsequent research trajectory. See Durantaye.

6 The term "infancy" can be understood as more of a state that we dwell in rather than a chronological space that we regress to. In many ways, it comes to mirror the Christian language concerning one's "rebirth" that similarly follows a regressive pattern of thought. Cf. Watkin 13.

7 Agamben's "linguistic turn" engaged in relation to Kant is something which he is inspired to pursue based on the reflections of Walter Benjamin on language. See, among other places, Agamben, *Infancy* 50–1.

8 It should be noted here, however, that it is precisely this issue of appearance (and of representation then) that needs to be nuanced in relation to Agamben's own formulations. This is where, I would add, the Pauline "division of (representational) divisions" plays such a fundamental role in Agamben's attempt to go beyond – though without discarding completely – the realm of representations on the whole.

9 The charge of "political nihilism" in Agamben's work has been leveled by Ernesto Laclau, "Bare Life or Social Indeterminacy?" and William Rasch, "From Sovereign Ban to Banning Sovereignty," both found in Calarco and DeCaroli 22 and 107 respectively. Catherine Mills also draws attention to the viability of his end to politics in the conclusion to her *The Philosophy of Agamben*.

10 And, he continues:

> This is why Protestant theology, which clearly separates the profane world from the divine, is both wrong and right: right because the world has been consigned irrevocably by revelation (by language) to the profane sphere; wrong because it will be saved precisely insofar as it is profane. (90)

11 There is, of course, a deep resonance in Agamben's thought with that of Gilles Deleuze precisely on this point. See Deleuze, *Expressionism*, as well as his essay "Immanence: A Life." Agamben deals with these texts in his essay "Absolute Immanence" in *Potentialities*.

bibliography

Agamben, Giorgio. *The Coming Community*. Trans. Michael Hardt. Minneapolis: U of Minnesota P, 1993. Print.

Agamben, Giorgio. *Homo Sacer: Sovereign Power and Bare Life*. Trans. Daniel Heller-Roazen. Stanford: Stanford UP, 1998. Print.

Agamben, Giorgio. *The Idea of Prose*. Trans. Michael Sullivan and Sam Whitsitt. Albany: State U of New York P, 1995. Print.

Agamben, Giorgio. *Infancy and History: On the Destruction of Experience*. Trans. Liz Heron. London: Verso, 1993. Print.

Agamben, Giorgio. *The Kingdom and the Glory: For a Theological Genealogy of Economy and Government*. Trans. Lorenzo Chiesa with Matteo Mandarini. Stanford: Stanford UP, 2011. Print.

Agamben, Giorgio. *Language and Death: The Place of Negativity*. Trans. Karen E. Pinkus and Michael Hardt. Minneapolis: U of Minnesota P, 1991. Print.

Agamben, Giorgio. *Nudities*. Trans. David Kishik and Stefan Pedatella. Stanford: Stanford UP, 2010. Print.

Agamben, Giorgio. *The Open: Man and Animal*. Trans. Kevin Attell. Stanford: Stanford UP, 2004. Print.

Agamben, Giorgio. *Potentialities: Collected Essays in Philosophy*. Trans. Daniel Heller-Roazen. Stanford: Stanford UP, 2000. Print.

Agamben, Giorgio. *Profanations*. Trans. Jeff Fort. New York: Zone, 2007. Print.

Agamben, Giorgio. *Remnants of Auschwitz: The Witness and the Archive, Homo Sacer III*. Trans. Daniel Heller-Roazen. New York: Zone, 2002. Print.

Agamben, Giorgio. *The Sacrament of Language: An Archaeology of the Oath*. Trans. Adam Kotsko. Stanford: Stanford UP, 2010. Print.

Agamben, Giorgio. *The Signature of All Things: On Method*. Trans. Luca D'Isanto with Kevin Attell. New York: Zone, 2009. Print.

Agamben, Giorgio. *State of Exception, Homo Sacer II, 1*. Trans. Kevin Attell. Chicago: U of Chicago P, 2005. Print.

Agamben, Giorgio. *The Time that Remains: A Commentary on the Letter to the Romans*. Trans. Patricia Dailey. Stanford: Stanford UP, 2005. Print.

Badiou, Alain. *Saint Paul: The Foundation of Universalism*. Trans. Ray Brassier. Stanford: Stanford UP, 2003. Print.

Bartoloni, Paolo. "The Stanza of the Self: On Agamben's Potentiality." *Contretemps* 5 (2004): 8–15. Print.

Bertozzi, Alberto. "Thoughts in Potentiality: Provisional Reflections on Agamben's Understanding of Potentiality and its Relevance for Theology and Politics." *Philosophy Today* 51.3 (2007): 290–302. Print.

Boer, Roland. "The Conundrums of Giorgio Agamben: A Commentary on a Commentary on the Letter to the Romans." *Sino-Christian Studies* 3 (2007): 7–36. Print.

Bretherton, Luke. "The Duty of Care to Refugees, Christian Cosmopolitanism, and the Hallowing of Bare Life." *Studies in Christian Ethics* 19.1 (2006): 39–61. Print.

Calarco, Matthew. *Zoographies: The Question of the Animal from Heidegger to Derrida*. New York: Columbia UP, 2008. Print.

Calarco, Matthew, and Steven DeCaroli, eds. *Giorgio Agamben: Sovereignty and Life*. Stanford: Stanford UP, 2007. Print.

Chiesa, Lorenzo. "Giorgio Agamben's Franciscan Ontology." *The Italian Difference: Between Nihilism and Biopolitics*. Ed. Lorenzo Chiesa and Alberto Toscano. Melbourne: re.press, 2009. 149–63. Print.

Colilli, Paul. "The Theological Materials of Modernity (On Giorgio Agamben)." *Italica* 85.4 (2008): 465–79. Print.

Crockett, Clayton. "The Truth of Life: Michel Henry on Marx." *Words of Life: New Theological Turns in French Phenomenology*. Ed. Bruce Ellis Benson and Norman Wirzba. New York: Fordham UP, 2010. 168–77. Print.

Daly, Mary. *Beyond God the Father: Toward a Philosophy of Women's Liberation*. Boston: Beacon, 1973. Print.

Deleuze, Gilles. *Expressionism in Philosophy: Spinoza*. Trans. Martin Joughin. New York: Zone, 1990. Print.

Deleuze, Gilles. "Immanence: A Life." *Two Regimes of Madness: Texts and Interviews 1975–1995*. Ed. David Lapoujade. Trans. Ames Hodges and Mike Taormina. New York: Semiotext(e), 2006. 384–89. Print.

Derrida, Jacques. *On the Name*. Ed. Thomas Dutoit. Trans. David Wood, John P. Leavey, Jr., and Ian McLeod. Stanford: Stanford UP, 1995. Print.

Deveaux, Sherry. *The Role of God in Spinoza's Metaphysics*. London: Continuum, 2007. Print.

Dickinson, Colby. *Agamben and Theology*. London: Clark, 2011. Print.

Dickinson, Colby. *Between the Canon and the Messiah: The Structure of Faith in Contemporary Continental Thought*. London: Continuum, 2013. Print.

Dickinson, Colby. "Canon as an Act of Creation: Giorgio Agamben and the Extended Logic of the Messianic." *Bijdragen* 71.2 (2010): 132–58. Print.

Dombrowski, Daniel A. *A Platonic Philosophy of Religion: A Process Perspective*. Albany: State U of New York P, 2005. Print.

Durantaye, Leland de la. *Giorgio Agamben: A Critical Introduction*. Stanford: Stanford UP, 2009. Print.

Jantzen, Grace. *Becoming Divine: Towards a Feminist Philosophy of Religion*. Bloomington: Indiana UP, 1998. Print.

Johnson, David E. "As If the Time Were Now: Deconstructing Agamben." *South Atlantic Quarterly* 106.2 (2007): 265–90. Print.

Keller, Catherine. *Face of the Deep: A Theology of Becoming*. London: Routledge, 2003. Print.

Marion, Jean-Luc. *God without Being: Hors-Texte*. Trans. Thomas A. Carlson. Chicago: U of Chicago P, 1995. Print.

Mason, Richard. *The God of Spinoza: A Philosophical Study*. Cambridge: Cambridge UP, 1997. Print.

Meillassoux, Quentin. *After Finitude: An Essay on the Necessity of Contingency*. Trans. Ray Brassier. London: Continuum, 2008. Print.

Meyere, Job de. "The Care for the Present: Giorgio Agamben's Actualisation of the Pauline Messianic Experience." *Bijdragen* 70.2 (2009): 168–84. Print.

Mills, Catherine. *The Philosophy of Agamben*. Montreal: McGill-Queen's UP, 2009. Print.

Murray, Alex. *Giorgio Agamben*. London: Routledge, 2010. Print.

Murray, Alex, Nicholas Heron, and Justin Clemens, eds. *The Work of Giorgio Agamben: Law, Literature, Life*. Edinburgh: Edinburgh UP, 2008. Print.

Negri, Antonio. "Sovereignty: That Divine Ministry of the Affairs of Earthly Life." *Journal for Cultural and Religious Theory* 9.1 (2008): 96–100. Print.

Norris, Andrew, ed. *Politics, Metaphysics, and Death: Essays on Giorgio Agamben's* Homo Sacer. Durham, NC: Duke UP, 2005. Print.

Phillips, Dewi Z., and Mario von der Ruhr, eds. *Religion and the End of Metaphysics*. Tübingen: Mohr Siebeck, 2008. Print.

Presutti, Fabio. "Manlio Sgalambro, Giorgio Agamben: On Metaphysical Suspension of Language and the Destiny of its Inorganic Re-absorption." *Italica* 85.2-3 (2008): 243–72. Print.

Ross, Alison. *The Aesthetic Paths of Philosophy: Presentation in Kant, Heidegger, Lacoue-Labarthe and Nancy*. Stanford: Stanford UP, 2007. Print.

Spinoza, Baruch. *Ethics, Treatise on the Emendation of the Intellect, Selected Letters*. Trans. Samuel Shirley. Cambridge: Hackett, 1992. Print.

Surin, Kenneth. *Freedom Not Yet: Liberation and the Next World Order*. Durham, NC: Duke UP, 2009. Print.

Vattimo, Gianni. *After Christianity*. Trans. Luca D'Isanto. New York: Columbia UP, 2002. Print.

Wall, C.T. *Radical Passivity: Levinas, Blanchot and Agamben*. Albany: State U of New York P, 1999. Print.

Watkin, William. *The Literary Agamben: Adventures in Logopoiesis*. London: Continuum, 2010. Print.

Welch, Sharon D. *A Feminist Ethic of Risk*. Rev. ed. Minneapolis: Fortress, 2000. Print.

Wittgenstein, Ludwig. *Tractatus Logico-Philosophicus*. Trans. C.K. Ogden. London: Routledge, 1996. Print.

Zartaloudis, Thanos. *Giorgio Agamben: The Idea of Justice and the Uses of Legal Criticism*. London: Routledge, 2010. Print.

Žižek, Slavoj. *The Ticklish Subject: The Absent Centre of Political Ontology*. 2nd ed. London: Verso, 2009. Print.

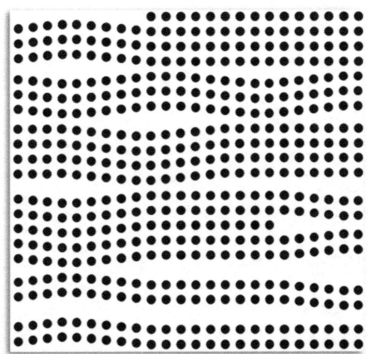

> But that the existence of a human being who lives merely for enjoyment (however busy he might be in this respect) should have a value in itself even if as a means to this he was as helpful as possible to others who were likewise concerned only with enjoyment, because he participated in all gratification through sympathy: of this reason could never be persuaded.
>
> Kant, Critique of the Power of Judgment 93[1]

introduction

In a radio conference broadcast in 1965, one of the thinkers that would shortly afterwards appear at the theoretical forefront of the students' movement, namely Herbert Marcuse, presented an interesting diagnosis concerning the contemporary political conjuncture.[2] Marcuse claimed that contemporary Western, post-revolutionary society can no longer be analyzed in the classical – Marxist – terms of a violent physical, i.e., military, oppression and dominance of one class over the other. Modern societies no longer have to maintain the repressive statist form of dictatorship, only functioning by relying upon a material system of production that includes the few and exploits the many. The newness of the modern (capitalist) political society is now based upon a new model of non-violent inclusion of (nearly) anyone into the material sphere of production, itself based on a global avoidance of the reduction of labor forces to a constantly perpetuated struggle for survival and to and on a reduction of alienation to the necessary minimum of sustaining the maintenance of collective wealth. All this is achieved by the specific state form of modern (capitalist) society; that is,

frank ruda

IDEALISM WITHOUT IDEALISM
badiou's materialist renaissance

by democracy. For Marcuse, it is precisely the democratic framing of the contemporary political situation – its *democratic condition*, as I put it – which introduces a yet unknown stability of domination he later calls "repressive tolerance."[3]

That for Marcuse the democratic guise of domination nonetheless remains a strict form of domination, although it abolishes any physical violence, springs from one implication that Marcuse marks when he states that the democratic frame of political society suspends any thinkable political alternative to it. Thereby it suspends all possible forms of rational and emancipatory, singular or collective political self-determination by immediately assimilating any critical or revolting position.

Criticism and subversion belong to and are assimilated by the very society that is supposed to be criticized or subverted. Modern political society under the emblem of democracy is thus a closed society; a political world in which any self-determination and self-organization of the people or the workers by definition always remains bound to the rationality of the already existing order and its laws. For Marcuse it is precisely this closeness of the political situation, the suspension of any true political alternative or choice and the installation of a fully fixated regime of what is and will be possible that ultimately leads to a total absence and loss of any emancipatory capacity.[4] Marcuse only mentions in passing that this contemporary political situation implies an understanding of what a true "life" is and should be; a life proper for mankind. It is this conception that determines not only how subjects should lead their life but also the material options of different ways of life that are imaginable. This fixation of these ways of life, as Marcuse indicates, leads to the fact that subjects are only able to maneuver within the given order, in the present state of things, and without knowing it they take for granted that which is declared as possible therein. It is a life that is conceived of as essentially determined by its own proper material needs, material interests and desires meaning in the end, determined by its finitude. This form of life remains what Marcuse calls a "comfortable edifice of dependence [*Hörigkeit*]."[5] For him such a situation has a fatal effect on any form of life living in it. It directly leads to the loss of any capacity to negate, of the ability to simply say "no" to the possibilities or options offered by the state of things. Life under the democratic paradigm lacks the capacity of determinate negation. As a result one can claim that where negation is the proper motor of any form of dialectics – especially of any form of materialist dialectics – the democratic framing of life leads to an absence of dialectics.

It is precisely here that one can find a systematic link and an important difference to the analysis of contemporary situations as present in the works of Alain Badiou, especially in his attempt to fundamentally rework materialist dialectics.[6] Furthermore, for Badiou, what is essentially at stake in contemporary situations is a (materialist) conception of what it means to live, of what living truly can mean. However, what distinguishes his materialist diagnosis from any form of orthodox Marxist or renewed-orthodox Marxist analysis is the thesis that what is lost under the present circumstances is the capacity of determinate negation: for Badiou what is lost, rather, is the capacity of what I call *determinate affirmation*. Determinate affirmation, that is to say, to say "yes" to something, to a choice, not only marks a subjectively necessary category but also is closely linked to a reworking of negation too.[7] This is a task for philosophy. Philosophy, under the present conjuncture, has to rethink dialectics and to rethink materialism. My central thesis in what follows is that it is precisely in the work of Badiou that one can grasp the task of philosophy today and this task consists in introducing a *materialist re-naissance* here and now. However, to grasp under which conditions this has to take place, a few further preliminary remarks are needed. This is to better understand the one decisive question that for Badiou any philosopher has to answer: what is the philosophical situation today?

One can resume one essential aspect of this situation today in the following formula: God is dead and idealism died on the very same day. Today, these not only seem to be quite self-evident statements, their evidence, if one follows Badiou, comes from the fact that they have been historically proven correct by Georg Cantor amongst others.[8] As Badiou has argued, the development and history of philosophy can be understood as what he called a "creative repetition":[9] there is always something unchanging in the form of the philosophical gesture, but there also can be transformation inside philosophy due to "the pressure of some events and their consequences" that bring along a "necessity for transforming some aspects of the philosophical gesture."[10] This is why one can say that as soon as one of the conditions of philosophy, namely mathematical science,[11] offers the insight that there cannot be a set of all sets[12] (and this is precisely the proof of God's death), the old (ideological) battle between idealism and materialism that determines philosophy gains a new face.

The split that separated idealism from materialism reappears inside materialism. This is arguably an abstract yet still possible rendering of how one might historically conceive of the distinction between democratic materialism and materialist dialectics, between a materialism that insists solely on the given material sphere and a dialectical approach that emphasizes an exception to this very sphere, which is introduced on the very first pages of Badiou's *Logics of Worlds*.[13] If idealism is impossible the only thinkable option is materialism. But as materialism still is an "ideological atmosphere,"[14] one could assume that the repetition of the distinction between idealism and materialism within materialism brings forth an idealist materialism – a bad one – and a good and proper materialist materialism. Nevertheless, I will attempt to argue that the contemporary inscription of the distinction between idealism and materialism into the domain of materialism itself should be understood in a different and more dialectical way. To cut a long story short: I will claim that one can and should differentiate between two different forms of materialism but that the inscription of the distinction of idealism and materialism into materialism also contains a moment of reversal. Therefore, I will argue that democratic materialism can be understood as a materialism without idea, a materialism without idealism and that any materialist dialectics, at least following Badiou, as a philosophical enterprise should instead be conceived of as what I will call an *idealism without idealism*. In order to justify this claim a short detour is helpful, since there have already been attempts made to develop a materialist-dialectical thought in close proximity to idealism.

It was the early Marx in his argument with Hegelian dialectics who was in a structurally similar position. He attempted to formulate a materialist position by working through Hegelian dialectic. One first outcome of this endeavor was the famous Feuerbach theses.

I will therefore first investigate the 11th thesis[15] on Feuerbach, as it presents in a slogan one of the most crucial issues that any materialist-dialectical approach has to take into account: the question of change. This is why I will initially reconstruct in a short and rather sketchy manner three different paradigmatic readings of Marx's 11th thesis on Feuerbach that all center on the theme of how the task of philosophy should be understood in relation to a materialist notion of change and what this change means. What is at stake here is that any materialist thought, via Marx, is confronted with how to conceive of the relation between change and philosophy. In a second step I will then show how, starting from the philosophical coordinates that Alain Badiou provides, one can begin to draw a diagonal towards these three readings. This will lead me to a short discussion of a certain number of Badiou's statements and to a short reconstruction of his reading of Hegel in *Logics of Worlds*. I will eventually conclude by gathering a certain set of coordinates that have to be taken into consideration for a Badiousian reading of the 11th thesis that can be conceived of as an axiom of contemporary renewed materialism.

change the world, change interpretations, changing interpretations

What followed the first publication of the Marxian thesis on Feuerbach are many different attempts to present original and coherent reconstructions of Marx's thesis 11, which is, as Georges Labica put it, apart from the fragments of the pre-Socratics, "the shortest document of our occidental philosophical tradition."[16] But at the same time the relevance and validity of the thesis as such was never called into question: The 11th thesis has been read as containing the "ingenious germ of a new world-view, Weltanschauung," as Karl Korsch formulated, that "hammers to the ground all joists of the hitherto bourgeois philosophy."[17] Wolfgang Fritz Haug insisted that the theses in general and the 11th thesis in particular are "discursive events that become more and more significant the more we move away from them."[18] One can easily distinguish three different ways to read Marx's 11th thesis on Feuerbach. All of them were quite influential throughout history, although it is at the same time not always possible to separate each of these three readings from the others in all respects. The first and maybe the most classical reading insists on the necessary transition from "interpretation of the world" to "changing it": this first way of reading thesis 11 I want to call a *transformative reading*. Its decisive feature lies in the emphasis that interpretation is nothing but a form of contemplation *ante rem* and should be replaced by a practice – also by a philosophical practice of cognition – *in rem*. Paradigmatically one can find such a reading in the first volume of Ernst Bloch's *Principle of Hope* in which he claims that against the hitherto contemplative pseudo-philosophical interpretations of the world, the 11th thesis invites us to "set sail" to arrive at "a new, an active philosophy, one of which, in order, to achieve change, is as inevitable as it is suitable."[19] The *transformative reading* does not necessarily imply the dissolution of philosophy. Rather, it insists on the need to develop a new, a different – one might say materialist – philosophy; a philosophy of praxis that is able to revolutionize the world. Therefore, it sides with Engels' inclusion of the "but" between the two sentences of the 11th thesis ("Philosophers have hitherto only interpreted the world in various ways; BUT the point is to change it"). In this sense the 11th thesis articulates an axiom of any true philosophical praxis to come: one first has to change the very notion of change – from mere abstract interpretation to active practical intervention – and consequently this will produce a change of philosophy. Philosophy has to leave behind the "interpreting donkeys of induction," as Engels once put it, assume its proletarian-revolutionary task and replace the empty discourse of varying interpretations with real and true change. This is the proper materialist task of philosophy that the 11th thesis encapsulates.

Hence, there will be no real change as long as, again Bloch put it, as there is no "philosophical change [...] thus a change according to the stipulations of the analyzed situation, of dialectical tendencies, of objective laws, of real possibilities."[20] Only by becoming a philosophy of praxis, this transformative reading insists, can real change occur. This change will realize a true materialist stance by sublating the proletariat and will sublate the proletariat by realizing philosophy, to borrow this expression from Marx himself. Philosophy itself, by becoming practical, by introducing real change and not only varying interpretations, can relate to, or more precisely: it is and can become an actual material truth filling the lack of practical change by introducing a move from theory to praxis. This first reading can therefore be rendered in the following formula: replace the abstract and idealist speculation that seeks to reduce the world to a unifying principle, comprehend the necessary dialectical laws of history and consequentially change the very notion of change. Thereby you will not only change philosophy but you will also change the world.

Competing with this *transformative reading* of the 11th thesis, one can find a second one that I want to call a *reversing reading*. This second reading starts from a different angle: it starts by emphasizing, to put it in the words of Günther Anders' *Outdatedness of Human Beings*, who is a paradigmatic figure of this reading, that: "It does not suffice to change the world. We do it anyway. And to a large extent that happens even without our involvement. In addition we have to interpret this change."[21] While the first reading insists on the necessity of a transformative replacing of the absence of change with the primacy of real change, this second reading emphasizes the actuality of ongoing change. That is to say: the world is constantly changing and what we therefore urgently need are renewed and adequately transformed interpretations. Although there seems to be a conservative subtext to this rendering of the Marxian thesis 11, there also seems to be, to a certain extent, an implied reference to the old Hegelian model of philosophy as owl of Minerva – an owl that begins its flight when the day turns to dusk. Philosophy has to change because the world itself changes and its task is not only to keep up with the transformation of the world but also to render it comprehensible. As Theodor W. Adorno put it in his posthumously published *Lectures on the Negative Dialectics*: "To interpret means to point at something, not necessarily to recognize and accept it. My thesis: Interpretation is criticism. Without interpretation in this sense, there can be no true practice [...]"[22] This second reading of Marx's thesis agrees with the first one concerning the idea that it is necessary to transform philosophy. But its proponents disagree with regard to what philosophy should be and should become after this transformation, because, as again Adorno put it, "this vantage point from which philosophy appears to be obsolete has itself become obsolete in the meantime. And it would be ideological in its turn, namely dogmatic, if we were not to concede this."[23] The *reversing reading* defends the idea of a transformation of philosophy but its foundation lies in the very principle of the world (i.e., in change) to which philosophy relates. Changing philosophy under given conditions in a necessary first step to keep up with what is anyhow happening in the world: for the world is a constantly changing one and its change is the result of multifold practices, technologies, modes of production and so forth. Hence, philosophy has to change but this first and foremost means it has to change its own proper medium, that is: the interpretation it gives of the world. As Elias Canetti once put it: "The reality has changed to such an enormous degree that a first presentiment of it puts us in the state of perplexity [...] Therefore we need interpretation."[24] If the central motive of the first reading of Marx's thesis was to realize a materialist philosophy in the form of a real practice, the central Leitmotif of the second reading is that one first has to understand the change already happening in the world to be able to intervene in it, and it therefore posits a primacy of interpretation.

Now, one can find another reading that claims neither that philosophy has to change *for* the world to change (as the *transformative reading* does), nor that philosophy and its interpretations of the world have to change *because* the world itself has already changed (as the *reversing reading* does). The third reading, which I want to call an *exaggerating reading*, produces another twist in its rendering of Marx's 11th thesis. As, for example, Slavoj Žižek, whom I consider amongst others to be a proponent of this reading, claims: "The past is never known 'as such', it can become known only in the process of its transformation, since the interpretation itself intervenes in its object and changes it."[25] This reading envisages the task formulated in the 11th thesis also, as the first reading does, as a task of philosophy and it shares with the second reading that change has to be related to interpretation. But the essential punch-line put forward here is expressed in the idea that only through exaggerated interpretations will the world actually change. This idea can also be found in Adorno. Just recall his dictum that psychoanalysis is only true in its exaggerations.[26] Only exaggerated interpretations can break with the onesidedness and seemingly natural order of the world and produce actual change in it. The excess of "exaggeration" is supposed to undermine the falsity of any contended balanced or stable totality of the world. And the undermining effect manifests itself precisely by means of interpretation. Hence interpretation of the world is intervening in it. Thereby philosophy can only act upon the world and change it, as also Heidegger, in an interview commenting on Marx's thesis 11 involuntarily implied, via its interpretation.[27] This is also why the exaggerating reading necessarily has to claim that it is right now precisely not the task to change the world.

For this would only lead to remaining stuck in the ideological coordinates of the world, which prevent any real change from happening. As Žižek asserts:

> the first task today is precisely NOT to succumb to the temptation to act, to directly intervene and change things, but to question the hegemonic ideological coordinates [...] If, today, one follows a direct call to act [...] it will be an act WITHIN the hegemonic ideological coordinates [...] The kind of

activity provides the perfect example [...] of doing things not to achieve something, but to PREVENT from something really happening, really changing [...] It fits the formula of "Let's go on changing something all the time so that, globally, things will remain the same."[28]

Not to fall for the spontaneous temptation to act within the world but to withdraw from it and to interpret it, this is the true task of any materialist philosophy. Only via interpretations can the world change because it is only via interpretations that philosophy can relate to what will have been possible in the past and seems to be foreclosed in the present. By this relation to the past, this past will shed its proper light on the contemporary world and open up new possibilities of change within it.

To summarize: either materialist philosophy changes the world by becoming actively and practically engaged in the process of changing it (this is the *transformative reading* oriented towards the *future* realization of philosophy) or interpretations have to change because the world itself has already changed (this is the *reversing reading* that is oriented towards the *present* actuality of change in the world) or finally only exaggerated interpretations are able to change the seemingly stable coordinates of the given world (this is the *exaggerating reading* that is oriented towards that which in the present world is foreclosed from the *past*).

This sketchy and not exhaustive formalization of different possible readings of Marx's thesis 11 provides a sufficient arsenal for constructing another type of reading of Marx, a reading that in some sense lies diagonal to the other three. I will simply call it a *materialist-dialectical reading*. My central claim is that for constructing this new type of reading the works of Alain Badiou offer hugely helpful tools. In them one can find passages that seem to be connected to all three readings delineated above, and to properly comprehend why this is the case it is necessary to reconstruct their internal relationship. This is not only instructive to understanding Badiou's philosophical position in a more adequate manner but also because thereby one can derive an interesting proposal of how to comprehend a contemporary renewal of materialism. My guiding question in the following selective reconstruction of Badiou is therefore: is there a fourth type of reading Marx's thesis 11?

I will seek to show that a fourth type of reading Marx's thesis, the materialist-dialectical reading neither claims, as the *transformative reading* does, that philosophy should be realized as practical intervention into the world that would be able to directly change it, nor does it claim, as the *reversing reading* does, that the only task of philosophy is always to offer renewed different interpretations of the change (always already) taking place in the world. Finally, it will also not claim, as the *exaggerating reading* does, that it is only via interpretations that the world itself and its past can be changed. I will demonstrate that starting from Badiou's conception of philosophy, reading the 11th thesis implies that (1) philosophy itself has to change and has to perform an active gesture, an act that is properly philosophical but cannot be rendered in terms of interpretation; (2) that in the contemporary situation this act is directly related to the world, or better, its absence (I will return to this below); (3) that one can conceive of this philosophical act in a way that is different from the *transformative* and *reversing reading* of the 11th thesis as it is neither critical nor always already determined by the change occurring in the world; and (4) that one can take up the *exaggerating reading* by insisting that the philosophical act can help to counter the hegemonic ideological coordinates by returning to a seemingly obsolete moment from the past, namely to idealism. But this return is only a means for a renewed assertion of materialist thought.

the philosophical act between change and interpretation

I want to start from four complex statements which can be found in Badiou's oeuvre whose systematic combination will help to construct the aforementioned fourth type of reading Marx.[29]

(1) The first statement is from a brief text called *Philosophy as Creative Repetition*. It reads: "The philosophical act is always in the form of a decision, a separation, a clear distinction" and it continues that this is the reason why it "always has a normative dimension. The division is also a hierarchy."[30] Philosophy, for Badiou, as one can see here, is an act; it is an active inscription of a line of demarcation that always also implies a hierarchy between the two sides it demarcates. To give an example of such lines of demarcation one can think of the philosophical distinctions between truth and opinion or between ethically good and bad actions, etc. Such an act of demarcation is also present in the beginning of one of Badiou's magnum opuses, namely *Logics of Worlds*. Therein he starts by delineating two different axioms of a materialist conviction, or, more precisely, of a materialist ideology. This book starts with the very act of introducing a hierarchic distinction between two forms of materialism that rely on two different axioms: on one side the axiom is: "There are only bodies and languages" – this is the axiom of what he calls democratic materialism – and on the other there is the axiom of what he calls materialist dialectics which is: "There are only bodies and languages, except that there are truths."[31] According to Badiou, what remains in the very center of philosophical practice is the active inscription of a hierarchical distinction (and this may also be the distinction between idealism and materialism or that between two different forms of materialism). The first element relevant for a reading of the 11th thesis from a Badiousian perspective is the philosophical act, the philosophical decisive gesture of demarcation.

(2) The second quote is from the 2007 book on *The Meaning of Sarkozy* in which Badiou claims:

> Why am I justified in saying that the real axiom of the dominant politics is that the unified world does not exist? Because the world that is declared to exist and that supposedly has to be imposed on everyone, the world of globalization, in uniquely a world of objects and monetary signs, a world of the free circulation of products and financial flows [...] In their crushing majority, the women and men of the supposed "world" [...] have no access at all to this world.[32]

This quotation is an analysis of the ideology of the contemporary historical situation. The decisive action of philosophy (the first element) therefore has to be linked to the precise historical coordinates within which it is situated. And this situation today can be described as follows: (1) it is governed by the "phallic name of our present," as Badiou put it in one of his seminars. And this name is democracy;[33] (2) it is introduced and maintained precisely after the historical disappearing of idealism. And this is done by means of a materialist conviction that represents the contemporary ideological form of capitalism: democratic materialism that I mentioned above; and (3) the two first elements relate to an even broader category that Badiou names contemporary nihilism.[34] The contemporary form of nihilism *on the one hand* implies a reduction of human beings to their animal substructure: if for democratic materialism there are only bodies and languages and any individual is nothing but a finite body with a specific potential to enjoy that should be realized in a particular language, a particular cultural practice appropriate to it, human beings are reduced to their individual interests that are culturally mediated, reduced to their needs and small private fetishisms.

This is why the nihilism put forward by the democratic materialist ideology is incorporated in two different versions of hedonism today: the libertarian and the liberal.[35] If the libertarian one defends an enjoyment without boundaries, the liberal one differs from it only slightly by its presupposition that enjoyment is basically purchasable. Hence, there is no contradiction in being at the same time both a liberal libertarian hedonist and a democratic materialist. For democratic materialism it is the instant that counts, the very moment in which the body enjoys. This is what Badiou called in his seminars the "the prostitutional element"[36] in democratic materialism. Anyone is reduced to the commercial capacities of their body. It should already be evident that for Badiou the fundamental framework needed for such a conception of materialism is perfectly well provided by capitalism, which is the regime that fully takes into account that man is an animal. An animal whose passions are oriented towards objects and it is precisely these objects that are endlessly circulating. This implies that in the current situation there seems to be no passion that is not centered on an object. In fact it is in this sense that Badiou defines capitalism as "the only regime which absolutizes the idea that man is an animal."[37] It thereby produces a very specific animalist conception of life: life as survival; a life that Badiou in his seminars, flirting with Agambenian or Benjaminian terminology, also calls an "empty life."[38]

On the other hand, if the contemporary historical situation within the hegemonic democratic materialist coordinates and within the nihilism put forward by capitalism is determined by the absence of a common world, this implies that the most elementary symbolic places are abolished (the places of antagonistic positions towards that which is to live, for example). The supposed common world is constitutively structured by a split, a division between the included and the "excluded." "Excluded is the name for all those who are not in the real world,"[39] as Badiou put it, or even more rigidly in an earlier variant of the same claim: "Excluded is the sole name for those who have no name, just as 'market' is the name of a world which is not a world."[40] Therefore, on the one hand there is, in the given historical coordinates, a radical reduction of human beings to their animality whose passions are centered on always circulating objects (i.e., commodities) and there is nothing but these objects, nothing that would not enter into circulation (i.e., commodified). The general (and abstract) equivalence of circulating objects thus relates to the general equivalence of human animals and their passions, desires and needs that themselves circle around the circulating objects. And: the given historical situation is one in which the supposed symbolic coordinates no longer construct the transcendental of a common, of a single, world. This is due to the fact that the seeming equivalence of all different languages and bodies, individuals and communities is based on an antecedent and more fundamental split that separates the pleasures of wealth from the desires of the poor, and in this way the transcendental of the world of globalization is effectively only sustainable under the condition of a separation of two different worlds. This fundamental split – that delineates two radically separate degrees of existence[41] (i.e., the rich and the poor) – separates those who are more different than others and also those who do not share the same norms of circulating objects and animals from the ordinary, normal human being. The contemporary situation, in which the philosophical act has to take place, is hence, according to Badiou, a situation which is marked by the absence of a world. A situation of an absent world under the given capitalist ideological – that is democratic materialist – coordinates, i.e., a situation of nihilism. The second element that therefore seems to be essential for a reading of the 11th thesis from a Badiousian perspective is the concrete analysis of concrete historical situations that relates philosophy to the present "world" or situation.

(3) The third quotation that I want to refer to is again taken from *The Meaning of Sarkozy* and it reads like this:

> We must assert right at the start the existence of a single world, as an axiom and a principle [...] And that the internal consequences are inevitably political actions based on the indifference of differences, which means: politics is an operator for the consolidation of what is universal in identities [...] To assert therefore that "there is only one world" is a principle of action, a political imperative.[42]

Within the wordlessness of given capitalist conditions and their democratic materialist ideology this quote indicates a precise point of affirmation. Being embedded into a specific historical situation, the affirmation of the existence of one and only one world is a very precise counter-affirmation to the very given coordinates of this situation.

I want to call such an affirmation, with reference to its formal structure, a *determinate affirmation*. One can therefore conceive of the philosophical determinate affirmation, that there exists one and only one world, as a philosophical act, a decisive philosophical gesture which first and foremost affirms the primacy of that which universally is the same and common to all the different identities within the situation. It does so by affirming an indifference to differences. It thereby inscribes a hierarchy between universality (what all particular identities have in common) and particularity (the particular identities). But, what is also important in this quote is that it not only implies an act of philosophy that could be qualified as an act of determinate affirmation. At the same time this determinate affirmative act of philosophy produces an important result: it can provide a principle of orientation that can guide action, political action. That is to say: what happens to the given situation if one seeks to act in full accordance with this affirmation, in accordance with the affirmation that there is something like one world (from which no one is excluded per se). Such a philosophical determinate affirmation can offer orientation or the possibility of a cognitive mapping, as Fredric Jameson[43] once put it. It can do so by affirming a concrete point that can be upheld no matter what. This point of orientation opposes the given hegemonic coordinates. A philosophical act which here and now affirms the very existence of a world can become an imperative for political organizations which consequently attempt to conduct any of their actions in accordance with this imperative or principle. A determinate affirmation thereby in its formal structure is always a determination of a clear and precise point. The term "point" here means first and foremost this: either you share this affirmation or you do not. All differences of the existing world are for a moment condensed in this decision.

So a philosophical act is not only a matter of an inscription of a line of demarcation but it also contains an affirmation of a concrete point. In this case one is dealing with a *point of existence*, with the affirmation of the existence of one world. The third element that is relevant for a Badiousian reading of the 11th thesis is a *determinate affirmation*, an affirmation of a concrete point that cannot in any sense be deduced or derived from the given ideological coordinates.

(4) The fourth statement I want to dwell upon is the 15th point from Badiou's *Third Sketch for a Manifesto of Affirmationism*. It reads: "It is better to do nothing than to work officially in the visibility of what the West declares to exist."[44] This quotation at first glance might seem to be somehow out of context with regard to the three others. Nonetheless, I contend that it strongly relates to them. Not only is the name that Badiou refers to here – "the West" – the signifier that introduces the fundamental split into the "world" which makes it into a non-world, moreover: to do nothing does not simply mean to stop acting. Rather, it implies not to follow the given and hegemonic coordinates of what a meaningful action is any longer. This statement therefore can also be read as a counter-affirmation against the present state of things, again in terms of determinate affirmation: it not only claims that one should resist the temptation to act but rather that *one should do nothing*. This "nothing" can only be understood in relation to the visibility that, as Badiou claims, the West generates. One might put this as follows: what exists for democratic materialism is primarily circulating objects and animals, bodies and languages, or again: individuals and communities. Therefore, what Badiou emphasizes when he claims one should do nothing can also be rendered as: one should actively *do no-thing*.

To do no-thing then means not to produce or re-produce objects (some-thing-s) that then circulate on the market. Doing no-thing also means to produce something which has neither an objective exchange value nor an objective use value precisely because it is not an (objective) object and thus cannot be reified. To do no-thing in this precise sense can mean to do something that is not considered to be useful at all, at least not useful if one shares the perspective of the given declaration of existence. To do no-thing can mean to do something that subtracts itself even from the exchange and use-value category and that can thereby counter the objective abstraction of equivalence exchanges and the real abstraction that reduces human beings to their animality. But, as one might immediately ask: what is considered not to be useful still differs according to the historical coordinates in which it takes place. In any given situation, some-things, some forms of practice, seem not to be useful at all. They, say, take the form of a utopian project or might even appear suspicious. But at the same time, what exactly appears not to be useful – it might be an abstract mathematical investigation, a philosophical enterprise, or something comparable – changes with the historical specificity of the situation. One therefore has to ask: what is considered to be not useful or maybe even to be a suspicious type of activity today? A first tentative answer could be: what seems to be not useful today is everything that challenges the reality principle and the naturalized evidence of the democratic materialist ideology. The fourth element that is relevant for a reading of the 11th thesis from a Badiousian perspective is the counter-affirmation of actions that engage in allegedly useless, futile, maybe even dull practices and can therefore, from the perspective of the given situation, only appear as if one were doing nothing.

To summarize, the four elements thus far gathered, which play a crucial role in a possible Badiousian reading of the 11th thesis, are: (1) a philosophical act that is an inscription of a hierarchical distinction; (2) an element of concrete analysis of the concrete contemporary situations and hegemonic ideological coordinates that relates philosophy to the present world; (3) a determinate affirmation that cannot be deduced from these given ideological coordinates; and (4) an active form of doing nothing, of doing no-thing. I want to propose that it is precisely the last of the four elements that gives consistency to the diagonal that I seek to construct with regard to the first three readings I presented at the beginning. I want to render this more plausible by drawing on a very simple insight: one thing that is certainly not complying with the axiom and the consequences of democratic materialism and that seems completely obsolete today is precisely to engage in the reworking of an idealist position. I want to substantiate this claim in the following and final part of this article.

materialist dialectic or: idealism without idealism

In his recent seminars, from 2005 onwards, Badiou has remarked that, faced with desperate or even disastrous times, what is often needed is "a new renaissance" that "renews the fundamental questions of existence; questions which today do not seem to have any sense any longer."[45] He then elaborates this idea of a "renaissance" in a later session of his seminar, by stating the following: "has idealism become the support of emancipatory thinking today? This temptation always exists but it is futile to go along this path because idealism is a truly dead configuration."[46] Idealism is a dead configuration since scientific practice has forever falsified its basic axioms (namely that there could be something like one totality, one type of infinity, etc.). Yet any renaissance, if it is a true rebirth, implies to a certain degree a resurrection of the dead; it brings back the dead in a new guise, in a new appearance and in a new body. Against this background one might not be surprised that two of the most crucial references of Badiou's whole oeuvre are Plato and Hegel – thinkers most people today would qualify as idealists.

I am not suggesting here that Badiou simply returns to idealism but that Badiou's *renaissance of materialism* nonetheless, and maybe paradoxically, can be read as a *renaissance of idealism*. But why should that be and what is the precise form that this renaissance takes? In one of his books Badiou characterized the contemporary situation as follows: "Just as in around 1840, we are faced with an utterly cynical capitalism, which is certain that it is the only possible option for a rational organization of society." And he continues by comparing this contemporary situation to the one that "Marx and his friends"[47] were facing in their time. Somehow deviating – not really to the left and not really to the right – from the path that leads Badiou to return to and to renew Plato,[48] I want to claim that this comparison between the situation of Marx in 1840 and our present situation contains a further implication. When the early Badiou in *Peut-on penser la politique?* suggests that "we have to redo the [Communist] Manifesto,"[49] what seems nowadays to be necessary for its preparation – and at the same time fits perfectly the historical development of Marx's own thought – is to redo Marx's thesis on Feuerbach, including, of course, the 11th. This becomes even more evident when one recalls Badiou's claim that the contemporary situation is not only structured by the absence of a common world but also by the complete absence of any active truth procedures – reactive and obscure subjects and their ideology rule.[50] Put simply: except for all that there is, nothing is happening. Nothing new under the sun. But as only a proper collective endeavor could provide orientation in politics, what we are facing is also the absence of any proper ethical orientation. Badiou proposes that in such a situation the only thing that philosophy can do is to propose what Badiou calls, with reference to Descartes, a "morale provisoire,"[51] a provisory moral.

Its first axioms one can find amongst others in *The Meaning of Sarkozy*. I will return to this. But what can be stated here is: Badiou's own project can therefore be said to also work for a redoing of the Marxian thesis on Feuerbach under present conditions. As Georges Labica and Pierre Macherey have shown in great detail,[52] Marx criticized Feuerbach for his problematic conception of materialism. Initially Feuerbach rightly criticized Hegel for his idealist conception but somehow he threw out the baby with the bath water. If in the 1840s the bath water was idealism and the baby dialectics, somehow under present conditions, as Badiou seems to suggest, this gesture has to be repeated but with a certain twist. For, after the death of idealism any materialist thought has to agree, according to Badiou, with the axiom of democratic materialism – that there are only bodies and languages; but the thing to be avoided is to repeat the Feuerbachian mistake of throwing out the baby with the bath water. This means materialist thought has to avoid getting rid of the dialectic. It is precisely necessary to throw out idealism but to keep the dialectics: this is the first necessary step to take to be able to repeat and to renew the Marxian gesture of the Feuerbach thesis under present conditions.

This also crucially implies that contemporary idealism not only threw out the idealist bath water but also the seemingly idealist baby. Under present conditions marked by the death of God and the disappearance of idealism, one might even be tempted to repeat the famous Engelsian slogan from his *Ludwig Feuerbach and the End of Classical German Philosophy*: "Enthusiasm was general; we all became at once Feuerbachians."[53] Today, it seems, "Enthusiasm is general; we all became at once democratic materialists." But if, as Pierre Macherey rightly remarked, for Marx, working through Feuerbach was a necessary transition – a transition not to get away forever from but to return to: Hegel. Return to Hegel after first being able to distance oneself from him via Feuerbach.

Hegel again becomes the main point of reference for any contemporary materialist (following Badiou) today, that much of a reference has he been for Marx. Already in Marx the return to idealism – against Feuerbach and against the old materialism of Democritus and Epicure – was associated with a *return to dialectical thinking*. Already Marx turned to Hegel again, to renew his thought after Feuerbach, and Feuerbach himself therefore was nothing but a "necessary correction"[54] that made it possible to remain a Hegelian without being an idealist, or, in short: to stick to dialectics in a non-idealist, that is, in a materialist, way. This is why it seems to be especially instructive that Badiou maps his own theory again to the systematics of Hegel in *Logics of Worlds*.[55] This bears the marks of an attempt to renew, to redo dialectics at a time in which the "night of non-dialectical thinking came over us"[56] and at a time which is structured by the death of idealism, its axioms and its implications. Turning back to Hegel and thereby repeating the

Marxian gesture seems to establish a position of a *Hegelian without Hegel*. Such a stance itself aims for what Badiou named a renewal of the dialectic as such – a renewal that, precisely because idealism is dead, seeks to formulate a fully new dialectical framework in which determinate negation is replaced with determinate affirmation and the famous Hegelian sublation with a praxis of subtraction.[57] If Hegel's idealism endeavored to demonstrate that the One exists as in the form of the totality (of history), as its own temporal self-exposure, at this point it is quite interesting to see how Badiou maps his very own system onto Hegel's. If Hegel's One can only become a totality by positing itself twice, first as immediate and then as repetition of this immediate-as-the-result, any dialectic after the death of idealism has to do away with this move. Badiou claims that the four terms that are crucial for any Hegelian dialectics is structured as follows: "the beginning (the Whole as pure edge of thought), the patience (the negative labor of internalization), the result (the whole in it and for itself)" but the complete thinking of this triple implies "the Whole itself, as immediacy-of-the-result" that "still lies beyond its own dialectical construction."[58] Badiou's renewed rendering of this idealist dialectics now reads like this: "the thinking of the multiple [...] the thinking of appearing [...] and true-thinking (post-evental procedures borne by subject-bodies)" and one needs to add the "vanishing cause, which is the exact opposite of the Whole: an abolished flash, which we call the event [...]"[59] If Marx in his theses on Feuerbach tried to put forward a dialectics without Hegel, Badiou's renaissance of idealism as renewal of materialism can be characterized in terms of a formula that he once used to describe his enterprise. He called his own philosophy a "metaphysics without metaphysics"[60] and I would like to suggest that one should read Badiou's renaissance of idealism, the philosophical act by which he reinscribes the very distinction of idealism and materialism into materialism as a means to renew materialism, as an *idealism without idealism*.

To conclude, I want to give at least one possible direct rendering of what a Badiousian reading of the 11th of Marx's theses might look like. This might be considered to be a starting point of any materialist philosophical thought today: The philosophers have only interpreted the world, in various ways; the point is to affirm it. Or to give a more precise version of this: The philosophers have only interpreted the world, in various ways; the point is to affirm its existence.

notes

For their discussion of a first version of this text, I would like to thank Bruno Besana, Lorenzo Chiesa, Mladen Dolar, Oliver Feltham, Peter Hallward, Ozren Pupovac, Rado Riha, Jelica Sumic-Riha, Alberto Toscano, Jan Völker, and Slavoj Žižek.

1 Immanuel Kant, *Critique of the Power of Judgment* (Cambridge: Cambridge UP, 2000) 93.

2 Cited from the German version of the broadcast *Der Mensch in einer sozialisierten Welt* [*Human Being in a Socialized World*].

3 See Herbert Marcuse, *Repressive Tolerance*, available <http://www.marcuse.org/herbert/pubs/60spubs/65repressivetolerance.htm>.

4 For this see also Herbert Marcuse, "Democracy Has/Hasn't a Future ... a Present" in idem, *The New Left and the 1960s* (London and New York: Routledge, 2004) 87–99.

5 Marcuse, *Der Mensch in einer sozialisierten Welt*; my translation.

6 For the Badiousian notion of materialist dialectic see Alain Badiou, *Logics of Worlds, Being and Event 2* (London and New York: Continuum, 2006) 1–40.

7 I have presented a systematic reading of Badiou's attempt to introduce different conceptions of negation and his reworking of dialectics elsewhere: Frank Ruda, "Remembering, Repeating, Working through Marx: Badiou and Žižek and the Re-actualizations of Marxism," *Revue Internationale de Philosophie* 2012/3, no. 261 (2012): 293–320.

8 For this see Alain Badiou, *Being and Event* (London and New York: Continuum, 2005)

81–89, 142–60; idem, *Theoretical Writings* (London and New York: Continuum, 2004) 3–67; idem, *Briefings on Existence: A Short Treatise on Transitory Ontology* (Albany: State U of New York P, 2006) 21–33. The idea that the death of God has been proven by Cantor can be rendered in the following way: Cantor demonstrated that there can be different sizes of infinity (say the set of natural numbers and prime numbers are of the same size). Thereby he sought to demonstrate that there is an infinity of infinities (of infinite sets of numbers). If this were to be true – and Badiou contends it is – this makes it impossible to still defend the idea of an infinity that could encompass all infinities, the latter being a very simple definition of God. For this see also Shaughan Lavine, *Understanding the Infinite* (Cambridge, MA and London: Harvard UP, 1998).

9 Alain Badiou, *Philosophy as Creative Repetition*, available <http://www.lacan.com/badrepeat.html>.

10 Ibid.

11 On science as a condition of philosophy see Alain Badiou, "Philosophy and Mathematics" in *Conditions* (London and New York: Continuum, 2008) 93–112; idem, *Being and Event* 1–22.

12 For this see also Alain Badiou, *Logics of Worlds* 153–55.

13 Ibid. 1–40. The axiom of democratic materialism is: "There are only bodies and languages," or in its second formulation: "There are only individuals and communities"; the axiom of materialist dialectics is: "There are only bodies and languages, except that there are truths" or "There are only individuals and subjects, except that there are subjects." The materialist dialectics therefore combines a materialist stance and a dialectics of exception.

14 Ibid. 11.

15 Although it is well known, I want to mention it here again: "Philosophers have hitherto only interpreted the world in various ways; the point is to change it."

16 Georges Labica, *Karl Marx, les "Thèses sur Feuerbach"* (Paris: PUF, 1987) 5; my translation.

17 Karl Korsch, *Marxism and Philosophy* (1923), available <http://www.marxists.org/archive/korsch/1923/marxism-philosophy.htm>.

18 W.F. Haug, "Die Camera obscura des Bewusstseins" in *Die Camera obscura der Ideologie*, ed. Projekt Ideologie-Theorie (Berlin: Argument, 1984) 18; my translation.

19 Ernst Bloch, *The Principle of Hope*, vol. 1 (Cambridge, MA: MIT P, 1995) 278.

20 Ibid. 281.

21 Günther Anders, *Die Antiquiertheit des Menschen*, vol. 2: *Über die Zerstörung des Lebens im Zeitalter der dritten industriellen Revolution* (Munich: Beck, 1980) 265; my translation.

22 Theodor W. Adorno, *Lectures on Negative Dialectics: Fragments of Lecture Course 1965/1966* (Cambridge and Malden, MA: Polity, 2008) 44.

23 Ibid. 42.

24 Elias Canetti, "Realismus und neue Wirklichkeit" in *Das Gewissen der Worte* (Munich and Vienna: Hanser, 1983) 66; my translation.

25 Slavoj Žižek, *The Plague of Fantasies* (London and New York: Verso, 1997) 90.

26 See Theodor W. Adorno, *Minima Moralia: Reflections on a Damaged Life* (London and New York: Verso, 2005) 29.

27 A video recording of this can be found at <http://www.youtube.com/watch?v=jQsQOqa0UVc>.

28 Slavoj Žižek, *In Defense of Lost Causes* (London and New York: Verso, 2008) 48.

29 Here, I do not presuppose any previous knowledge of Badiou's thought. In what follows I will provide all the references and explanations needed. However, this section of the article is not meant to present an introduction to Badiou; rather, its task is to construct the mentioned fourth type of reading Marx.

30 Badiou, *Philosophy as Creative Repetition*.

31 See idem, *Logics of Worlds* 1–40.

32 Idem, *The Meaning of Sarkozy* (London and New York: Verso, 2008) 55.

33 See, for example, Alain Badiou, *Séminaires sur: S'orienter dans la pensée, s'orienter dans l'existence (2004–2005)*, available <http://www.entretemps.asso.fr/Badiou/04-05.2.htm>; my translation. Here, one should remember that the term "phallic signifier" was introduced by Jacques Lacan. The phallic signifier is a signifier that embodies the lack of something; in this case

"democracy" embodies, for Badiou, the lack of any real political action.

34 Alain Badiou, "The Caesura of Nihilism," paper presented at the Society for European Philosophy, University of Essex, 10 Sept. 2003. Unpublished MS.

35 For this see also Frank Ruda and Jan Völker, "Thèses sur une morale provisoire communiste" in *L'Idée du communisme 2*, eds. Alain Badiou and Slavoj Žižek (Paris: Ligne, 2011) 215–37.

36 See Alain Badiou, *Séminaires sur: S'orienter dans la pensée, s'orienter dans l'existence (2005–2006)*, available <http://www.entretemps.asso.fr/Badiou/05-06.2.htm>; my translation.

37 Alain Badiou, Frank Ruda, and Jan Völker, "Wir müssen das affirmative Begehren hüten" in Alain Badiou, *Dritter Entwurf eines Manifest für den Affirmationismus* (Berlin: Merve, 2008) 45–46; my translation

38 Badiou, *Séminaires sur: S'orienter dans la pensée, s'orienter dans l'existence (2005–2006)*.

39 Idem, *The Meaning of Sarkozy* 56.

40 Idem, "Philosophy and the 'War against Terrorism'" in *Infinite Thought: Truth and the Return to Philosophy* (London and New York: Verso, 2003) 162.

41 For this see idem, *Logics of Worlds* 109–40.

42 Idem, *The Meaning of Sarkozy* 60–68.

43 Fredric Jameson, "Cognitive Mapping" in *Marxism and the Interpretation of Culture*, eds. Cary Nelson and Lawrence Grossberg (Urbana: U of Illinois P, 1983) 347–57.

44 See Alain Badiou, *Manifesto of Affirmationism*, available <http://www.lacan.com/frameXXIV5.htm>.

45 Idem, *Séminaires sur: S'orienter dans la pensée, s'orienter dans l'existence (2005–2006)*.

46 Ibid.

47 Alain Badiou, *The Communist Hypothesis* (London and New York: Verso, 2010) 258–60.

48 More recently this has become even overly explicit in his seminars: "For Today: Plato!" See Alain Badiou, *Séminaires sur: Pour aujourd'hui: Platon!*, available <http://www.entretemps.asso.fr/Badiou/seminaire.htm>.

49 Idem, *Peut-on penser la politique?* (Paris: Seuil, 1985) 60.

50 For these notions see idem, *Logics of Worlds* 43–78.

51 Idem, *Le Courage du présent*, available <http://www.editions-lignes.com/Le-courage-du-present.html>.

52 See Labica, *Karl Marx, les "Thèses sur Feuerbach"*; Pierre Macherey, *Marx 1845– Les "Thèses sur Feuerbach"* (Paris: Amsterdam, 2008).

53 Friedrich Engels, *Ludwig Feuerbach and the End of Classical German Philosophy* in Selected Works, vol. 2 (Moscow: Progress, 1973) 368.

54 Macherey, *Marx 1845–* 116–17.

55 See Badiou, *Logics of Worlds* 141–52.

56 Idem, *Peut-on penser la politique?* 17.

57 For this see idem, "On Subtraction" in *Conditions* 113–28.

58 Idem, *Logics of Worlds* 144.

59 Ibid.

60 Alain Badiou, "Metaphysics and Critique of Metaphysics," *Pli: The Warwick Journal of Philosophy* 10 (2000) 290.

I

One of the trends emerging in the recent move in Continental philosophy towards systems proclaiming to be both immanent *and* rigorously materialist is the return to the idea of the philosophical subject. The most obvious example is the work of Alain Badiou, whose materialist dialectics is a conceptual reintroduction of an anti-humanist philosophy of the subject into post-Althusserian materialism. While in general I am in favour of an enthusiastic celebration of the return of the subject into materialist philosophy, this return carries with it as many problems as it does possibilities. In this essay I would like to outline what I consider to be one of the most crucial problems afflicting recent materialist (and immanent) theories of subjectivity, primarily in dialogue with the development of a theory of subjectivity in the work of Alain Badiou. I will outline the stakes of this problem by tracking the modifications and developments in Badiou's account of subjectivity over the course of his major works, beginning with his *Theory of the Subject*, to the most formal exposition of his ontology in *Being and Event*, and finally in his most recent work *Logics of Worlds*. Through this chronological account of Badiou's systematic development, I will show how he begins with a Lacanian-influenced theory which attempts to introduce a theory of the subject into Marxist materialism, then moves to a purely conceptual theory of non-individual subjectivity articulated through the language of set-theory, and finally arrives at a materialist phenomenology of the subject as pulled into existence through the experience of immanent affects produced by truths.

My primary claim in regards to Badiou's theory of subjectivity will be that while in

michael o'neill burns

PROLEGOMENA TO A MATERIALIST HUMANISM

many ways he succeeds in articulating the most comprehensive theory of subjectivity in contemporary materialist philosophy, this theory suffers from a tension between conceptual and affective thought. By this I mean to say that Badiou attempts to have his (materialist) cake and eat it too by arguing for a purely formal, non-individual, anti-humanist subject which can be articulated through mathematical formalism, while at the same time wanting to ground this subject in its affective response to external events and phenomena. I will call this problem the *internal–external* problem of materialist subjectivity. This problem is the one created by the tension between theories which attempt to ground subjectivity purely in response to external events, as Badiou articulates most clearly in *Being and Event*, and theories which attempt to ground subjectivity in purely internal processes which subsequently allow this internal subject to emerge in response to external events.

It will be my contention that while Badiou offers a theory which explains both the conceptual and affective aspects of subjectivity, his theory operates in the purely external realm, and because of this he fails to explain why it is that the (always) human subject is able to respond to the affects produced by external events, and subsequently transverse the field of subjective points which accompany the process of faithful subjectivity, and in his terms, truly live.

In contrast to Badiou's external theory of subjectivity, I will then examine a recent materialist articulation of what I would consider a purely internal account of the subject as it is developed in the work of Catherine Malabou. This account utilizes the neurological and biological sciences to provide an account of the emergence and operation of internal (or, more properly speaking, neuronal) subjectivity. While relying on a materialist and scientific account of neural structure, Malabou provides a purely materialist account of human freedom and the capacity for subjectivity akin to the external theorization of subjectivity offered by Badiou.

After arguing for the necessity of this recent engagement with the neurosciences to properly articulate a materialist theory of internal subjectivity, I will consider the way in which this account of internal subjectivity seems to perfectly complete Badiou's systematic account of external subjectivity. The problem with this synthesis arises, however, from the fact that in both his published writings and recent interviews Badiou consistently fails to recognize the natural sciences as a part of the scientific truth procedure which is reserved for what he deems to be purely mathematizable sciences. It will be my contention that as long as Badiou decides to leave the natural sciences outside the bounds of what counts as a properly true articulation of the scientific, his theory of the subject, which is the lynchpin of his entire systematic ontology, will ultimately fail. As I will show, if Badiou were to allow the natural sciences into the realm of the scientific truth procedure, he would be able to articulate a theory of subjectivity which would be able to account for both aspects of the split in materialist theories of subjectivity. By beginning with a neuroscientific account of the internal (and individual) subject, he could then more rigorously explain why this pre-collective neuronal subject would possess the capacity to experience the affects of an event, and subsequently respond to this affective experience by beginning the faithful subjective process of saying "yes" to the event and joining in the activity of the collective subject-body, living for an idea in the way Badiou argues is equivalent to truly living.[1]

Finally, I will follow Adrian Johnston's recent call for "materialist and humanist to unite"[2] and briefly conclude by arguing for what I see as the necessity to boldly proclaim the time for a properly materialist humanism which proudly announces the uniqueness of human freedom and subjectivity, while equally acknowledging that this unique freedom is not the product of any divine transcendence or metaphysical priority, but rather merely the accidental product of a series of material and biological processes. It is my contention that this brand of materialist humanism can provide the grounds to think about the pursuit of equality, justice, and radical political activity without setting up a transcendent hierarchy in which humans (and far too often particular humans) have an absolute ontological priority over others. My argument will end by briefly showing how the recent work of Quentin Meillassoux, who loosely follows his former teacher Badiou in many ontological respects, opens up the space to further develop a humanism that adequately embraces the insights of twenty-first-century Materialism.

II

Badiou's first major theoretical work, *Theory of the Subject*, contains many of the developments found in *Being and Event* (1988) and *Logics of*

Worlds (2006) in their germinal form, including the "materialist dialectic" he will return to twenty-four years later. That said, this work lacks the systematic nature found in Badiou's later works, as it was initially written as a set of lectures covering a wide range of topics. Another important aspect of this work is the role of mathematics. While Badiou will later go on to make the famous assertion that mathematics equals ontology, at this point the role of mathematics is purely analogical, and thus the formal accounts of subjectivity present in this work cannot be equated with an actual description of ontological structure. Rather, this structural account has more to do with psychoanalytic concepts gleaned from Lacan than it does with any sort of set-theoretical ontology. While this work covers a wide array of philosophical, political, and psychoanalytic ground, I will only be concerned with the model of subjectivity that Badiou develops in this work. In basic terms, Badiou strives in this work to develop a theory of formal subjectivity which could supplement the scientific (and anti-humanist) reading of Marx posed by Althusser and his students.

In many ways this work utilizes the psychoanalytic tradition to attempt to supplement Marxist materialism with a formal theory of the subject. To quote Badiou:

> We demand of *materialism* that it include what we need and which Marxism, even without knowing it, has always made into its guiding thread: a theory of the subject.[3]

Along with this, Badiou goes on to note that this "materialism centered upon a theory of the subject (which is a conceptual black sheep) is equally necessary for our most pressing political needs."[4] For Badiou, the point of articulating a rigorous materialism is overwhelmingly political in nature, and he considers the lack of a theory of the subject to be a crucial deficiency in the Marxist materialism of his time. It could be said that this concern with being able to think about subjectivity in materialist terms stems from Badiou's focus on theorizing the novel, or new, and the manner in which he considers subjectivity the body supporting novelty in concrete political sequences.

While in Badiou's later work politics becomes only one of four distinct truth procedures, early on in *Theory of the Subject* Badiou makes the claim that "every subject is political. This is why there are few subjects and rarely any politics."[5] Thus the dialectical interaction between the subject and matter is necessarily political, as the freedom of this subject is first and foremost the freedom to reinscribe itself into the real of materiality. Along with this, it is crucial to note that this political subject in no way signifies an individual human consciousness, but rather the collective form of subjectivity embodied in the political party and its support of a novel political sequence. Badiou will thus argue that the proletariat "is the subjective name of the new in our time."[6]

An important aspect of this theory of the subject, and one which will serve as important in tracking the development from this text to *Logics of Worlds*, are the "four concepts of the subject" which Badiou develops to describe the process of subjectivization experienced by every properly political subject. These four concepts are: anxiety–courage–superego–justice, all of which Badiou gleans from Lacan's psychoanalytic account of subjectivity.[7] These concepts describe different stages of the process of becoming subject. Initially this subject (or, party) faces anxiety at the uncertainty of its projected future, as there is no certainty accompanying their political sequence. Courage is the moment at which the subject decides to forge ahead in the face of this anxiety-inducing uncertainty and continue forth in its political process. The superego is the point at which the party is tempted by an external structure (offering consistency) to give up its impossible project. Justice, the final concept, signifies the point at which the party fights the temptation to be reinscribed into the structure of power and instead creates its own structure of absolute equality. These are the concepts which must necessarily mark any full process of subjectivization for Badiou, although it is crucial to note that in a properly Maoist fashion, the revolutionary subject-party is never a "complete" process, as the concept of justice remains open and must be constantly reconsidered and worked out.

To summarize, the subject in *Theory of the Subject* is always political, always collective, and must necessarily be a material configuration and process. Along with this, the subject is marked by four fundamental concepts: anxiety–courage–superego–justice. It is important to note that at this point these are not affects which pull the subject forward into a process but rather concepts marking the existence of the subject in its process of subjectivization. This early development of Badiou's theory of the subject is important as it hints at formal and affective tendencies which will be pushed to their respective limits in Badiou's next two major works.

While *Theory of the Subject* was more or less a set of coherent lectures on the possibility of a materialist theory of subjectivity to supplement Marxism, Badiou's next major work, *Being and Event*, is a full-scale systematic ontology with a formal theory of subjectivity, both grounded in the axiomatics of set-theory. While mathematics had a purely analogical function in *Theory of the Subject*, in *Being and Event* mathematics serves as the formal language of ontology as such. In other words, set-theory becomes the language by which we can speak of reality in-itself. This emphasis on formal ontology does not take away from Badiou's emphasis on subjectivity, and in this work he casts aside the necessarily human and political implications of the subject as described in *Theory of the Subject* in favour of a purely formal account of the subject given in the language of set-theory.

In this work Badiou defines the subject as "any local configuration of a generic procedure from which a truth is supported."[8] From this definition he proceeds to list what the subject is not: a substance, a void point, the organization of a sense of experience, or an invariable of presentation.[9] This subject only emerges through a relationship to an event, and a subsequent fidelity to this event. Badiou notes that this subjective process is the "[...] liaison between the event (thus the intervention) and the procedure of fidelity (thus its operator of connection)."[10] Because of its liaison between the two terms, the subject is neither the intervention nor the operator of fidelity, but instead exists as the advent of their two.[11]

This position exemplifies the external tendencies of Badiou's account of subjectivity, in which the role of the subject is to support the truth presented by an event wholly external to the subject. The subject is thus the middle term between the intervention of an event into the situation and the procedure by which the consequences of this event are collectively worked out. In this sense, the subject does not exist prior to the evental intervention, i.e., it only exists in its relation to an external force which essentially draws it into existence. There is no account given of any form of pre-evental subjectivity, as this would lead to an account of pre-subjective consciousness which would be little more than "the organization of a sense of experience," something which we have previously noted Badiou argues is absolutely non-subjective.

It is important to note that during the period of *Being and Event* there were only two subjective responses to the truth emerging through an event: the positive faithful procedure, and the negative procedure.[12] In this sense Badiou sets up a very hard line on the nature of subjectivity – either one is a subject or one is not. The faithful subjective procedure would consist of the subject naming the event, and subsequently supporting the truth of the event through a subjective fidelity. This fidelity is never forced, but must be chosen by the subject, and thus decision serves as a crucial category for the subjective process in Badiou. Along with the emphasis on subjective decision, it must be noted that the event will always remain unverifiable in the present situation, and thus the subject has no way of knowing for sure whether the truth emerging through this event is actually true. We must here note that the negative subject does not in any sense witness an event and then make a decision to not follow its consequences; it simply does not recognize the event. If *Theory of the Subject* laid the groundwork for both formal and affective accounts of subjectivity, *Being and Event* represents the most rigorously formal account given by Badiou over the course of his three major works.

While *Being and Event* exemplifies the most formal tendency in the development of Badiou's theory of subjectivity, his theory takes an affective turn in his most recent major work *Logics of Worlds*. While I have already explicated the four concepts of the subject that Badiou introduces in *Theory of the Subject*, I will now show how these four concepts reappear in *Logics of Worlds* as the four affects of the subjective process. Rather than serving as merely conceptual descriptions of the process of the becoming-subject of the party, this theory of affects provides an account of how it is that the pre-subjective human animal finds itself drawn into the process of becoming-subject through an internal response to external affects. Along with the addition of a theory of subject affect, *Logics of Worlds* also contains a materialist theory of life. While going to great lengths to distinguish this theory of life from any bio-political notion of the term, Badiou's theory of life signifies the possibility of a subject to "truly live" by continuously creating a new present through the consistent affirmation of the consequences of an event and the creation of a new world.

It is worth noting that while Badiou's theory of affect as developed in *Logics of Worlds* seems to take more seriously the role of the pre-evental (or, internal) subject, this pre-evental individual is little more than a human animal in Badiou's terms. To put it bluntly, while the post-evental subject is able to transcend the state of any given situation through the faithful working out of a truth, the pre-evental human animal is only able to operate in the terms provided by the situation. Thus, while the post-evental subject participates in the creation of justice, the human animal can hope for little more than survival.

Whereas Badiou's *Being and Event* was concerned with the *being* of the subject, *Logics of Worlds* is concerned with the *appearing* of the subject, and how a singular truth can appear in subjective form in distinct worlds. He provides an updated definition of the subject early on in *Logics of Worlds* as "an operative disposition of the traces of the event and of what they deploy in the world."[13] *Logics of Worlds* also provides a theory of four distinct modes of subjectivity: the faithful subject, the reactive subject, the obscure subject, and the resurrected subject (who repeats a truth in a new world). It is crucial at this point to note that for Badiou the subject is still *non-individual* just as it was in *Theory of the Subject* and *Being and Event*. Thus in *Logics of Worlds* Badiou claims that the subject-body is the collective formation that "imposes the readability of a unified orientation onto the multiplicity of bodies."[14]

Along with this phenomenology of subjective appearance, Badiou also provides a theory of affect which accounts for the gripping of a subject by an event. Badiou theorizes these affects as being the anthropological form of local signs of the present as embodied in the subject. For each type of faithful subject Badiou assigns a unique affect: for the political subject, it is *enthusiasm*, for the subject of art, it is *pleasure*, for the subject of love, it is *happiness*, and for the scientific subject, it is *joy*.

Badiou supplements these affects characterizing the individual generic procedures with a universal process of four affects which signal the incorporation of a human animal into the process of becoming-subject. These affects are *terror, anxiety, courage*, and *justice*. It is worth noting the way in which these four affects of the subject mirror the four concepts of the subject found in *Theory of the Subject*: anxiety, courage, superego, and justice.

The first, *terror*, "testifies to the desire for a great point."[15] This point serves as the decisive discontinuity which brings about the new in an instantaneous fashion, and completes the subject in the process. The second, *anxiety*, "testifies to the fear of points,"[16] in which the human animal fears the choice between two hypotheses which come with no guarantee. The third, *courage*, "affirms the acceptance of the plurality of points."[17] The final affect is *justice*, which "affirms the equivalence of what is continuous and negotiated, on the one hand, and of what is discontinuous and violent, on the other."[18] To justice, all categories of action are thus subordinated to the absolute contingency of worlds.

Badiou goes on to note, "all affects are necessary in order for the incorporation of a human animal to unfold in a subjective process, so that the grace of being immortal may be accorded to this animal."[19] Thus, the human animal must go through each affect to enter into the process of "becoming-subject."

While it is intriguing to see Badiou relying so much on language of affect in *Logics of Worlds*, one is left wondering what or who is actually feeling these affects. And along these same lines, how does a/the subject "feel" an affect? This is especially troubling as Badiou has already defined the subject as an "operative disposition." One could then pose the question, just how does an operative disposition feel an affect? It seems as if Badiou here wants to attribute specifically human forms of affect (i.e., anxiety, courage) to a purely formal structure. While Badiou has included the category of the "human animal" in *Logics of Worlds* (a category he first introduced in his *Ethics*), he still has not explained why it is that humans have access to the affects accompanying events as well as the capacity to experience and subjectively respond to these affects in an act of decision. We can see at this point that Badiou's theory of subjectivity still remains largely external in so much as a majority of his theorization of subjectivity takes place after the event, while in the pre-eventual the not-yet-subject is little more than a human animal.

As I have already stated, *Logics of Worlds* contains a theory of life which in some ways can be seen to accompany his theory of affects. In the introduction to the work Badiou claims: "my idea is rather – at the cost, it's true, of a spectacular displacement – to bring this word [life] back to the centre of philosophical thinking, in the guise of a methodical response to the question 'What is it to live?'"[20] Shortly after he provides a description of what it might mean "to live": "[…] to live is to participate, point by point, in the organization of a new body, in which a faithful subjective formalism comes to take root."[21]

Badiou's formulation of the question "What is it to live?" finds its home in the final chapter of *Logics of Worlds*, which bears this question as its title. Here, Badiou connects the possibility of life to the trace of a vanished event, noting that this trace signals the subject towards life.[22] He goes on to note that it is not just the recognition of this trace which provides the possibility of life but that one must "incorporate oneself into what the trace authorizes in terms of consequences."[23] Badiou then provides a response to a previously unanswered question: "what is life?" To this he responds with: "life is the creation of a present [but this is a continuous creation]."[24] Thus, for Badiou, life is the process by which the subject works out the consequences of a truth point by point. As we have seen, his description of the process of life is more or less parallel to the process of becoming subject, so living for Badiou is just another name to describe the process of faithful subjectivity. While the addition of theories of both life and affect in this later work may seem to edge Badiou closer to bridging the divide between external and internal theories of materialist subjectivity, his lack of a theorization of the pre-eventual human animal leaves his theory firmly on the side of external (or, conceptual) philosophy. It seems as if this inability to bridge this gap stems from a strong conviction against any humanist or anthropocentric conceptions of philosophy, and an equally strong commitment to philosophical materialism (one which crucially leaves out naturalism as a resource for materialism). Throughout his corpus Badiou has avoided any substantial discussion of consciousness, humanism, or serious interaction with the natural or biological sciences, and it seems as if this avoidance is what leaves him unable to get past the conceptual, or external, account of subjectivity.

The crucial question remains: what is it about the structure of the human animal that enables it to experience the affects produced by events, and how is this human animal able to freely decide to enter into the process of becoming-subject opened up by these events? In some ways it could be said that while Badiou has clearly utilized much of his master Sartre's later work as found in the *Critique of Dialectical Reason*, he has avoided reckoning with the account of internal consciousness found in Sartre's major early work, *Being and Nothingness*.

Now that I have outlined the development of Badiou's theory of subjectivity and pointed to ways in which this theory fails to go beyond a purely external theory of subjectivity, I will move on by considering recent attempts to theorize subjectivity as an internal process which occurs within the individual human animal.

III

While I have shown that over the course of his three major works Badiou has gradually refined his theory of the subject to get closer to crossing the gap existing in recent materialist articulations of the subject between the external (philosophies of concept) and the internal (philosophies of affect), there still exist major difficulties with his recent turn to considering the subject in the terms of "life" and "affect."

A major problem which follows on from this is Badiou's theorization of the "human animal." For Badiou, before the emergence of a faithful subject-body, there are merely human animals, without an orienting idea, and subsequently not truly living. The question is, then, what is it about this "human animal" that enables it to make a decision in the wake of an event? And equally, what is it about this "human animal" that allows it to feel the affect of these events, and subsequently respond with a living commitment to an idea? While Badiou sometimes relies on a notion of "grace" to describe this transition from the "human animal" to the "living-and-faithful subject," this notion seems to risk collapsing the whole process back into a mystical and religious trope. While Badiou is justified in wanting to avoid an appeal to a sort of phenomenological consciousness which structures the pre-subjective human animal, it seems equally problematic to attempt to argue that a structural formalism is able to "feel" affects such as happiness, joy, and enthusiasm and then respond to these feelings with decision, belief, and commitment that enable this formalism to "become immortal" in the ongoing process of "living for an idea."

While I will not argue that Badiou should adopt a notion of the pre-subjective that relies on a phenomenological account of consciousness, I would like to explore the possibility of another sort of pre-subjective (or, pre-eventual) account of the human through a discussion of the recent neuroscientific account of subjectivity provided by Catherine Malabou. While committed to a form of dialectical materialism similar to that of Badiou, and employing a largely Hegelian ontology, Malabou's recent work is an attempt to consider the dialectical structure of the brain. Through a serious consideration of recent developments in neuroscience, Malabou is able to arrive at a theory of internal subjectivity which seems surprisingly close to the structure of Badiou's external account of subjectivity.

In Malabou's work *What Should We Do with Our Brain?* she puts forward the proposition that we are, in fact, subjects of our own brains.[25] Rather than considering neuronal function as a causal and deterministic biological process, Malabou utilizes the notion of plasticity to paint a picture of the neuronal structure of the brain as one of a constant process of destruction, modification, and rebuilding. Malabou notes: "our brain is, in part, what we do with it"[26] and that the brain in fact "has no center."[27] In language that sounds remarkably similar to that used by Badiou when developing his systematic ontology, Malabou notes that cerebral space is constituted by cuts, voids, and gaps which make it possible to consider the brain as a non-totalized structure.[28] And in this sense, neuronal function privileges *events* over *laws* in a way that once again mirrors the language used in much of Badiou's work to describe the eventual nature of truth.

In a manner which also seems to speak to problems contained within Badiou's own thought, Malabou connects this picture of the brain to a critique of political ideology, arguing that a certain neuronal ideology can keep us from realizing the potential of our brains to transform themselves, and subsequently of our selves to transform the world. Malabou argues that "the plasticity of the brain is the real image of the world"[29] and that "the screen that separates us from our brain is an ideological screen."[30] Thus, the neuronal ontology expressed by Malabou at the internal level seems to mirror the ontology developed by Badiou to argue for the capacity of subjects to be the bearers of the truly novel. Malabou goes on:

> To produce consciousness of the brain is not to interrupt the identity of brain and world and their mutual speculative relation; it is just the opposite, to emphasize them to and to place scientific discovery at the service of an emancipatory political understanding.[31]

In the context of her discussion of the emancipatory political potential of rethinking our understanding of the neuronal self, she emphasizes a non-vitalist understanding of life that once again seems to be perfectly compatible with Badiou's definition of life and a continual affirmation of a continuous series of points:

> What we are lacking is life, which is to say: resistance. Resistance is what we want.[32]

She goes on to explain the crucial difference between plasticity, the concept which she connects with resistance, and flexibility, a concept she associates with the ontology of contemporary capitalism:

> Paradoxically, if we were flexible, in other words, if we didn't explode at each transition, if we didn't destroy ourselves a bit, we could not live.[33]

Thus life for Malabou is the ability to resist structures up until the point of destruction, in a process of destruction and continuous creation, rather than a process of merely being flexible in the face of determining structures.

One of the most important concepts for Malabou's theorization of subjectivity is freedom,[34] and the account of neuronal subjectivity she develops is one which avoids both the deterministic view of the functioning of the brain which all but eliminates the possibility of freedom and transformation, and one which holds onto some mythical "remainder" to provide a ground for freedom. Rather, she develops a materialist reading of the brain as a dialectical process in which voids and gaps allow an account of the free human subject without relying on an appeal to either religious tropes or a phenomenological account of consciousness. The seeming instability (or, inconsistency) of the brain is at the heart of this freedom, and Malabou goes on to speak in language once again in line with Badiou's ontological (and political) project:

> Only an ontological explosion could permit the transition from one order to another [...][35]

Before ending this study, Malabou provides her most concise materialist account of human thought:

> A reasonable materialism, in my view, would posit that the natural contradicts itself and that thought is the fruit of this contradiction.[36]

Thus, rather than following Badiou in avoiding any discussion of the grounds of pre-eventual human thought, Malabou relies on the natural sciences to develop a theory in which thought is the result of a dialectical and material process occurring within the brain itself, and thus she can rightly argue that we are first and foremost subjects of an event internal to our own neuronal structures.

It seems that if Badiou were willing to concede ground to the neurosciences (or, in particular, Malabou's particular utilization of the neurosciences) he would be able to offer a type of minimalist anthropology (or humanism) that would still be rigorously materialist and not cause a lapse into viewing the subject as either a substance or as a phenomenological consciousness. Along with this, we see that this addition of an account of the pre-political neuronal self only further encourages the emancipatory project that has been the consistent aspect of Badiou's entire philosophical trajectory.

Thus, when we consider Malabou's theory of neuronal subjectivity in tandem with Badiou's theory of subjectivity, we can see how Malabou's account of freedom as a dialectical process occurring in the brain itself provides a sort of pre-eventual internal subjectivity which would subsequently explain just how it is that this pre-eventual internal subject can materially respond to the affects accompanying an event. This subjective experience of affect and subsequent participation in the creation of a new present thus follows the same structure as Malabou's internal account of subjectivity but on the external and collective level. What Malabou is offering is something crucial to the furthering of the project of any twenty-first-century materialism which hopes to have socio-political relevance, and that is a sort of minimalist materialist anthropology which adequately explains the capacity of individual human subjects to respond to external events and join in the creative activity of collective subjectivity.

IV

At this point the stakes of my argument should be clear; mainly, that any fully immanent and materialist theory of subjectivity which aims at any sort of socio-political efficacy must be able to account for not only the manner in which a novel event can pull the individual into the process of becoming-subject in its affirmation of an external truth, but must equally be able to account for why the neuronal structure of the individual human being contains the potential to respond to the affects accompanying an event with reflection and decision. To take things a step further, it is my aim, contra Badiou, to reintroduce a minimal form of humanism into contemporary materialist discourse. While I remain in full agreement with Badiou that the sort of liberal humanism espoused in contemporary "human rights" discourse serves as little more than a distraction from any attempt to move past the deadlock of contemporary market capitalism towards actual justice, this aversion towards positively theorizing the human leaves a glaring blind spot in his theory of subjectivity. Rather than an actually existing "either/or" between a radical anti-humanism and a boring liberal humanism, a proper employment of the neurobiological sciences (as seen in the work of Malabou) can give us the grounds to acknowledge the unique capacities of human beings in *purely materialist terms*, with no recourse to theological concepts or sentimental pseudo-mystical humanism. This sort of materialist humanism can thus provide a bridge between internal and external accounts of subjectivity which possesses both conceptual and affective rigour, while providing better grounds for political action than telling individuals that before they become an element of a subject they are little more than a pre-subjective human animal.

While this essay has been an attempt to both clearly articulate a problem existing in contemporary materialist philosophy as well as outline the stakes of this tension between internal and external accounts of materialist subjectivity, I will end by briefly highlighting the emerging position of Quentin Meillassoux, a French philosopher who stands in clear relation to both Badiou and Malabou. While his ontological position is warranting continued discussion throughout contemporary philosophy, I will here briefly outline the potential for his recent work to contribute to the development of a materialist humanism.[37]

The work of Meillassoux seems to lay the groundwork for a rigorously immanent materialism which brings both the external and internal strands of thought together through considering the development from matter, to life, to thought as a series of reorienting (and *ex nihilo*) events all encompassing a contingent break from the previous world.[38] Thus, the transition from matter to life is not a dialectical transition but rather a radical break in which something completely new emerges. Similarly, thought is not to be considered as a potentiality contained in matter and life simply waiting to be actualized, but rather as something which wholly breaks with these worlds. Following this, Meillassoux finds it reasonable to conclude that "the thinking being is the ultimate being" in the worlds of matter–life–thought, but not because human thought carries any hierarchical significance.[39] On the contrary, because the emergence of human thought is wholly contingent, with no higher "reason" lying behind this event, humanity is extraordinarily unique for *no good reason whatsoever*. Thus for Meillassoux the thinking being is the ultimate precisely because this being "knows his own contingency."[40]

The special place of human thought allows Meillassoux to then speak of the fourth world which would follow the previously mentioned worlds of matter–life–thought – *justice*.[41] This is the one advent that Meillassoux argues would be as irreducible and radically novel as the previously outlined shifts from matter to life and from life to thought. While this world has yet to emerge, we can hope for its advent, and this hope has the ability to affect our orientation in this world. This messianic brand of materialist leads to the creation of a vectorial subjectivity in which the activity of subjects in this world points towards the world of justice to come. Because the fourth world serves as the real possibility of emancipation, this real possibility engenders political action in the current world, as Meillassoux states:

> If the fourth world can have an effect upon present existence, it can do so *only* in the case of an eschatological subject, moved by the desire for universal justice.[42]

Differing with his former teacher Badiou, Meillassoux goes on to argue that the primary aim of this world of justice is not, in fact, a political aim, but rather:

> I believe that what remains once the advent of justice has occurred is precisely what Marx had promised – and perhaps this is in truth his most extraordinary promise, even if today it is held in contempt even by his most inventive heirs: there will be *a communist life*, that is to say, *life finally without politics*.[43]

Thus for Meillassoux the ultimate end of human thinking and activity is not politics but life, and that the love of life is precisely what is "at stake in the ultimate transformation of the eschatological subject."[44] Rather than focusing on an abstract and mathematical form of political equality, Meillassoux affirms particularly human pursuits such as love, friendship, art and thinking as the ultimate aims of his militant form of subjectivity.[45]

While Meillassoux has yet to publish a systematic account of his philosophy which would give us a more comprehensive idea of the connection between his ontological project, his divinology, his theory of subjectivity and his political philosophy, this account of the unique (and ultimately reasonless) place of human thought in relation to the previous worlds of matter and life provides a further exemplification of what the place of a materialist humanism would be in contemporary philosophical discourse. In particular, this account allows us to acknowledge that human thinking does possess a special place in its immanent development out of matter and life while equally acknowledging that there is absolutely no reason for this unique capacity. Thus the ability of human thinking to realize its own absolute contingency provides a way out of either grounding the unique capacities of humans in any form of divine transcendence or in a stale liberal human rights discourse.

V

While thus far this essay has consisted of a constructive synthesis of internal and external theories of materialist subjectivity, I would like to conclude with some speculative remarks as to what I see as the crucial issue to the future of materialism as it pertains to theories of subjectivity and the human. It is my contention that one of the most crucial failures in contemporary immanent materialism is the disavowal of anything resembling humanism. This is most obvious in Badiou, who develops an ontology of subjectivity that depends entirely on the receptivity and activity of human subjects, while at the same time dismissing any confusion of his theory with a humanism as if the mere intimation of a humanist philosophy would be the pinnacle of philosophical embarrassment. While recognizing the failures of previous humanisms grounded in transcendent principles and hierarchical structures, contemporary materialism, and in particular its engagement with the natural sciences, provides the possibility of once again affirming the uniqueness of human subjectivity and its creative capacity for the production of novelty. If the return of metaphysics and the turn to materialism in recent Continental philosophy have offered us anything, it is the chance to reverse the worst tendencies exhibited by Continental philosophy after the "end" of metaphysics, particularly the tendency to frame projects only as critical responses to previous philosophies rather than affirming the productive and novel capacities of philosophical speculation itself.

Here I am in full agreement with a remark made by Adrian Johnston during the conclusion of a recent presentation in which he noted that the contemporary developments in the natural sciences have given materialists and humanists more reason than ever to unite and proudly proclaim that the day is ours.[46] If contemporary materialism hopes to remain politically relevant in a manner that is not only theoretically satisfying but also practically relevant, we must avoid the temptation of an anti-humanism that is reacting against the worst tendencies of twentieth-century humanism and instead be unashamed in our affirmation of the unique capacities of human thought and action. For no metaphysical or theological reason whatsoever, human thought holds a unique place amongst the variety of configurations of matter which currently exist, and it is time that materialist philosophers admit this fact and move forward rather than waste any more time pushing the conceptual and political limits of a stale and reactionary anti-humanism.

notes

1 For an extremely detailed account of Badiou's relation to the natural sciences see Adrian Johnston, "What Matter(s) in Ontology." While my own argument covers much of the same ground, and relies on many of Johnston's insights, I am more concerned with the human and affective aspects of Badiou's theory of subjectivity and, in particular, a theory of materialist subjectivity which has both affective and conceptual aspects.

2 Johnston concluded his presentation at the 2010 "Real Objects or Material Subjects" conference at the University of Dundee with this remark. For his elaboration on this comment see "Materialism, Subjectivity and the Outcome of French Philosophy."

3 Badiou, *Theory of the Subject* 182.

4 Ibid. 189.

5 Ibid. 28.

6 Ibid. 71.

7 While these four concepts are gleaned from Lacan, there is also an interesting comparison to be made between this and Sartre's account of the development of political groups in his *Critique of Dialectical Reason Vol. 1*. In many senses, Badiou could be seen as reading Sartre's account of group formation in Lacanian terms against the background of an Althusserian materialism. This would seem to be a reasonable assumption to make as Badiou himself has claimed that Sartre, Lacan and Althusser are his three masters and primary influences.

8 Badiou, *Being and Event* 391.

9 Ibid.

10 Ibid. 239.

11 Ibid. 393.

12 Ibid. 394.

13 Badiou, *Logics of Worlds* 33.

14 Ibid. 3.

15 Ibid. 86.

16 Ibid.

17 Ibid.

18 Ibid.

19 Ibid. 87.

20 Ibid. 35.

21 Ibid.

22 Ibid. 507.

23 Ibid. 508.

24 Ibid.

25 Malabou 1.

26 Ibid. 30.

27 Ibid. 34–35.

28 Ibid. 36.

29 Ibid. 39.

30 Ibid. 40.

31 Ibid. 53.

32 Ibid. 68.

33 Ibid. 74.

34 Ibid. 69.

35 Ibid. 72.

36 Ibid. 82.

37 For a discussion of the systematic nature of Meillassoux's ontology and its relation to his divinology and political thinking, see my "The Hope of Speculative Materialism."

38 Meillassoux 461.

39 Ibid. 462.

40 Ibid.

41 Ibid. 461.

42 Ibid. 463.

43 Ibid. 473.

44 Ibid. 474.

45 Ibid. 477.

46 For Johnston's elaboration on this comment, see "Materialism, Subjectivity and the Outcome of French Philosophy."

bibliography

Badiou, Alain. *Being and Event*. Trans. Oliver Feltham. London: Continuum, 2007. Print.

Badiou, Alain. *Logics of Worlds*. Trans. Alberto Toscano. London: Continuum, 2009. Print.

Badiou, Alain. *Theory of the Subject*. Trans. Bruno Bosteels. London: Continuum, 2009. Print.

Burns, Michael O'Neill. "The Hope of Speculative Materialism." *After the Postsecular and Postmodern: New Essays in Continental Philosophy of Religion*. Ed. Anthony Paul Smith and Daniel Whistler. Newcastle: Cambridge Scholars, 2010. 316–34. Print.

Johnston, Adrian. "Materialism, Subjectivity and the Outcome of French Philosophy." *Cosmos and History* 7.1 (2011): 167–81. Print.

Johnston, Adrian. "What Matter(s) in Ontology: Alain Badiou, the Hebb-Event, and Materialism Split from Within." *Angelaki* 13.1 (2008): 27–49. Print.

Malabou, Catherine. *What Should We Do with Our Brain?* Trans. Sebastian Rand. New York: Fordham UP, 2008. Print.

Meillassoux, Quentin. "The Immanence of the World Beyond." Trans. Peter M. Candler, Jr., Adrian Pabst, and Aaron Riches. *The Grandeur of Reason*. Ed. Connor Cunningham and Peter M. Candler. Norwich: SCM, 2010. 444–78. Print.

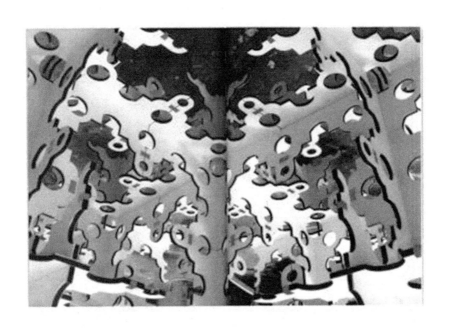

This paper is concerned with the possibility of a materialist, or immanent, transcendence that is outlined in Theodor Adorno's philosophy. There are two questions that I will address relating to the concept of immanent transcendence. First, how does transcendence arise given a purely negative philosophy? Second, in what sense can we speak of transcendence as an experience? This concept of material, or immanent, transcendence will be interrogated in relation to a series of themes within Adorno's philosophy that coalesce around the concept of life.

I want to articulate why metaphysical questions merge with questions about the possibility of living through an analysis of three interlocking themes concerning the question of life, which I have termed in the title of this article as mere life, damaged life and ephemeral life. The term "mere life" is one used originally by Benjamin in his essay on the "Critique of Violence" and later adapted and used by Giorgio Agamben when he writes of "bare life."[1] Here, I will try to link this concept of "mere life [bloßes Leben]" with the account that Adorno and Horkheimer give of self-preservation in *Dialectic of Enlightenment*. The term "damaged life [beschädigten Leben]" is one Adorno uses to refer to the reified life of individuals under capitalism and forms the subtitle of his book *Minima Moralia* which is the attempt at a series of reflections from damaged life.[2] The term ephemeral life refers to Adorno's attempt to give an account of the possibility of a metaphysical experience, a metaphysical experience that contrary to the tradition of metaphysics will lie in the particular, the transitory and the non-conceptual. In *Negative Dialectics*, Adorno writes, in a gloss on

alastair morgan

MERE LIFE, DAMAGED LIFE AND EPHEMERAL LIFE
adorno and the concept of life

Karl Kraus's famous slogan that the "origin is the goal," that "there is no origin save in ephemeral life [*Kein Ursprung außer im Leben des Ephemeren*]," and it is this idea of ephemeral life that I take as key to an understanding of metaphysical experience.[3]

In the lectures on metaphysics, Adorno begins with an account of five fundamental propositions of traditional metaphysical thought:

(1) All metaphysics is concerned with a thinking of the absolute.
(2) This absolute is conceived as the intelligible, either beyond or beneath all empirical contents of thought.
(3) A metaphysics can conceive the absolute in terms of an absolute being or as an

absolute idea, as a principle of sufficient reason.
(4) The absolute is that which grounds a systematic and unified field of knowledge.
(5) The means of accessing the absolute is through speculative reason – a form of thinking that is fundamentally transcendent.

Adorno writes in his lectures on metaphysics that:

> [...] the question whether it is still possible to live is the form in which metaphysics impinges on us urgently today.[4]

He writes that this is a "metaphysical question" but that it has "its basis in the total suspension of metaphysics."[5] It is a metaphysical question because it relates to a possibility of living that cannot be easily articulated or traced given his general account of the destruction of experience in modernity. However, it has its basis in the suspension of metaphysics, because any attempt to think the absolute as beyond experience can no longer have any meaning given the destruction of experience in the concentration camps. To try and construct a meaning that does not measure itself against the concrete experience of suffering results in an illegitimate theodicy.

How can something be both a total suspension of metaphysics and still remain a metaphysical question? Adorno will try to argue that it can be so through a transformation, or a decay in the fundamental concepts of metaphysics, which will allow a new metaphysics to arise that in the demise of its traditional propositions can merge with materialism. Adorno returns to these five propositions of metaphysics that were outlined above in the final section of *Negative Dialectics* that is entitled "Meditations on Metaphysics."[6] Here, he attempts a rescue and critique of the central questions of metaphysics in the moment of their demise, following the catastrophe of Auschwitz. He recasts the central propositions of metaphysics in the following way:

(1) All metaphysics is concerned with experiencing an absolute.
(2) The absolute appears within experience, but only at the limits of experience, and is not exhausted by experience.
(3) The absolute is both a temporal experience and can arise only in temporal phenomena.
(4) The absolute grounds the possibility of reconciliation.
(5) The means of accessing the absolute is through speculative experience.

At first glance, when comparing this list of propositions with the propositions of traditional metaphysics, two things are immediately apparent. First, the centrality of the concept of an absolute to Adorno's recasting of metaphysics. This is the commonality between these two lists. If we can take seriously the idea that Adorno is engaged in what could be loosely termed a metaphysical philosophy, then it lies in this attempt to experience the absolute. However, equally glaring is the replacement of a concept of intellectual ideas with a concept of experience.[7] The absolute is no longer to be conceived as beyond all experience, but only to appear within experience. If this is the case, then how can we still speak of an absolute? We can list a series of attributes of the absolute – namely its being perfect and complete, unchanging, unconditioned, independent of any relation – and realise that none of these attributes can still apply if applied to a temporal experience. If we take proposition (3) from Adorno's recasting of the metaphysical tradition seriously and the absolute arises as a temporal experience, and through temporal phenomena, then such an absolute must be conditioned, adulterated, and subject to change, and therefore no longer an absolute.

The means beyond such an incoherent position lies in Adorno's concepts of immanence and transcendence. The immanent context of life is understood through a philosophical anthropology where everything living reverts to the dead, through an account of mere life and damaged life in capitalist societies. Transcendence lies in the possibility of escape from such an immanent context, a possibility that is radically removed to the margins. The absolute becomes the possibility of difference, the possibility of something different, of something other. If we understand reconciliation in the particular sense developed in Adorno's philosophy, as not a unity of subject and object but as the condition in which that which is different remains in its difference, then the absolute becomes an experience within the immanent context of damaged life, of the possibility of reconciliation.[8]

The problem with this position is that we secure a concept of the absolute as something that is shown in a moment of transcendence from within an immanent context, but at the cost of materialism. The absolute just becomes the pure possibility of an escape.

transcendence as pure possibility

Transcendence as the pure possibility of escape becomes a regulative principle of a belief in the possibility of something other than the reified context. This is a regulative ideal in the Kantian sense, and Adorno appears to argue that such ideas are necessary for any thinking that is going to raise itself above the immanent context. For example, in *Negative Dialectics*, Adorno writes that the experience of transcendence is really an experience of a radical finitude:

> [...] nothing could be experienced as truly alive if something that transcends life were not promised also. The transcendent is, and, it is not.[9]

These transcendental ideas are therefore both regulative and beyond experience, thinkable but never experienceable, but providing the horizons against which any genuine free thought is possible. However, there is a subtle difference here in Adorno's terminology which should move us away from just considering the concept of transcendence as equivalent to the notion of a transcendental idea, namely of the notion of something that is thinkable but never experienceable. Adorno is concerned with an experience that exists in a space of indeterminacy with regard to actuality, thus his use of a concept like promising. However, this is not just an experience of radical finitude or of pure possibility arising through the awareness of radical finitude, but an experience of appearing and disappearing meaning.

The problem for such a concept of transcendence is that Adorno elsewhere denounces it as a mystification and argues for a metaphysics that is concerned with everything material and temporal.[10] Such an understanding of transcendence ends in a dual idealism. An idealism of finding hope, only in a complete eschatology, and the idealism of construing the most regulative ideas as those which, in principle, cannot be experienced.

A more positive reading given of Adorno's metaphysical experiences is that they do not have any determinate content, but that does not mean that they don't have an experiential content. Nothing is communicated in the metaphysical experience itself, but that what is shown but not said is an ineffable experience that reflects back onto reified life. James Gordon Finlayson has argued for a position on Adorno's concept of transcendence between both the actuality and the non-actuality of metaphysical experiences, through a notion of the ineffable and an idea of showing rather than saying.[11] When we try to think what cannot be thought, such as the actuality of a concept of reconciliation that would not involve annexing the alien, we cannot acquire a determinate idea of such a situation, but what we can reflect upon is the state of being in an ineffable experience itself. Trying to think that which is beyond thought does not communicate any determinate content other than the very foundering experience of an attempt at transcendence. However, what this attempt at transcendence reveals are certain fundamental human virtues or attitudes. In the very failure of identification, there is a consciousness of fallibility, a modesty about human potential and an affective openness towards the world.

Finlayson's construction of a space between actuality and possibility as the experience of the ineffable is rooted in Adorno's texts and offers an illuminating interpretation. My concern with it is that it still remains too

Kantian, for a reconciliation with materialism. The showing of the failure of the metaphysical itself still requires an attempt to think transcendence in terms of the ineffable, the absolutely other. The ineffable is still the realm of the unconditioned, of that which is absolutely and not only historically beyond experience. There is no content to the ineffable experience itself, only a showing of the immanent context as immanent. What transcendence does here is allow an experience of immanence which cannot be given any content, other than the historically conditioned nature of the immanent context of life, which can then sublate itself into the possibility of something wholly other, or radically different.

However, there is another way of trying to understand this changed concept of metaphysical experience, which involves an attempt to trace within distorted life an actuality of transcendence; an actuality which may be difficult to discern, but can only be encountered through distortion, and through contact with the most ephemeral and damaged objects. I want to try to delineate some themes for trying to think this understanding of transcendence through distorted life by outlining a concept of what I have termed ephemeral life, but first it is necessary to give an analysis of mere life and damaged life, which together give us an understanding of Adorno's concept of immanence.

mere life

What is mere life, or life itself, for Adorno? In the first instance, mere life is the process of human self-preservation that Adorno and Horkheimer read in *Dialectic of Enlightenment* as being at the heart of enlightenment thinking. The process of enlightenment is centrally concerned with a process of life as self-preservation. In the philosophical anthropology outlined in *Dialectic of Enlightenment*, Adorno and Horkheimer outline a transformation from a mimetic form of self-preservation that is predominant in primitive societies to a self-preservation that arises through the domination and use of nature in enlightenment thinking and practice. Mimetic practices animate the natural world and attempt to adapt the human organism to the natural object in order to ward off the threat of nature. This is a completely entrapped form of mimesis, which can only maintain self-preservation through the transfer of human powers to the natural world.[12] With the increasing rational control and use of nature, there is a promise of the escape from such a mythic fear, but Adorno and Horkheimer famously argue for a return of mythic fear at the heart of enlightenment thought. Enlightenment is "mythical fear radicalised," as in the attempt to ward off all threats to life through the rational control and domination of nature nothing is allowed to remain as external or non-identical to the human subject.[13] The pursuit of self-preservation as an end in itself produces three forms of domination, of objects, of the relationships between people and of the relationships of individuals to themselves. This pursuit of self-preservation becomes systematised with the rise of capitalism and of the commodification of these three elements of living as processes of absolute fungibility, where everything is exchangeable and usable. A politics that has at its heart the pursuit of mere life, of life as self-preservation, reverts to a politics of death, a thanatopolitics, in two ways. First, everything material, or non-identical with the attempt to dominate and use nature, is suppressed and cast aside, therefore objects, relations and the self become petrified. Adorno writes in the Kierkegaard study of the self as a space of "objectless inwardness."[14] Thus life becomes both object and subject of a process of petrification in the service of mere life, of self-preservation. Second, there is the process of a constant attempt to suppress and expel anything that is constructed or considered as different, and to classify it in terms of a threat to life, which must be completely annihilated.

Therefore, Adorno and Horkheimer write that:

> The human being's mastery of itself, on which the self is founded, practically always involves the annihilation of the subject in whose service that mastery is maintained, because the substance which is mastered,

suppressed and disintegrated by self-preservation is nothing other than the living entity, of which the achievements of self-preservation can only be defined as functions – in other words, self-preservation destroys the very thing which is to be preserved.[15]

This quotation points to another, more positive, connotation of mere life, as the living entity. Certainly, there is a gesture towards a concept of natural life in *Dialectic of Enlightenment* that doesn't conceive of nature purely in terms of myth or second nature, but in terms of life itself. However, I think it is a mistake to conceive Adorno and Horkheimer's project in terms of an affirmation of nature itself, or a positive concept of mere life. J.M. Bernstein, in an essay critiquing Giorgio Agamben's concept of bare life, points to a concept of the "sweetness of life" itself, excavated from a passage in Aristotle's *Politics*.[16] Aristotle writes that:

> [...] there is probably some kind of good in the mere fact of living itself. If there is no great difficulty as to the way of life, clearly most men will tolerate much suffering and hold on to life (zoë) as if it were a kind of happiness and a natural sweetness.[17]

Bernstein mobilises a concept of the "sweetness" of mere life as a way of solving a problem that he reads in Agamben's work, in that Agamben remains within a context of bare life as something that is both included and excluded within the law, without an understanding of how that inclusive exclusion is a severing of the claims of the sweetness of life. This means that bare life becomes the only norm. This is problematic, for Bernstein, as it means that there can be no movement beyond bare life, and therefore in his analysis, for a truly normative ground, we need to understand bare life as a severing of the claims of mere life or the sweetness of life.[18]

This account is fundamentally opposed to Walter Benjamin's understanding of the concept of mere life in the "Critique of Violence" essay, where mere life is equated with the guilt context of living. Mere life is always already caught up within myth as the "eternally mute bearer of guilt."[19] For Benjamin, it is the reduction of humans to their mere life that should be resisted at all costs, rather than considering mere life as raising a claim of the authority of nature. Mere life is already caught up and entwined within a generalised guilt context of the living.[20]

Adorno attempts to stake a position between these two approaches towards mere life; namely mere life as already guilty, and mere life as a normative claim and an authority in itself. I think that Adorno broadly shares Benjamin's argument in the "Critique of Violence" essay that the human should on no account be identified or reduced to its mere life. Rather, Adorno and Horkheimer gesture towards a positive concept of enlightenment which they describe as "nature made audible in its estrangement."[21] The process of separation from nature, in the name of self-preservation, is necessary. There is no nostalgia for a return to an animistic fearful mimetic relationship to nature. Therefore, mere life should not be affirmed in itself. However, the promise of enlightenment thinking is the promise of a thought which would enable self-preservation without domination. The possibility of living is itself only raised through the separation from nature, but if it is to preserve itself as living it must relate to the material as that which escapes all conceptuality and all identification. Therefore, mere life is always already caught up within the context of guilt, which is conceived as the drive for self-preservation which can never be actualised other than in terms of a mythical fear. However, within a primitive mimetic relation to nature there lies the potential for a non-dominating relation with objectivity that becomes suppressed as mythical fear is radicalised in identity thinking. If one can speak of the claims of mere life then it is only in the terms of the trace or potentiality that lies in mimesis of a relation to objectivity that would preserve the object in its non-identity with thought, and would release an openness and vulnerability to objectivity in a non-dominating and non-fearful manner. However, this does not mean that Adorno wants to affirm a concept of life as some kind of foundational ground or norm.

This is a point that Deborah Cook makes in her book *Adorno on Nature* when she writes that Bernstein's approach to Adorno's work runs the risk of a deification of the object. For Cook, there is a turn towards the object in Adorno's work, but this is a turn towards a possibility of relating to objectivity in a different manner rather than an immersion in nature as a foundational ground and set of norms.[22]

Therefore, if the human should not be identified completely with mere life there is nevertheless an element of something that escapes subjectivity that must resound even in the most conceptual thought, if philosophy is not to mimic the petrification that occurs in the service of mere life as self-preservation. It is these material elements within thought that become speculative or transcendent when trying to think about the possibility of life. They become transcendent because of Adorno's account of damaged life, to which I now turn.

damaged life

In his series of reflections from damaged life, entitled *Minima Moralia*, Adorno attempts what Axel Honneth has described as a "physiognomy of the capitalist form of life."[23] Adorno tracks down, in everyday forms of life in capitalist society, the damage and suffering inflicted by the commodification of life in pursuit of self-preservation. The three forms of domination (a domination in terms of objects, interpersonal relations, and the self) are tracked down in a myriad of examples of everyday life. Adorno reads the everyday life of capitalism in ruthlessly negative terms. There is no aspect of life that is immune to the processes of abstraction, identification, exchange and use which characterises all human relationships and relationships to the world, and that allows for no spontaneity or difference to arise. Life itself cannot be invoked as a means beyond this immanent context, because any attempt either to affirm or deny life just inscribes the person back within the empty space of a form of domination which from its outset is concerned with the construction of life as a dead space in the service of self-preservation. In many of the pieces in *Minima Moralia*, Adorno resists the invocation or affirmation of life as flourishing, as a form of sickness in itself. As he writes in an aphorism that has the title "The Health unto Death":

> The very people who burst with proofs of exuberant vitality could easily be taken for prepared corpses, from whom the news of their not-quite-successful decease has been withheld for reasons of population policy.[24]

Equally, there is no escape in a refusal of life's flourishing, in an attempt to construct a Stoic life that is beyond all affectivity, although he does acknowledge an element of freedom here:

> [...] one might compare this situation to that of the philosophy of late antiquity, in which, in response to the same question, people fell back on expedients such as ataraxy, that is the deadening of all affects, just to be capable of living at all [...] I would say that even this standpoint, although it emphatically embraces the idea of freedom, nevertheless has a moment of narrow-mindedness in the sense that it renders absolute the entrapment of human beings by the totality, and thus sees no possibility other than to submit.[25]

The idea of a life beyond use that Adorno writes about in several aphorisms only mirrors the complete exhaustion of life at the heart of a capitalist destruction of experience.

This critique of damaged life takes on an even more negative hue with Adorno's reflections on Auschwitz in *Negative Dialectics*. In the concentration camps, a form of living is created that erases any possibility of differentiating between what is living and what is dead. The death-in-life instituted in the camps is the apotheosis of the reversion of a politics of life to a thanatopolitics.

Given this account of a reversion of the living to the dead that arises at the heart of enlightenment thought how can the possibility of living arise? Adorno argues that within distorted life itself can be read the traces of a possibility of something different. Michael Theunissen argues here that we are dealing with a kind of magical sublation in Adorno's negative dialectics. As though, somehow, the negation of the negative life miraculously reverses into its opposite.[26] However, I think that there is a rich constellation of themes that can be excavated from Adorno's work to try to give some actual content to the idea of an immanent transcendence that attempts to merge metaphysics with materialism. This constellation of themes revolves around issues of particularity, transience, decay and non-conceptuality. It is here that a metaphysical experience arises in a moment of passing time and I want to outline these themes in the final part of the paper dealing with ephemeral life.

ephemeral life

I want to provisionally outline four components of ephemeral life. I am not suggesting that these are complete or exhaustive definitions, but rather should be seen as a set of problems for a deepening reflection on the question of speculative experience, and a series of trajectories for a thought that takes seriously the problem of a materialist transcendence.

First, there is the notion of what Adorno terms an intellectual experience, "geistige Erfahrung," which he defines as "full, unreduced experience in the medium of conceptual reflection."[27] Such a concept of intellectual experience requires a particular attentiveness to the object, through which the object of experience comes to appear in its non-identity with any concept. This requires, paradoxically, an element of both exaggerated and negative interpretation. The exaggerated element lies in the deployment of concepts around a particular object in which the object itself is never fully identified, but only illuminated. Adorno writes in the lectures on *Negative Dialectics* that the "contents of experience are no examples for categories." This is negative because it refuses any intentional interpretation, in terms of hoping to find within the object a readily available meaning or truth. How does such an experience survive the generalised destruction of experience? It harbours both the truth content of a mimetic relation to nature and of the separation of nature that we talked about in relation to mere life. Such an experience is withdrawn from any engagement with objects, thus is in some sense abstract, but at the same time not an attempt to identify or subsume objects under concepts. It is what Adorno terms "contemplation without violence." In his recent lecture on reification, Axel Honneth describes a form of empathetic engagement with oneself and the world as a mode of primordial recognition, that is the opposite of the reified contemplative stance of disinterested observation.[28] However, I don't think that what Adorno refers to here as attentiveness, and what Benjamin writes of as a "listening," should be read in terms of empathetic engagement, but rather as an immanent modification of reified thought.[29] If reification is characterised by a cognitive attitude that is removed from engagement with the world, and views others, the world and the self in terms of things to be manipulated in the service of self-preservation, attentiveness is a modification of such a contemplative stance that retains a critical distance but accompanies it with an affective concern, but an affective concern that is not fixed in an engaged manner on objects. Massimo Cacciari has written about this attitude in terms of a "profane attention" which is both a critical distance and also an affective stance. He describes a profane attention as being determined by a fundamental yet interior emotional attunement, which doesn't reach out to the world but is "inactive, as if it were limited to witnessing events "from behind tinted glass." Such attention is certainly not empathetic engagement, in that even in its affective mode it is withdrawn from any direct involvement with objects, but in some ways is a purification of the reified attitude. Cacciari writes, in an echo of Benjamin, that:

> The pinnacle of attention would be, therefore, a language deprived of "being", resolved in listening [...][30]

Adorno has his own name for such a critical attitude that is affective, dissolving of subjectivity, but yet still entails a critical relation to objectivity. He terms it, paradoxically, "distanced nearness."[31] It is most characteristic of the reception of certain artworks, but other experiences can bring about the development of such an attitude, which is really an immanent shift within reified thinking itself. However, this jolt is only brought about through the limit-experience of being confronted with objects, relations or aspects of the self which appear as suddenly beyond any straightforward grasp or identification.

This is a utopian hermeneutics which immerses itself in phenomena to uncover a historical process of decay and latent potentiality. In the lectures on History and Freedom, Adorno writes that this attentive interpretation

> always discovers what phenomena used to be, what they have become and, at the same time what they might have been, [and] retains the possible life of phenomena as opposed to their actual existence [...] Interpretation in fact means to become conscious of the traces of what points beyond mere existence – by dint of criticism – that is to say, by virtue of an insight into transience, and into the shortcomings and fallibility of mere existence.[32]

What is uncovered in phenomena is the absolute, which is the truth content contained within phenomena, a truth content that is only released in the moment of decay of objects which have been stabilised as second nature within a history of domination. Truth content refers to both the expression of suffering contained within the domination of objects in a history of mere life as self-preservation, and the possibility of a different history, or of a life of objects freed from domination, from exchange, even from use. There is a historical moment in the decay of phenomena when the concepts constructed in order to dominate objectivity can be attended to in order to release both a history of suffering contained in the entwinement of subjects and nature in the pursuit of self-preservation and the possibility of a different mode of relating with objects in a non-dominating fashion.

The second component of ephemeral life is already implicated in the first, as a turn towards the object, whilst remaining within the subject–object situation. It is often unclear what Adorno means by an object. There is certainly a sense in which the model of an object is always a socially or culturally produced object, although there are important references to the natural object in Adorno's works. The turn towards the object is in the hope of the releasing of a "process" stored in the object. However, what Adorno means by such a process is not a life force, or a force of becoming in itself, but the attempt to release the object from the process of reification, from the process of being turned into an inert dead thing. The process within the object is a historical process, a process of decay, of transience. There is thus an interplay between ephemeral and eternal elements within such an interpretation of objectivity in two forms. The object is read as natural, in the sense of being a mythic production of capitalism as reified second nature, but also as historical, as the sedimented repository of the needs and suffering of human beings. However, the eternal content also relates to an idea of a truth content to the object which is the expression of suffering. This truth content only arises in the decay of objects.

There is a central question in Adorno's philosophy as to what the project concerning the "primacy of the object" really means. To what extent does Adorno's philosophy remain within a correlationist framework, to use the terminology recently coined by Meillassoux? Meillassoux defines correlationism as the idea that subjects and objects cannot be considered as entities independent of one another. We cannot know what an object is in itself as our knowledge is always mediated by the form of our consciousness and our language, according to the correlationist.[33] Adorno's philosophy appears to be fundamentally non-correlationist in its emphasis on a material moment that is never exhausted within the givenness of experience. There is always something that exerts a force on experience but can never be conceptualised or fully encapsulated within experience. However, at the same time, the object that comes to life through an attentive interpretation always appears to be an object that is sedimented with the traces of historical and therefore human meaning. The object appears within Adorno's philosophy as an object constructed through human history, and as an object of human experience.

Adorno argues that what is given is constituted conceptually, but we don't then have to make the claim that it is exhaustively or thoroughly constituted conceptually. There is always a remainder, a material moment that escapes concepts. This does not have to be thought only in terms of a logical concept of the non-identical or a Kantian thing-in-itself, because conceptuality is itself a form of praxis, a means of relating and responding to the material world, that exists independently of concepts. The categories that constitute the given are historically produced through the process of self-preservation, but there remain traces of a life of objects that are not exhausted by the encounter with subjectivity. Perhaps we could ascribe to Adorno the position that Graham Harman ascribes to Heidegger, of a "correlationist realism," "that human and world must always come as a package, but [also] that being is not fully manifest to humans." Harman terms this a "monstrous hybrid doctrine."[34] However, I don't see why this needs to be considered in such a manner. Adorno's argument is that experience is given conceptually, that experience is conceptual all the way down (to use McDowell's terminology),[35] but that conceptuality is not an invariant structure but a historical practice that has its principal underpinning in the drive for self-preservation. Precisely because the underpinning of conceptual experience is self-preservation, then a force of external nature or reality is presupposed within experience itself. Experience originates in warding off threats and in a fearful and then dominating relation to objectivity. Any talk of experience as a matter of dealing with affordances in the environment, or as Axel Honneth has recently discussed in Heideggerian terms of a primordial empathetic engagement in the world, already renders the material world as inert stuff that can be manipulated. However, understanding conceptual practice as originating in a drive for self-preservation gives us a primary understanding of materiality itself as active and exerting a force on human experience.

Nevertheless, there is still the problem that the conceptual determination of experience, as it is consolidated in the commodity form of the object within capitalism, is so complete that nothing else can arise. In this sense, Adorno does argue for a fundamental and thorough, if historical, conceptual determination of the given. However, immanent to this determination of materiality through self-preservation there are always residues or remnants of a different mode of being with objects.

This is the third aspect of ephemeral life; an experience of involuntary elements of the self, of a fundamental non-cognitive, affective and embodied access to the world, which is open and receptive in a passive sense to objectivity. Adorno describes the initiating moment of such experiences as somehow involuntary. They are not the process of an attempt to think the whole but a shock caused by an intrusion of suffering, or the material moment within thought. In a sense here I am saddling Adorno with an old-fashioned sense of humanism, that the block to reified thinking returns us to a set of fundamental human qualities. However, these human qualities are not necessarily those which separate us completely from animals and nature. There is a similarity in what I am outlining here to Honneth's argument that reification is a forgetting of primordial human qualities, but I would not construct those qualities in terms of empathetic engagement to the world or a fundamental form of recognition, that Honneth relates to Heideggerian care and Dewey's pragmatism. Primarily, Honneth's account of such a pre-reflective foundation for experience downplays two central aspects of such experience outlined in *Dialectic of Enlightenment*. First, this experience is fundamentally passive. Prior to any particular stance, or response to affordances in the environment, there is a fundamental passivity of human pre-reflective and affective experience. Second, this passivity is accompanied by a vulnerability of the individual to threats, to suffering and to death. It is this passivity and vulnerability, and the possibility for suffering, that lies at the heart of the undergoing of experience, but it also initiates the very process of enlightenment, whose originating, motive principle is life as self-preservation.

Instead, I would look to a pre-reflective ipseity of experience, which has been most fully considered in phenomenology and in writers such as Merleau-Ponty, Henry and Levinas.[36] This is a fundamental pre-reflective passive, receptive, affective openness to the world, the self and others. However, I am not suggesting that this is unaffected by reification, as though this exists as a pre-existing potentiality that can be recovered whole, once reification is demystified as a false mode of praxis. Rather, such a fundamental pre-reflective mode of being in the world is a potentiality which itself has been scarred by reification.[37] However, what cannot be completely erased by reified experience is a fundamental openness, vulnerability and passivity constitutive of an ipseity of experience. What this passivity of experience preserves is a relation to something non-identical and material to conceptuality, an element impinges in an involuntary manner on experience. Adorno writes of this in terms of a yielding to impulse in which there is an openness to something other than the subject, but also the promise of a different way of relating to objectivity. He writes that:

> [...] as long as we obey our impulses we shall find ourselves once again in the realm of objects from which we had withdrawn by an absolute necessity, albeit perhaps only in appearance. Thus, the phantasm of freedom may be said to be something like a reconciliation of spirit, the union of reason and nature as it survives in the impulse [...][38]

This begins to sound dangerously like a rather traditional concept of reconciliation and close to a philosophy of irrationalism, of a lauding of fundamental experiences. I think it is important to try and read this in terms of fundamental limit experiences (one could list some of the experiences that Levinas writes of such as fatigue, enjoyment, pleasure, effort, suffering), in which there is no apparent divide between subject and object, but where there is also a primacy to that which is objective, a primacy given to otherness, to a modelling of the subject upon the other.[39]

However, these experiences cannot rest in themselves but must be taken up conceptually, in terms of an immanent modification of the longing for reconciliation between subject and object. Metaphysical experience is constituted by an experiential dialectic internal to the longing for reconciliation. It is in what Adorno terms as the "vital need" in thinking for a state in which subject and object would no longer be dissevered that a new understanding of reconciliation as a state in which the alien exists as other can be glimpsed. Here we can outline a fourth element of ephemeral life, which would lie in forms of life in which the operations of damaged life could not take hold. Adorno theorises these in terms of metaphysical experiences, which consist of a hope for completion, but are able to rest in a lack of fulfilment, that in their emptiness give an imperfect image of a possibility of relating to difference in a non-dominating manner. Adorno writes of experiences such as fruitless waiting, the Proustian place-name, and the déjà vu. What is constitutive of the experience of the place-name in Proust is that the hopes invested in the name disappear when one arrives there, but that somehow this is not an experience of disappointment but an experience of being able to rest in non-fulfilment, in a non-identity with the desire for an absolute reconciliation, which can then open up a space for a different idea of reconciliation, one that would not be about annexing that which is other but about a non-dominating relationship with objectivity.

conclusion

Unfortunately, this appears, through a long detour, that we have just returned to a fundamental problem with the idea of an immanent transcendence that we began with. Namely, that transcendence just becomes an empty experience of finitude as finitude, and therefore ceases to be an experience with any content at all. I think that this is certainly one of the problems with the manner in which metaphysical experiences are constructed in the "meditations on metaphysics" at the end of *Negative Dialectics*.[40] However, I do think that there can be a content given to the idea of a metaphysical experience that is both transcendent and experiential. The transcendent moment of a return to a passive, receptive openness to the world can only be recuperated by an attentive responsiveness to such an experience, to an attentive reading of the traces of possibility. However, such an attentive responsiveness cannot be thought of as somehow transcendent to human cognition in an absolute sense. This is the problem with Adorno's emphasis on the total negativity of identity thinking. Such an attitude of attentiveness cannot be derived from an attempt to think what is beyond thought, or through a remembering of some primordial empathetic engagement with the world, but only as an immanent possibility within reified thought itself. Transcendence rests in a relation between a certain limit-experience, not only but often of a distorted life, which blocks all attempts at identification, and brings us into contact with a fundamental affective openness towards the world. However, this can only be experienced in a non-dominating way through a cognitive attitude of attentive interpretation, which remains both disinterested yet concerned and that can decipher within the negative life the possibility of something different.

notes

1 Walter Benjamin, "Critique of Violence," trans. Edmund Jephcott and Kingsley Shorter, in *One Way Street and Other Writings* (London and New York: Verso, 1998) 153; Giorgio Agamben, *Homo Sacer: Sovereign Power and Bare Life*, trans. Daniel Heller-Roazen (Stanford: Stanford UP, 1998).

2 T.W. Adorno, *Minima Moralia: Reflections from Damaged Life*, trans. E.F.N. Jephcott (London: Verso, 1997).

3 T.W. Adorno, *Negative Dialectics*, trans. E.B. Ashton (London and New York: Routledge, 1990) 156; idem, *Negative Dialektik – Gesammelte Schriften*, vol. 6 (Frankfurt: Suhrkamp, 1996) 158.

4 T.W. Adorno, *Metaphysics: Concept and Problems*, trans. E.F.N. Jephcott (Cambridge: Polity, 2000) 112.

5 Ibid.

6 *Negative Dialectics* 361–408.

7 Adorno is consciously pitting himself against Kant's formulation of metaphysics as concerned with "mere ideas" and it is this move from ideas to experience that is both key and extremely problematic for Adorno's recasting of metaphysics. For Kant's argument for the concept of metaphysical ideas as merely regulative see Immanuel Kant, *Critique of Pure Reason*, trans. Norman Kemp Smith (Basingstoke: Macmillan, 1989) 532–33.

8 *Negative Dialectics* 191.

9 Ibid. 375.

10 For one of many examples see *Negative Dialectics* 407: "No absolute can be expressed otherwise than in topics and categories of immanence [...]"

11 James Gordon Finlayson, "Adorno on the Ethical and the Ineffable," *European Journal of Philosophy* 10:1 (2002): 1–25.

12 Max Horkheimer and T.W. Adorno, *Dialectic of Enlightenment: Philosophical Fragments*, trans. Edmund Jephcott (Stanford: Stanford UP, 2002) 2–34.

13 Ibid. 11.

14 T.W. Adorno, *Kierkegaard: Construction of the Aesthetic*, trans. Robert Hullot-Kentor (Minneapolis: U of Minnesota P, 1999) 27.

15 *Dialectic of Enlightenment* 43.

16 J.M. Bernstein, "Bearing Witness: Auschwitz and the Pornography of Horror," *Parallax* 10.1 (2004): 2–16. See also idem, "Intact and Fragmented Bodies: Versions of Ethics 'after Auschwitz,'" *New German Critique* 33.1 97 (2006) 32.

17 Aristotle, *The Politics*, ed. Stephen Everson (Cambridge and New York: Cambridge UP, 1990) 60, 1278b.

18 Bernstein concentrates mainly on Agamben's book on Auschwitz; see Giorgio Agamben, *Remnants of Auschwitz – The Witness and the Archive* (New York: Zone, 1999).

19 Walter Benjamin, "Critique of Violence," trans. Edmund Jephcott and Kingsley Shorter, in *One Way Street and Other Writings* 153.

20 Ibid. 132–56.

21 *Dialectic of Enlightenment* 31.

22 Deborah Cook, *Adorno on Nature* (Durham: Acumen, 2011) 31, 75.

23 Axel Honneth, "A Physiognomy of the Capitalist Form of Life: A Sketch of Adorno's Social Theory," *Constellations* 12.1 (2005): 50–64.

24 Adorno, *Minima Moralia* 59.

25 *Metaphysics* 112.

26 Michael Theunissen. "Negativity in Adorno," trans. Nicholas Walker, in *Theodor W. Adorno: Critical Evaluations in Cultural Theory*, vol. 1, ed. Simon Jarvis (London and New York: Routledge, 2007) 178–98.

27 *Negative Dialectics* 13.

28 Axel Honneth, *Reification: A New Look at an Old Idea*, with commentaries by Judith Butler, Raymond Geuss, and Jonathan Lear, ed. and intro. Martin Jay; trans. Joseph Ganahl (Oxford: Oxford UP, 2008).

29 See Walter Benjamin, "Franz Kafka: On the Tenth Anniversary of his Death," and "Max Brod's Book on Kafka and Some of my Own Reflections" in *Illuminations*, trans. Harry Zorn with an introduction by Hannah Arendt (London: Pimlico, 1999) 108–44. For the reference to listening, see 141:

> The main reason why this listening demands such effort is that only the most indistinct sounds reach the listener. There is no doctrine that one could absorb, no knowledge that one could preserve.

For the reference to attentiveness, see 130:

> Even if Kafka did not pray – and this we do now know – he still possessed in the highest degree what Malebranche called "the natural prayer of the soul": attentiveness.

For Adorno's reference to the concept of attentiveness, in relation to Benjamin's Kafka study, see Theodor Adorno and Walter Benjamin, *The Complete Correspondence, 1928–1940*, trans. Nicholas Walker (Cambridge, MA: Harvard UP, 1999) 66–73.

30 Massimo Cacciari, *Posthumous People: Vienna at the Turning Point*, trans. Rodger Friedman (Stanford: Stanford UP, 1996) 206. Cacciari's essay is concerned with Robert Musil's "The Man without Qualities."

31 *Minima Moralia* 89–90. Adorno writes that:

> Contemplation without violence, the source of all the joy of truth presupposes that he who contemplates does not absorb the object into himself: a distanced nearness.

32 T.W. Adorno, *History and Freedom – Lectures 1964–1965*, ed. Rolf Tiedemann; trans. Rodney Livingstone (Cambridge: Polity, 2006) 138.

33 Quentin Meillassoux, *After Finitude – An Essay on the Necessity of Contingency*, trans. Ray Brassier (London and New York: Continuum, 2008) 5, 36.

34 Graham Harman, *Prince of Networks: Bruno Latour and Metaphysics* (Prahran, Vic.: re.press, 2009) 180.

35 See John McDowell, *Mind and World* (Cambridge, MA and London: Harvard UP, 1994).

36 I give a rather preliminary outline of this approach in the chapter "Suffering Life" in A. Morgan, *Adorno's Concept of Life* (New York and London: Continuum, 2007).

37 More work is needed here on thinking the concepts of reification and ipseity together, but I think that many of the pieces in *Minima Moralia* can be read as reflections upon a fundamental distortion of sensory experience through the operations of commodification and the way that the culture industry functions through the human sensorium. One could join these analyses with Benjamin's notion of *Erlebnis* as shock experience in modernity. Such an infiltration of power into the very heart of life itself has, of course, been massively extended in recent years, with forms of biopower and biopolitics that take a transformation of affectivity itself as the main focus for a project of transforming human life.

38 *History and Freedom* 237.

39 See Emmanuel Levinas, "There Is: Existence without Existents," trans. Alphonso Lingis, in *The Levinas Reader*, ed. Sean Hand (Oxford and Malden, MA: Blackwell, 1989).

40 *Negative Dialectics* 361–408.

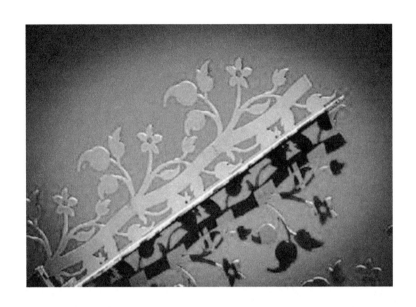

Matter is not Soul; it is not Intellect, is not Life, is no Ideal-Principle, no Reason-Principle; it is not limit or bound, for it is mere indetermination; it is not a power, for what does it produce?
Luce Irigaray[1]

[...] And yet beneath
The stillness of everything gone, and being still,
Being and sitting still, something resides [...]
Wallace Stevens[2]

patrice haynes

CREATIVE BECOMING AND THE PATIENCY OF MATTER
feminism, new materialism and theology

introduction

Since the late 1990s a shift has begun to take place in feminist thought, and critical theory more generally, which sees increasing attention paid to questions concerning the materiality of bodies and nature as that which is more than a passive medium for the determinations of social forces. For sure, the appeal to the discursive, by anglophone feminists drawing on postmodern and poststructuralist philosophies, exposed the extent to which language and culture are implicated in power and politics, and thus actively work to establish and buttress social norms regarding gender (as well as a whole range of identificatory categories such as race, class and sexuality). However, in recent years a growing number of feminists have expressed concern that the intense preoccupation with social constructivism typical of postmodern and poststructural feminism has fuelled a certain wariness, even antipathy, towards matter and materiality as that which exceeds socio-cultural discourse.[3] Although "the body" has been a signature topic in feminist writings since the publication of Simone de Beauvoir's *The Second Sex* in 1949, it may be argued that feminist theory tends to examine discourse *about* the body rather than the material reality of bodies and corporeal practices.[4] In particular, Judith Butler's *Gender Trouble* and *Bodies That Matter* are often cited as paradigmatic examples of the eclipse of matter in feminist theorizing in favour of what could be called "linguistic idealism."[5] Seeking to reclaim matter to feminist theory is a growing group of feminist scholars whose work, often informed by the physical and biological sciences, is helping to drive a materialist turn in theory more generally, a turn which has been gathering momentum and is variously dubbed "new materialism,"[6] "post-constructionism,"[7] "transcorporeal feminism,"[8] or "material feminism."[9]

Below I will highlight what we might think of as the main nodal points for the various analyses, methodologies and aspirations proceeding under the "new materialist" banner. However, for the moment I want to draw attention to perhaps the most salient feature of new materialist thought: the agential character of matter. Contra the conception of matter as inert, passive, featureless stuff – the legacy of Cartesian dualism and Newtonian mechanism – new materialists propose a non-reductive account of matter as that which possesses agency and productive forces of its own.[10] Matter is thus considered to be lively and dynamic, the fount of emerging forms. Such a non-reductive materialism not only confounds dualistic accounts of form and matter, mind and body, organism and machine, it is also, for the most part, posthumanist and post-theological in orientation, for it refuses to restrict creative agency to persons alone, whether human or divine.

I believe that recent accounts of matter as that which is efficacious and self-organizing are important interventions in theory because they seek to do justice to matter and materiality. Moreover, a non-reductive formulation of matter is particularly pertinent for feminist theory since it resists hylomorphism and its gendered associations, namely, the socio-cultural connection made between the female and passive, indeterminate matter in contradistinction to the active, male form that gives shape to matter.

Nonetheless, while I welcome the re-conception of matter by new materialists, it is my view that the tight focus on the liveliness and vitality of matter must be careful not to neglect the correlate of agency: namely, patiency. Whereas the term "agency" denotes the capacity for action or doings, and implies positive notions such as autonomy and independence, the term "patiency," by contrast, denotes that which is acted upon (by others) or that which simply endures (through actions and events), and thus carries negative connotations such as passivity and dependence. The trouble is that the valorization of matter's agential qualities risks uncritically anthropomorphizing nature (understood here as the material world), inasmuch as it comes to mirror the humanist model of personhood, with its agential understanding of persons.[11] Thus, rather than arriving at a posthuman ontology,[12] new materialists may be charged with simply *extending* the paradigm of the human person to the whole of nature, a move which preserves, rather than defeats, humanism. Furthermore, by prioritizing activity (agency) over passivity (patiency), new materialism inadvertently sustains a dualistic interpretation of the active/passive distinction, a dualism which is traditionally cashed out according to gendered stereotypes: while man is linked with vibrant, creative productivity, woman is aligned with less favoured qualities such as passivity, reproduction and inertia. The radical promise of new materialism for feminist theory is thereby betrayed.

In her essay "On Not Becoming Man: The Materialist Politics of Unactualized Potential," which appeared in the 2008 volume *Material Feminisms*, Claire Colebrook sees the appeal to vitalism by a number of (new) materialist feminists as something of a double-edged sword. On the one hand, vitalism offers feminists a way to oppose the Cartesian view of matter as lifeless, mathematizable *res extensa*, a view that would go on to pave the way for Newtonian mechanics. On the other hand, the vitalist tradition poses difficulties for feminist thinkers to the extent that it affirms "an expressive and creative life force,"[13] which is understood in opposition to the dumbness and passivity of inorganic, mechanical nature. In a similar vein to my comments above, Colebrook warns feminists that a simple appropriation of traditional vitalism can only reinforce time-worn gender binaries concerning the active male and the passive female. Seeking to circumvent this bind, Colebrook offers an innovative reading of Gilles Deleuze and Félix Guattari as advancing a "new vitalism," which she will also describe as a "passive vitalism." Whilst traditional, active vitalism posits life as the ultimate organizing principle by which matter can be directed towards some particular end, Colebrook maintains that the striking move of passive vitalism is that it admits of "a matter that fails to come to life,"[14] that is, matter conceived *and acclaimed* precisely in so far as it is unactualized potentiality, unproductive, virtual.

This paper enters into conversation with Colebrook, taking seriously both her criticisms of the ventures with vitalism by feminist new materialists and the passive vitalism she elaborates as an alternative response to the "linguisticism" which dominated poststructuralist feminist theory for much of the 1980s and 1990s. However, I will argue that theology also offers a way to counterbalance an over-emphasis on the agency of matter by new materialists. While I will suggest that a theological materialism need not regard matter as ceaselessly productive, I will also claim that matter's moments of passivity need not point to a life perpetually at odds with itself (as Colebrook's passive vitalism implies), but instead to a certain patiency of matter indicative of its "coming to be" as distinct from its "becoming."[15] It is with this notion of "coming to be" that a passage between theology and (a non-reductive) materialism may be charted.

To reach this position, I first outline the new materialist re-conception of matter as that which is, in some sense, agential. I then consider Colebrook's passive vitalism, a theory which seeks to exorcise the remaining spectres of humanism from new materialism, particularly as these continue to feed gendered, dualistic thinking. Finally, I indicate how theology can articulate a non-reductive materialism whereby the affirmation of divine transcendence neither inhibits the becoming of material creation nor assumes that pure, self-forming activity must be the hallmark of lively matter. A theological materialism, thus, offers a basis from which to challenge an uncritical humanism[16] and its concealed allegiance to patriarchal norms.

matter: creative becoming

In Western philosophy it is the capacity for agency that traditionally serves to mark human persons as distinct from the rest of nature. Richard Taylor puts it thus: "Persons are unique, in that they sometimes act. Other things are merely passive, undergoing such changes as are imparted to them, but never really performing even simple actions as people do."[17] While the meaning of the word "agency" may seem fairly straightforward, on closer scrutiny this is far from the case. The term is operative in a range of contexts including metaphysics, ethics, and political theory. Yet for all its fuzziness, the concept of agency is typically considered to encompass notions of selfhood, rationality, choice, intention, will, autonomy and independence, all of which effectively serve to delimit its application to persons alone.

It is precisely the idea that personhood is a condition of agency that new materialists wish to deny. If a more *distributive*[18] understanding of agency is to be achieved, thus enabling the acknowledgement of matter's agential power, then the tie between agency and agent, doing and doer must be undone at the ontological level. With Nietzsche, new materialists hold that ontologically "there is no 'being' behind doing, acting, becoming."[19] The siren song of language must be resisted; the traps of grammatical structure avoided, if matter is to be envisaged as lively and vibrant rather than an inert substance capable only of mechanical motion.

Diana Coole and Samantha Frost contend that a non-reductive materialism is marked by a materiality that "is always something *more than 'mere' matter*: an excess, force, vitality, relationality, or difference that renders matter active, self-creative, productive, unpredictable."[20] The danger here, though, is that the articulation of a non-reductive materialism retains the standard view that matter must be supplemented by something other than itself, which serves to vitalize it. For without such a supplement, matter continues to be "'mere' matter": passive, dead stuff devoid of all quality (save extension and motion on the Cartesian–Newtonian model).

Accordingly, Jane Bennett warns new materialists against repeating the mistake of nineteenth-century vitalists who, wrestling against the dominant mechanistic model of nature, refer to "a vital principle that while profoundly implicated in matter, is not 'of' matter."[21] In order to avoid imagining agency as some sort of immaterial force indissociable from matter, while nevertheless distinct from it, agency itself must be materialized. For new materialists like Bennett and Karen Barad, "Agency is not an attribute but the ongoing reconfiguring of the world."[22] Importantly, then, rethinking agency demands an ontological shift, one congruent with a materialist, posthumanist understanding of agency. In what follows I will delineate several significant aspects of the ontological topography envisaged by new materialist thought.

First, is a commitment to a metaphysics of process. Drawing on a range of thinkers – including naturalists such as Democritus, Epicurus, Spinoza, Darwin and Niels Bohr, vitalists such as Bergson and Deleuze, the phenomenologist Merleau-Ponty, historical materialists inspired by Marx,[23] and feminist philosophers such as Luce Irigaray, Judith Butler and Donna Haraway – new materialists jettison a substantialist ontology and instead posit a world of creative becoming. Such a world is at bottom characterized by myriad and complex processes of materialization. Consequently, objects (whether things, structures or thinking subjects) do not pre-exist the various processes they subsequently undergo. Rather, they emerge from creative processes that yield not sharply individuated entities with a fixed set of properties but differential zones which, though determinable, are never completely determinate.

To reiterate, for new materialists reality just is emerging materiality. As Barad puts it: "The world is an ongoing open process of mattering through which 'mattering' itself acquires meaning and form in the realization of different agential possibilities."[24] Such a vision resonates somewhat with the ancient Greek understanding of nature (*phusis*) as creative becoming. Importantly, the avowal of nature's capacity for self-formation must not overlook the *materiality* of this process. Commenting on Heidegger's understanding of being as *phusis*, Irigaray criticizes his phenomenological ontology for ultimately privileging form (*morphē*) and language over the potentiality of matter (*hylē*), and thus the reality of sexual difference.[25]

In a similar manner, although in a different context, Barad argues that while Butler attempts to offer a non-reductive theory of matter – one which encompasses both the mediation of matter by discourse and the material reality necessarily implicated by such discourse – she, nevertheless, ends up perpetuating the idea of matter as the shadowy effect of (active, form-giving) signification.[26] Certainly, Barad, like Butler, appreciates that at one level matter is the sedimentation of its ongoing discursive history. However, wishing to resolve the problems she finds in Butler's work, Barad also insists that the matter inherent in the activity of materialization is not to be figured negatively as the outer limits of discourse. More positively, it is to be recognized as a productive power capable of modifying in non-trivial ways processes of materialization. Barad suggests the term "entanglement" as a metaphor for the relationship between matter and meaning, which are less like two distinct elements and more like differentiated phases of an open becoming.[27] On this account, matter and meaning mutually engender each other. Here we can note – and this is our second point – that new materialists emphasize a *monistic* ontology, thereby refusing dualistic oppositions between matter and meaning, matter and form, body and mind, etc., which have dominated the history of Western thought.[28]

Third, by avowing a process ontology, new materialists also avow a *relational* ontology. Thus, the ontological baseline is not discrete things but rather the network of relations in and through which varying agential sites (i.e., things) emerge. Concerned that her rhetoric of "thing-power" is problematic, in so far as it suggests that materiality is characterized by distinct, stable objects, Bennett's vital materialism draws on the work of Spinoza and Deleuze and Guattari in order to emphasize the notion of assemblage.[29] According to Bennett, the world is "a dynamic flow of matter-energy that tends to settle into various bodies, bodies that often join forces, make connections, form alliances."[30] The term assemblage captures the idea that bodies, that is, material objects, do not exist and act in isolation from each other but establish dynamic, protean groupings which constitute the rich, diverse ecologies that are the very condition of any particular thing. Moreover, Bennett tells us, the word "assemblage" does not refer to an organic whole governed by a predominant organizing principle but instead points to an unsystematic, yet more or less coherent, arrangement of interconnecting elements.

While Bennett's notion of assemblage may still carry undertones of individual things interrelating with each other (such that relations are predicated on things), Barad coins the term "intra-action" precisely in order to convey the ontological primacy of relations and thus the derivative nature of things. According to Barad, "reality is not composed of things-in-themselves or things-behind-phenomena, but of 'things'-in-phenomena,"[31] where phenomena are differing processes of materialization which produce various distinctions by virtue of specific intra-actions.[32] Such intra-actions enact what Barad calls "agential cuts" which institute fissurings and ruptures within the flow of phenomena (which would otherwise remain ontologically indeterminate), and so establish differentiations which introduce *"exteriority-within-phenomena,"*[33] that is, boundaries separating "components" in phenomena in ways that matter ontologically, epistemologically and ethically.[34] Importantly, Barad's relational ontology (which she labels "agential realism") "refuses the representationalist fixation on 'words' and 'things' and the problematic of their relationality."[35] Instead, it emphasizes the entanglement of matter and meaning in terms of agential intra-actions: processes of materialization in which notions such as "materiality" and "discourse," "subject" and "object," "human" and "non-human," emerge together as "entangled agencies"[36] that articulate not just human bodies and experiences but an entire (more than human) world of differentiated becoming.

Barad's focus on the idea of "intra-action," rather than interaction, alerts us to a further aspect of new materialist ontologies: the reinterpretation of traditional notions of causality. Where processes of materialization are characterized by the mutual constitution of emerging forms and distinctions, the expression of causal relations in terms of a linear series of efficient causes becomes wholly inadequate. As Frost puts it:

> to conceive of causation in singular, linear, and unidirectional terms is to elide the mutual and on-going transfigurations, the serendipitous, surprising, and sometimes anomalous developments that emerge through the kinds of interactions [or, indeed, intra-actions] highlighted by these new materialists.[37]

The relational ontologies advanced by new materialists are dis/organized by complex, multilayered causal processes which effect unpredictable ruptures, swerves, juxtapositions and groupings that resist analysis in the overly-simplified terms of mechanical chains of cause and effect. Instead of efficient causation, William Connolly suggests the term "emergent causality" as a more appropriate way to describe "the dicey process by which new entities and processes periodically surge into being."[38] Connolly importantly points out that the concept of emergent causality challenges the traditional, strict division between human agency, on the one hand, and a world of objects set in motion by external causes, on the other.[39] Emergent causality places the accent on the agentiality of material processes where no simple line can be drawn between cause and agent, or even between cause and effect. Thus, Connolly writes: "Emergent causality consists of resonances within and between force-fields [read: different levels of material processes] in a way that is causal but beyond the power to isolate and separate all elements in determinate ways. An element of mystery or uncertainty is attached to emergent causality."[40] Rethinking agency beyond the compass of human affairs demands a radical reinterpretation of causality in ways that are attentive to the self-transformative, capricious trajectories of lively matter.

The fifth point I wish to highlight regarding new materialist ontologies is the emphasis on immanence rather than transcendence. Connolly explains:

> By immanence I mean a philosophy of becoming in which the universe is not dependent on a higher power. It is reducible

neither to mechanistic materialism, dualism, theo-teleology, nor the absent God of minimal theology. It concurs with the [...] [view] that there is more to reality than actuality. But that "more" is not given by a robust or minimal God.[41]

The transcendent God of classical theism has traditionally been figured as the archetypal agent. On this account, the world is held to be the product of God's creative act. Moreover, not only is God's creative agency believed to sustain the existence of whatever is, it is also said that God is providential, directing all nature to the fulfilment of the divine *telos*. Divine agency provides the model for human agency. Unsurprisingly, then, new materialists generally reject the idea of divine transcendence. By liberating material immanence from the regimes of both divine and human sovereignty, new materialists can envisage matter as agential, and thus a world characterized by dynamic moments of creative transitions.

Although new materialists such as Connolly repudiate the idea of divine transcendence, they do not, however, endorse an uncritical positivism that would insist on a strict adherence to the actual. While material immanence (actuality) is all there is, for the new materialist, this is not a closed, mechanistic totality devoid of all novelty. Instead, it is an ever-shifting plane of creative materializations open to the spontaneous emergence of new formations. It is precisely due to the creative becoming of matter that new materialism may be viewed as, to use Rosi Braidotti's words, an "enchanted materialism."[42]

passive vitalism: between mechanism and vitalism

According to Colebrook, the exalting of materiality as that which is inherently agential and dynamic would seem, on the face of it, to be a welcome move for feminism because it overturns the customary image of inert matter, and in doing so collapses the gender hierarchy that figures woman as passive body and man as active mind. However, commenting on the frequent appeal to the vitalist tradition by feminists seeking to articulate a new materialism that would re-energize a feminist theory exhausted by an over-emphasis on discursive factors, Colebrook observes: "What we have *not* overturned, though, is a horror of the inert, the unproductive, and the radically *different*: that which cannot be comprehended, enlivened, rendered fertile or dynamic."[43] Against the current of those streams of contemporary feminism lauding material agency, Colebrook calls for a break with a "norm of life"[44] that privileges action, creativity and productivity over that materiality which remains unactualized potential. She argues:

> The true politics of matter lies not in matter now occupying the position that was once attributed to God (and the man who is made in his image) – the position of a being that has no determination or limit other than its own coming into existence – but in a matter that fails to come to life.[45]

It is not that Colebrook disagrees with vitalist and feminist critiques of matter as mere *res extensa*. More precisely, her target is the vitalist insistence that life must always be striving, always a potentiality (*dunamis*) on its way to actualizing a particular form (*energeia*). This ought to be of concern for feminists, Colebrook believes, precisely because it maintains the gendered dualism that is active male/passive female. As noted above, Colebrook discovers in Deleuze and Guattari's co-authored work, as well as in Deleuze's solo writings, an alternative, minor tradition of vitalism – a *passive* vitalism – which can be distinguished from the more dominant strand of active vitalism, a strand which, on Colebrook's account, includes figures such as Karl Marx, Henri Bergson, Michel Foucault, Jacques Derrida and Butler. How, then, does a passive vitalism escape a norm of life which demands creative activity of all things endowed with life? Moreover, why might the concept "becoming-woman" created by Deleuze and Guattari turn out to be, as Colebrook holds, "the anti-vitalist concept par excellence"?[46] It is to these questions that I now turn.

In her book *Deleuze and the Meaning of Life*, Colebrook summarizes the distinction between two forms of vitalism – one active, the other passive – in the following way:

> Vitalism in its contemporary mode [...] works in two opposite directions. The tradition that Deleuze and Guattari invoke is opposed to the organism as subject or substance that would govern differential relations: their concept of "life" refers not to an ultimate principle of survival, self-maintenance and continuity but to a disrupting and destructive range of forces. The other tradition of vitalism posits "life" as a mystical and unifying principle. It is this second vitalism of meaning and the organism that, despite first appearances, dominates today. The turn to naturalism in philosophy, to bodies and affect in theory, to the embodied, emotional and extended mind in neuroscience: all of these manoeuvres begin the study of forces from the body and its world, and all understand "life" in a traditionally vitalist sense as oriented towards survival, self-maintenance, equilibrium, homeostasis and autopoiesis.[47]

In contrast to the standard reading of Deleuze's philosophy as fundamentally life-affirming, a eulogy to life as pure, creative becoming,[48] Colebrook argues that while he agrees with active vitalism that determinate bodies, structures and meanings emerge from life, he also views life as that which can, perversely, refuse synthesizing processes of creation, refuse conscious meaning, continuity and expansion.

Put baldly, Deleuze's passive vitalism is that which affirms life without, however, instituting life as a normative value: life need not always live. Moreover, and crucially, for Deleuze, life or vitality is not circumscribed by the organism. For life exceeds the parameters of living, identifiable forms and so is not bound by principles of organization. Passive vitalism is thus the avowal of inorganic life. As Deleuze and Guattari put it in *A Thousand Plateaus*, "If everything is alive, it is not because everything is organic or organized [...] the life in question is inorganic, germinal and intensive [...] everything that passes *between* organisms."[49]

By focusing their attention on the notion of inorganic life, Deleuze and Guattari are able to develop a passive vitalism that enables them to bypass the opposition between (traditional, active) vitalism and mechanism. Although informed by a history reaching back as far as Aristotle, vitalism as a self-defined position arose at the turn of the twentieth century precisely in order to challenge the mechanistic approaches to the life sciences prevailing at the time. While mechanism struggles to explain the emergence of complex wholes and their capacity for transformation, vitalism, in its traditional form, postulates a vital principle or life-force as that which organizes matter towards a specific form whilst remaining irreducible to the material processes it guides. However, by situating itself in opposition to mechanism, traditional vitalism remains dedicated to a conception of life which takes the living organism as normative. Life is thus understood to be characterized by the capacity for self-organization and growth, as well as purposive striving towards the realization of predetermined forms. But this organicist or holistic model of life fails to appreciate what Deleuze (in both his single authorship and in his work co-written with Guattari) would describe as a virtual field of pre-individual singularities or forces, an inorganic life that is passive because its dynamism is not the intentional, purposive action of well-organized bodies but rather that of chance encounters, some of which produce various levels of organization ("molar" forms) and some of which remain "molecular," thus tending towards further variation rather than bounded wholes or identifiable systems.

Unlike traditional, active vitalism, Colebrook explains, passive vitalism enables us "to consider forces of composition that differ from those of man and the productive organism."[50] There are two important upshots to this. First, by invoking forces that exceed the limits of the organism, passive vitalism refuses the association of the inorganic with death: lifeless, unthinking mechanism. Instead, the living – i.e., determinate forms of life – are traversed by an inorganic vitality, that "powerful, non-organic Life which grips the world."[51] The basis for opposing the living organism with mere mechanism (death), *phusis* with *technē*, is thereby dissolved, enabling Deleuze to develop a machinic materialism (more on which below).

Second, passive vitalism is able to achieve a radical anti-humanism by thinking life beyond the image of the human. It is true, as Colebrook notes, that the Marxist theory of dialectical materialism reveals a vitalist impulse in so far as it counters Hegel's idealization of matter by recognizing the dynamism of material life: while human, social labour transforms nature in various ways over time, it is also the case that – and here is the dialectical move – bodily needs *irreducible* to labour inflect socio-economic history. The trouble is that Marxism aspires to fully humanize matter, harmonizing our material conditionedness with creative, free human activity.[52] Notably, Colebrook also argues that anti-dialectical forms of vitalism, inspired by Nietzsche and Bergson, remain anthropocentric even as they seek to affirm life in its pure, preconceptual immediacy, liberated from all theologico-humanist categories believed to subject life to stultifying, transcendent norms. This is because their refusal to countenance inertia, barrenness, and the non-living, coupled with their efforts to return all technical systems – language, concepts, perceptions, the rational subject – back to their constitutive origins, namely, creative life, belies a subtle commitment to the quite theologico-humanist demand for life to be fecund and productive.[53]

In addition to eluding the opposition between (traditional) vitalism and mechanism, as well as denying humanism, passive vitalism, Colebrook tells us, offers a novel way in which to rethink matter as "positive difference."[54] In common with new materialism, Deleuze and Guattari advance a monistic ontology whereby *matter is life itself*, is "creative force and difference,"[55] rather than an inert medium animated by life. Indeed, matter is understood by these two co-authors to be intensive, which is to say that it is not characterized by basic elements extended in space but by dynamic movements of differentiation. Importantly, difference is not to be understood here as the difference *between* two distinct things, which would be a negative difference (x is not y) premised on identity and negation. Rather, difference is continuous variation or endless becoming, a continuum comprising infinite singular events or positive differences. Moreover, for Deleuze and Guattari, the movements of intensive matter – inorganic life – are those of desire. This is not the desire *for* something that is lacking but a positive conception of desire as that which produces connections or relations. Importantly, as Deleuze explains, in his dialogues with Claire Parnet, "there is no subject of desire, any more than there is an object."[56] Thus, desire produces desire: a continuous intensification of differings and connectings.

At this point, Deleuze and Guattari's concept of the "machine" becomes relevant.[57] For machines, they contend, are just connections. However, while a mechanism is composed of parts contingently related to each other in ways that make possible a specific function, and an organism is composed of parts related together in an integral unity that is purposive and self-sustaining, a machine is composed of connections that are not subordinate to a specific function or an overarching unity. Consequently, connections – that is, desiring-machines – always carry the potential for further connections which in turn could actualize forces of desire differently.[58] A machinic materialism, then, alerts us to an immanent, processual reality from which actual bodies and spatio-temporal relations surface. Recalling Spinoza's *natura naturans*, this "plane of immanence" is

> a plane of absolute immobility or absolute movement [...] traversed by nonformal elements of relative speed that enter into this or that individuated assemblage depending on their degrees of speed and slowness. A plane of consistency peopled by anonymous matter, by infinite bits of impalpable matter entering into varying connections.[59]

Deleuze and Guattari's co-authorship directs our attention to a subterranean reality of flows and intensities that is not a chaotic materiality awaiting organization by predetermined, immaterial forms but a "body without organs," an inorganic life that is at once machinic in so far as it produces connections that yield various assemblages (actual bodies). While these often settle into stable and enduring forms they are, nevertheless, always open to molecular, indeterminate becomings given their immanent relation to an intensive, differential materiality. The appeal of Deleuze and Guattari's work for many contemporary theorists lies primarily in their articulation of a posthuman ontology in which difference and creative becoming are prioritized, thus promising exciting new modes of living and experiencing life which refuse all normative identities.

Colebrook's reading of Deleuze and Guattari's philosophy is fascinating precisely because she finds in their work a passive vitalism that resists (traditional conceptions of) life and productivity. The passivity of passive vitalism is at least twofold. First, it signals a vitality without a subject or an agent (or an object for that matter): there is no life "*of* this or that identifiable substance,"[60] for life is no more, and indeed no less, than positive difference or continuous variation. That relatively durable forms emerge is neither the result of a constitutive life-force or spirit working through matter nor entirely mechanistic processes but of myriad desiring processes, or what Deleuze and Guattari also call "passive syntheses," always already immanent in all actual bodies.[61] Intensive matter is dis/organized by unconscious and unintentional dynamics.

Second, passive vitalism affirms indeterminate becomings, that is, differential forces (also referred to as "multiplicities" or "singularities") that are not directed towards the realization of recognizable forms but instead signal a range of potential relations and affects. Such forces (of becoming-other) are contra life and immobilizing in so far as they diverge from the self-maintenance of organized forms. Passive vitalism thus brings to the fore detached, unactualized and unlived potentials that constitute what we might think of as a "deterritorializing vitality," a mode of life that tends towards a virtual, intensive materiality and thus towards the disorganization and disembodiment of the organism. The radical insight of Deleuze and Guattari's passive vitalism, Colebrook maintains, is that "Life does not strive to maintain and produce itself but is inflected and directed by powers from without."[62] Whereas new materialism promotes the reconception of matter as inherently lively and agential, Deleuze and Guattari write of "a viral power in [material] life that takes the form of a variability without self-reference, without meaning,"[63] a power characterized by stasis and sterility, thoroughly in tension with the dynamics and productivity of the organism.

Seeking to qualify the commonly held view that Deleuze is *the* philosopher of becoming, Colebrook is keen to point out that he never asserts the becoming of life per se. For Deleuze, as Colebrook makes clear, life is not a single generative power from which all becomings erupt. This is because there is only ever "*a* life," an indefinite yet particular becoming that is not, thereby, the becoming of life in general.[64] This is important both metaphysically and politically. It is the former because it rejects the view (often attributed to a certain reading of Bergson) that there is a pure becoming – life – that is all creativity and untrammelled flourishing that, inevitably, is frustrated and opposed by the creations it effects. Deleuze insists that becoming is always localized, a unique immanent encounter between pre-individual singularities by which new bodily relations and affective powers are actualized. Yet a life is always already a queer vitality since its creative impulse is bound up with "the unproductive, the sterile, the unengendered, the unconsumable,"[65] namely, the body without organs.

The emphasis on "a life" is politically significant because it contests the vision of the human as that which aspires to a pure becoming, thus free to actualize any kind of existence whatsoever, a vision beloved of the liberal tradition. Given such an aspiration, the political imperative must be the refusal of all normative images of humanity since these only ever serve to subjugate human beings. On such an account, the human is, to use Colebrook's words, "a sense of what might be, of potentiality or proper realization. To be human is to be burdened with giving oneself a world, with forming oneself and deciding on one's own being."[66]

Now, as a number of feminists have observed, the image of the human as unencumbered becoming is implicitly framed according to gendered values. It is man who is the subject of pure becoming, of self-productive life, the subject who casts the feminine as that material otherness through which he can ultimately arrive at himself as creative self-determination, the giver of forms. Woman, on the other hand, is (on Deleuze and Guattari's view) "a becoming that is not a becoming *of* a subject prior to its relations, nor is it a becoming toward realization."[67] Deleuze and Guattari's concept of "becoming-woman" thus gestures away from a humanist-masculinist macropolitics towards a micropolitics whereby life is not that which strives towards its fulfilment in man – who comes to recognize himself as self-determining life and, consequently, the very acme of life – but rather a flux of molecular processes prior to the rational subject and the organism, and thus prior to all acts and agency. It is because becoming-woman marks the first phase of deterritorialization, that is, the dissolution of stable, organized form epitomized by the "man-standard,"[68] which Colebrook suggests can be considered as "the anti-vitalist concept par excellence."[69] Moreover, becoming-woman emphasizes an immanent materialism: its orientation is directed towards the plane of immanence, away from the plane of transcendence, namely, illusory images of a fixed, originary ground as the basis of all becomings.

To sum up: Deleuze and Guattari's passive vitalism, as reconstructed by Colebrook, shares with new materialism a refusal of reductive accounts of matter as mere extended stuff to be vivified by an immaterial life-force. For Deleuze and Guattari there is only life – multiple differentiations – expressed as matter (and mind). However, the critical step taken by passive vitalism is that life is not envisaged as that which strives to actualize form, nor that which endeavours to increase its creative productivity. Instead, passive vitalism proposes the notion of an inorganic, machinic life, thereby liberating the concept of life from the bounds of the organism, as this serves to tie life to self-maintenance (against death) and productive relations. The dynamism of inorganic life is passive because it is not sustained by the intentional agency of the organism. Furthermore, inorganic life presupposes unactualized potentialities that remain inert, detached and unrelated to organized form. Passive vitalism invites us to elaborate a non-reductive, immanent materialism, where life is not all glorious, creative becoming but that which also deflects from the living, tending towards disorganization, disconnection and sterility.

Admitting life's "stupidity," its potential not to realize its productive powers, and appreciating that all living bodies presuppose a life which does not live (the body without organs), enables a feminist critique of the theologico-humanist imperative that life must thrive and be generative. Given passive vitalism, the passivity of the female body does not denote a materiality that easily and without resistance yields to the determinations of male form but rather matter as positive difference, indeterminate becomings without actualization or relation, thus deviating from life as creative, expansive production.

Colebrook also maintains that passive vitalism would reconfigure the relationship between nature (*phusis*) and culture (*technē*). Rather than understand culture as that which either breaks free of nature (social constructivism) or serves as nature's most complex self-expression (*naturphilosophie*), culture could be conceived as that non-human life which resists life. "Culture would not be an extension of nature," Colebrook explains, "but, *through its very materiality*, that which acts demonically in opposition to nature's potentiality."[70] Here, culture denotes those images, habits, quantifications, involuntary thoughts, pre-individual encounters and purposeless perversions comprising a passive dynamic prior to the conscious agency of subjects. In view of such a dynamic, ethics and politics would need to go beyond goal-directed activity, which presupposes the rational subject as agent, in order to take into account how varying molecular, desiring processes ceaselessly compose human bodies and social relations, which are consequently marked by unactualized potentialities and latent affects. According to Colebrook, the political is not the realization of life, whether this realization is understood to tend towards a particular normative framework (e.g., the discourse ethics of Jürgen Habermas) or away from all metaphysical gestures (Nietzsche and Bergson). Rather, the political must encompass a micropolitics that appreciates "all the ways in which an inappropriable non-life traverses bodies from the beginning."[71]

theology, life and matter

It is Colebrook's view that theology is committed to life as norm: the transcendent, creator God is the pure act from which all life endlessly flows. God is thus the ultimate agent. By contrast, and on a certain interpretation of classical theism, the material world is held to be empty of all life, lacking any creativity of its own. The transfer of divine agency to man, effected by secular humanism, does nothing to alter the impoverished status of matter, which remains no more than a passive medium for the imposition of (male) form. As we have seen, new materialism disputes this picture. However, I think Colebrook is right when she observes that the new materialist emphasis on the liveliness of matter simply repeats at the level of material reality the modern understanding of the human person as fundamentally agential. That said, while I welcome her attempt to highlight matter's passive dimension without, nevertheless, reducing this passivity to the simple reception of all-determining form, I wish to question her claim that theology is inevitably bound by the tenet that life must always be productive. In what follows, I hope to offer some preliminary suggestions on how a theological materialism could deliver a non-reductive materialism that upholds both the active and the passive aspects of matter, without running into the difficulties that, I maintain, attend passive vitalism.

Interestingly, Colebrook suggests that once vitalism is reconfigured beyond the constraints of organicism, it can be described as a "hyper-vitalism" as well as a passive vitalism.[72] For inorganic life swarms and heaves at the borders of determinate forms; as Deleuze and Guattari write: "The body without organs is not a dead body but a living body all the more alive and teeming once it has blown apart the organism and its organization."[73] The notion of a hyper-vitalism is significant because, I would argue, it helps to reveal how the philosophy of Deleuze and Guattari does not entirely distance itself from the vitalist longing for life to be productive and creative. For sure, their elaboration of a passive vitalism highlights unactualized potentials that remain unrelated and deflected from production. But this is precisely to lay bare the transcendental conditions of a *truly* creative life, where life is no longer figured as the creative becoming *of* some actual body but as a pure potential for creative differentiation.

For Deleuze and Guattari the problem with the vitalist tradition is not so much its stress on creative becoming but its organicist conception of life. However, a commitment to inorganic life produces a troubling tension with respect to the sorts of practical insights we can draw from this. On the one hand, for Colebrook, passive vitalism calls for a micropolitics charged with the twin tasks of (i) attending to the barely discernible, infinite, pre-personal desires constitutive of, as well as exceeding, all bodies; and (ii) aiming "to maximise the circumstances for the proliferation and pulverisation of difference."[74] On the other hand, pushed to its extreme, passive vitalism could support a sort of fatalism whereby humanity simply awaits its dissolution by the deterritorializing forces of inorganic life. Indeed, a motto for a politics informed by passive vitalism might be "let the desert grow [...],"[75] let organic, living bodies slip away into the anonymous flow that is non-human, inorganic life.

Of course, Deleuze and Guattari, in a rather Aristotelian manner, seek the middle ground: neither the stasis resulting from the hubristic insistence on viewing the world as it accords with human existence nor the death, destruction and chaos which would ensue by "wildly destratifying."[76] The problem is, as Anthony Paul

Smith rightly notes, that Deleuze and Guattari's thought appears to lack a mechanism, other than "vague suggestions of cautious experimentation," by which human life can become further open to unactualized potentialities and deterritorializing desires without, however, annihilating itself in the process.[77] Moreover, when a micropolitics such as Deleuze and Guattari's is underpinned by an ontology that places the accent on fragmentation and dissolution it becomes all too easy to end up endorsing either a passive anticipation for the unpredictable, revolutionary dynamics of inorganic life at best, or violently accelerating the arrival of the posthuman world at worst.

Colebrook's elaboration of Deleuze and Guattari's passive vitalism is important because it reveals how the construal of matter as inherently agential remains tied to humanist and masculinist assumptions. But, I contend, while passive vitalism avows the inert and the sterile, it does this precisely in order to liberate a creative life more superior than that which is delivered by vitalist positions which treat the agent – whether God, the human or life in general – as originary. Paradoxically, passive vitalism means that a truly creative life is to be achieved by resisting the imperative for life always to strive towards its self-maintenance and self-enhancement; yet this resistance must be careful not to incur the total destruction of that which lives, the organism. It is not that the human is displaced by the posthuman but rather it is through the human that posthuman, inorganic life is freed in ways that open up the creative transformation *of the human*. Indeed, despite the anti-humanist direction of passive vitalism, it strikes me that the human remains a central figure here, since it is the human that is best able to counter-actualize (that is, deterritorialize or disorganize) bodies through art and philosophy in ways that can (somehow) maintain a productive tension between destruction and creation.

In what follows I will make three points serving as no more than an overture for a theological materialism, the details of which I hope to develop elsewhere.[78] The first point concerns the claim, held by new materialists among others, that theistic accounts of divine creation necessarily rob the world of all integrity and contingency, reducing material finitude, and even human subjectivity, to no more than the passive effect of God's creative agency. The problem with this sort of criticism is that it assumes a *contrastive* account of the relationship between divine transcendence and worldly immanence.[79] Consequently, divine agency is construed as that which inevitably competes with worldly agency: the affirmation of God's supreme agency can only come at the expense of non-divine, creaturely agency, and vice versa. However, if we adopt a non-contrastive understanding of divine transcendence it is no longer possible to view God as one competing agent among others; rather, God's agency is wholly unique and, thus, cannot be contrasted with the agencies of this world, or with the agency of the world itself. Moreover, far from denying agency to creatures, God's creative agency can be understood as the very source of the creature's autonomy and efficacy. As Kierkegaard once wrote,

> Omnipotence, which can handle the world so toughly and with such a heavy hand, can also make itself so light that what it has brought into existence receives independence. Only a wretched and worldly conception of the dialectic of power holds that it is greater and greater in proportion to its ability to compel and to make dependent [...] the art of power lies precisely in making another free [...] only omnipotence can truly succeed in this.[80]

Although Kierkegaard, in the above passage, wishes to show how the total dependence of all creatures on God's sustaining love and power need not sacrifice *human* autonomy and productivity, there is no reason, as far as I can tell, why autonomy and productivity cannot similarly be extended to non-human life and, indeed, matter itself. Both theology and philosophy need to take seriously Kathryn Tanner's remark that "To exclude genuine created efficacy as a possible direct effect of God's agency is to misunderstand [...] the nature of the transcendence implied by the supremacy, sovereignty and holiness of God."[81] Divine transcendence defies any simplistic contrast between God's productive power and the productive power of nature.

My second point challenges Colebrook's assertion that theology commands life to be always active and fecund. It is undoubtedly the case that the God of classical theism is considered to be that eternal, inexhaustibly generative life from which all finite things proceed. However, it is worth considering how negative theology complicates this picture. For example, the German Dominican Meister Eckhart (c.1260–c.1327) evocatively appeals to images of barren desert, empty wasteland and desolate wilderness in order to convey the secret, innermost ground of the divine.[82] Indeed, for Eckhart, deeper than even the eternal life of the Trinity dwells the silent, inactive divine essence or Godhead. The divine ground emphasized by Eckhart's apophaticism is, I submit, not altogether dissimilar to Deleuze and Guattari's notion of inorganic life. This is because both denote the pregnant emptiness of pure potentiality, a groundless ground, a radical indeterminacy that is unlike any living thing because it is the immanent condition of all that lives.[83] Without wishing to labour the point, Eckhart's mystical theology intimates a life beyond the living, a life irreducible to the terms of human agency and the organism more generally.

As mystics such as Eckhart show, the theistic God need not only be regarded in terms of dynamic, vibrant life. Correspondingly, God's creation need not *only* be viewed as that which perpetually strives to live and expand itself. The work of William Desmond is pertinent here. In his efforts to construct a "metaxological metaphysics,"[84] he distinguishes between what he calls *passio essendi* and *conatus essendi*.[85] The latter term refers to the "endeavour to be" or the self-affirmation of living things, while the former refers to the "patience of being," the reception of being and life. While *passio essendi* and *conatus essendi* are always coupled together, there is, Desmond tells us, a certain priority to the *passio* for "we are given to be before we give ourselves to be."[86] Creation *ex nihilo* means that prior to any *becoming*, or process of self-determination, there is a *coming to be* by virtue of which we – that is, all of creation – receive the gift of our "being-between" (between being and becoming) from God, "an enigmatic endowing source."[87] Importantly, Desmond's ontological vision emphasizes the idea that "[t]he passion of life is not originally of our willing."[88]

For Desmond, both modern and postmodern thought tends to focus exclusively on *conatus essendi*, thus subduing the *passio essendi* to the point that "self-becoming [life] circles around itself in an entirely immanent enclosure" and, consequently, "there is no opening of the porous between [i.e., life] to an endowing source of life beyond all enclosed immanence."[89] By drawing attention to the coming to be of matter (and life more broadly), as well as its capacity for self-becoming, a theological materialism informed by Desmond's metaxological metaphysics can, I venture, retain both the new materialist re-visioning of matter as lively and self-determining and the passive vitalist insight that an unchecked desire for matter to be productive and creative betrays a tacit humanism that would shape the world in an all-too-human image.

Of course, whereas passive vitalism insists on absolute immanence, a theological materialism recovers a transcendent creator God to philosophy.[90] Desmond contends that theism posits a "superior" transcendence, namely, the absolute otherness of the divine. Divine transcendence is a superior transcendence, Desmond explains, because it is an original otherness prior to an "exterior" transcendence (i.e., the transcendence of finite beings external and irreducible to human thought and action) and to an "interior" transcendence (i.e., the transcendence of human self-othering or creative becoming).[91] Another way of putting this is to say that divine transcendence is "*transcendence itself*: an otherness reserved for God alone, and more than all holistic immanence."[92] When we conceive God's otherness to be beyond the immanent whole, we can then think divine creation not in terms of the *self*-othering of the divine but as "*the coming to be* of finite being,"[93] where finitude "is not its own determination, but is a released happening that is given its own promise of being creative."[94] On this account, the patiency of matter does not refer to a dynamism at odds with the organism but to the sheer "that it is" of material finitude, which Desmond calls the "idiocy of being."[95] Moreover, the patiency of matter can stun our thinking such that it can become porous to that which exceeds finite determination, namely, that original, enabling power by which finitude is given to be.[96]

Deleuze and Guattari's immanentism rejects the idea of an excess or reserve beyond the immanent whole – for the virtual and the actual rise and fall together, despite the arguable superiority of the former. While the circle of immanence envisaged by Deleuze and Guattari is that of an open, rather than closed, whole, such that difference is never reduced to identity (*à la* Hegel), I would argue that the dynamism of this whole is inevitably agonistic. Actual, finite determinations can only oppose and frustrate the a-teleological movements of inorganic life, which pull and push against the fixed boundaries of the organism, rendering these insecure. There is no space for the affirmation of differences in their lived, concrete actuality. The virtual power to differ – that life beyond (organic) life – configures the immanent whole towards creative dis/organization, always at the expense of the organism.

The American theologian David Bentley Hart summarizes my reservations well when he writes:

> Deleuzian affirmation is always an affirmation of the whole as force, never as gift or charity: not solely because a gift presumes a giver, but because being is *intrinsically* a violence whose intervals are not spaces where charity may be effectively enacted, but merely the shared ruptures between differences.[97]

By contrast, the divine transcendence of theism is an otherness other than the circle of immanence and as such, I hold, is able to grant each thing its space to be and become for its own sake (rather than as a medium expressing a virtual creative power).[98]

The final point I wish to make concerns the implications for feminism given a theological materialism. Colebrook, as we have seen, maintains that the passive vitalist concept "becoming-woman" can reinvigorate feminism in radically materialist directions. However, Deleuze and Guattari's becoming-woman is a concept which famously divides opinion among feminist theorists. For Colebrook, it serves to "queer" majoritarian politics of recognition, identity and representation by rethinking "woman," not as something which is and which demands recognition but as signalling positive potentialities (pre-personal desires) that "exceed and infinitely divide each body."[99] A micropolitics attuned to such positive potentialities offers the prospect of a "higher deterritorialization,"[100] open-ended, inhuman becomings which refuse any predetermined orientation.

Yet feminists such as Gillian Howie view the concept "becoming-woman" with suspicion.[101] The problem, Howie maintains, is not only that it advances a theory of difference with no room for concrete (molar) sexual difference but that it achieves its seeming liberation from sexual dimorphism in a way that quietly recovers sexual difference through the back door.[102] When Deleuze and Guattari identify becoming-woman with the schizo-processes of the body without organs, or with the inert, unproductive matter that is inorganic life, they continue to exploit, even if unwittingly, prevailing sexual difference stereotypes. Moreover, Howie argues, the process of abstraction by which the virtual body is approached and reconfigured could all too easily be described as a process of disembodiment, and thus a process "arguably at odds with any productive and beneficial social critique of invested desire."[103] While abstraction for Deleuze and Guattari is supposed to be a material practice – namely, the heightening of sensitivity to the not yet lived, positive potentialities constitutive of all molar forms – the shift away from actual bodies is quite at odds with feminist phenomenology, which seeks to consider women's experiences as these are lived and felt by embodied (inter)subjects situated in variable socio-historical contexts.

Theological materialism, I have begun to suggest, avows finite, lived actualities as those things which have been given to be and become. The transcendent God of theism does not simply affirm difference per se but actual things in their sensuous particularity. Leaving aside here the indefatigable debates concerning essentialism in feminist thought, it seems likely that "being a woman" is basic to my sensuous particularity. While highlighting the indeterminate powers and becomings composing and exceeding the human can remind us of how each thing always already contains the potential for creative renewal, this need not cast the lived body as a mere conduit for the erratic flux and flow of inorganic life. For Deleuze and Guattari, the specificities of the lived body are ultimately irrelevant; it is only the body's potential for becoming-other that matters. Theological materialism attempts to hold together the coming to be of things and their potential for becoming. *Passio essendi*, the patience of being, calls us to appreciate the existence of things in their sensuous particularity, for God wishes just those things to be, which means they are not simply for us.[104]

Moreover, it is worth noting that far from denigrating material immanence, divine transcendence deems creation to be good: the body *as it is lived*, as it is richly differentiated, is primordially affirmed as divine gift. Feminism need not shun theism on the (mistaken) grounds that it necessarily opposes the material world and its creative becoming. Indeed, theological materialism is committed to the sensuous particularity of embodied subjects and, thereby, avoids the flight from the lived which, I fear, is the upshot of the micropolitics of Deleuze and Guattari's passive vitalism.

conclusion

This paper has wanted to sound a note of caution in response to the keen emphasis on the agency of matter by new materialists. To be sure, rethinking the concept of agency, such that it may be said of matter, is a welcome step in so far as it acknowledges matter's form-giving powers, its capacity to be self-determining as well as determined, and so its moment of independence from human discursive practices. That said, I think feminist scholars ought to take heed of Colebrook's identification of a blind spot shadowing the feminist celebration of matter's liveliness and creativity. As we have seen, for Colebrook, the problem is that the agential conception of matter, particularly as it is informed by the vitalist tradition, simply extends the modern image of self-determining man to matter and leaves intact the norm of life, namely, that life should always be productive. The truly revolutionary idea, Colebrook argues, is that of matter understood as immanent, unactualized potential, as that which fails to come to life.

I share Colebrook's concern regarding the immense emphasis on the agentic capacities of matter by new materialist feminists – although I recognize that such an emphasis is understandable given the traditional, gendered construal of matter in Western thought. However, while Colebrook turns to the idea of a passive vitalism in the attempt to articulate a nonreductive materialism, I turn to the resources of theology. Although Colebrook claims that theology is of a piece with a masculinist humanism in so far as it upholds the "norm of life," I have argued that theology can uphold both the agency and patiency of matter. The contention that divine transcendence necessarily deprives material finitude of its own creative capacities can only be sustained given a contrastive understanding of the divine, which theists need not accept. Moreover, Desmond's metaxological metaphysics helpfully distinguishes between *passio essendi* (the patience of being) and *conatus essendi* (the endeavour to be), which enables us to think matter's passivity in terms of its coming to be and its activity in terms of its creative becoming. Whereas Colebrook posits a passive vitalism where material, immanent life is permanently at odds with the organisms it constitutes, a theological perspective, I have ventured, is one where God grants each thing its space to be and become. It may well turn out that the feminist insistence on the dignity of material reality is best achieved given the avowal of divine transcendence. At the very least, the prospect of a theologically oriented non-reductive materialism should not be foreclosed by feminists from the outset.

notes

1 Irigaray, *Speculum* 168. Here Irigaray is quoting Plotinus' *Enneads*.

2 Stevens 138.

3 This "nature-scepticism," as Kate Soper calls it, is driven by feminists wishing to obviate essentialist and determinist conceptions of biology, as these undermine notions of social transformation. Soper 121.

4 Almaio and Hekman 3. Sara Ahmed criticizes those who allege that feminism (from the second wave on) is steeped in "anti-biologism" or "biophobia." For Ahmed, the contention that social constructionism has become feminist dogma grossly reduces "the complex heterogeneity of modern feminism" (Ahmed 28).

5 For a critique of Butler's theory of performativity see, for example, Hull 57–63. Note, however, that in *Bodies That Matter* xvii, Butler herself cautions against the risk of "linguistic idealism."

6 According to Rick Dolphijn and Iris van der Tuin, the term "new materialism" or "neo-materialism" was coined by Rosi Braidotti and Manuel DeLanda – working independently of each other, and in different research areas – in the second half of the 1990s. Dolphijn and van der Tuin 153.

7 Lykke 131–36.

8 Almaio 237–64.

9 Almaio and Hekman.

10 Of course, in the wake of Einstein, contemporary particle physics upturns the mechanistic materialism of Newton. Rather than picturing atoms as invisible, solid corpuscles mechanically moving around empty space according to fixed natural laws, twenty-first-century theoretical physics instead views the fundamental features of matter in terms of "mass-energy," which include massless forces, waves, charges, virtual particles and mysterious "dark matter." The departure from classical mechanism, ushered in by Einstein's theory of relativity and quantum mechanics, may be viewed as the "progressive dematerialization" of our common-sense understanding of the material world. See McMullin 23ff. These developments in theoretical physics tend to provide grist to the new materialist mill. Moreover, new materialist thinking need not be viewed as extraneous in comparison to contemporary theoretical physics, not least because the former can ask how "these new conceptions of matter might reconfigure our models of society and the political" (Coole and Frost, "Introducing" 13).

11 For a discussion on the conception of persons as agents in Western philosophy, see Reader's seminal paper.

12 On the "avowed posthumanism" of new materialist thought, its refusal to privilege the human species over the rest of nature, see Coole and Frost, "Introducing" 20.

13 Colebrook, "On Not Becoming Man" 56.

14 Ibid. 59.

15 I obtain this distinction from William Desmond and will discuss it further in this paper. See Desmond, *God and the Between* 248–49.

16 While I am critical of the Enlightenment's construal of "rational man" (i.e., humanity), I do not, nevertheless, endorse a radical anti-humanism, which would seek to dissolve the notion of humanity altogether.

17 Richard Taylor cited in Reader 583. Taylor comes to disagree with this view.

18 Both Jane Bennett and William Connolly refer to the idea of "distributive agency." See Connolly 22; Bennett, *Vibrant Matter* 20–24.

19 Nietzsche 29.

20 Coole and Frost, "Introducing" 9; my emphasis.

21 Bennett, *Vibrant Matter* 138 n. 24.

22 Barad, "Posthumanist" 135.

23 Almaio and Hekman point out that "material feminism" (or "new materialist" feminism) must be distinguished from "materialist feminism" which takes its cue from Marx's emphasis on class agency. Almaio and Hekman 18. For a new materialist reading of Marx, see Edwards 281–98.

24 Barad, "Posthumanist" 135.

25 Irigaray, *Forgetting* 11–12.

26 Barad, "Posthumanist" 151 n. 26.

27 Barad, *Meeting* 271.

28 On the importance of the monistic tradition for new materialist ontologies, see Dolphijn and van der Tuin 153–54.

29 Bennett, *Vibrant Matter* 20–21.

30 Bennett, "Force" 365.

31 Barad, "Posthumanist" 135.

32 Barad's use of the term "phenomena" has its roots in Bohr's physics. For Bohr, there is no pre-existing distinction (or cut) between the knower (the agent of observation) and the known (the object). Rather, such a distinction is produced given the specific processes (intra-actions) of the scientific experiment. The word phenomena, for Bohr, thus articulates the interdependence of both knower and known, even as these may be temporarily distinguished under certain conditions.

33 Barad, "Posthumanist" 133.

34 Barad employs the term "ethico-onto-epistemology" in order to acknowledge the entanglement of what is usually taken to be distinct areas: ethics, ontology and epistemology. Barad, *Meeting* 185.

35 Barad, "Posthumanist" 132.

36 Barad, *Meeting* 33.

37 Frost 78.

38 Connolly 44. But note that Connolly does not abandon the notion of "efficient cause."

39 Ibid. 173.

40 Ibid. 174.

41 Ibid. 43.

42 Braidotti 60.

43 Colebrook, "On Not Becoming Man" 59.

44 Ibid. 58.

45 Ibid. 59.

46 Ibid. 78.

47 Colebrook, *Deleuze and the Meaning of Life* 137.

48 See, for example, Hallward.

49 Deleuze and Guattari, *Thousand* 550.

50 Colebrook, "Queer" 77.

51 Deleuze cited in Hallward 61.

52 Colebrook, "On Not Becoming Man" 60–64.

53 See Colebrook, *Deleuze and the Meaning of Life* 7.

54 Colebrook, "On Not Becoming Man" 71–77.

55 Colebrook, *Deleuze and the Meaning of Life* 152.

56 Deleuze and Parnet 58.

57 "[…] there is no matter apart from a dynamic, connecting and 'machinic' power" (Colebrook, *Deleuze and the Meaning of Life* 21–22).

58 Colebrook, "Introduction," *Deleuze and History* 11.

59 Deleuze and Guattari, *Thousand* 282.

60 Colebrook, "Introduction," *Deleuze and History* 21.

61 Deleuze and Guattari, *Anti-Oedipus* 28.

62 Colebrook, *Deleuze and the Meaning of Life* 133.

63 Ibid. 144.

64 See Deleuze 25–33.

65 Deleuze and Guattari, *Anti-Oedipus* 9.

66 Colebrook, "On Not Becoming Man" 79.

67 Ibid. 81.

68 Deleuze and Guattari, *Thousand* 321.

69 Colebrook, "On Not Becoming Man" 78.

70 Ibid.

71 Colebrook, "Politics" 705.

72 Colebrook, *Deleuze and the Meaning of Life* 38, 42.

73 Deleuze and Guattari, *Thousand* 34.

74 Colebrook, "Queer" 86.

75 This expression is used by Peter Hallward as a way to capture those Deleuzians who would declare: "who cares? Who cares about the

destruction of the human race? Why should we care? Let the capitalist movement of deterritorialization carry on to its logical conclusion [...]" (see Alliez et al. 164).

76 Deleuze and Guattari, *Thousand* 178. The co-authors are keen to stress that "[d]ismantling the organism has never meant killing yourself" (ibid. 177).

77 Smith 81.

78 For further insight into the idea of a theological materialism, see my book *Immanent Transcendence* 151–250.

79 On contrastive accounts of divine transcendence, see Tanner. She rightly argues that God's transcendence is "beyond relations of identity or simple contrast" (ibid. 66).

80 Kierkegaard, *Journals and Papers*, vol. 2, entry 1251. I am grateful to Simon Podmore for pointing me to this passage.

81 Tanner 87.

82 See, for example, Sermon 60 in Eckhart.

83 See Haynes, "Immanence."

84 Central to Desmond's work is the notion of the "between" or "*metaxu*," to use the Greek term. See Desmond, *God and the Between* 10, 3.

85 In particular, ibid. 248–49.

86 Ibid. 21.

87 Idem, "On the Surface" 45.

88 Ibid. 43.

89 Ibid. 45.

90 It is worth appreciating that the categories of absolute immanence and absolute transcendence invert into each other; they both invoke an irreducible otherness, a non-appropriable outside to every determination that is also the immanent condition of every determination.

91 Desmond, *Hegel's God* 3.

92 Ibid. 200; my emphasis.

93 Ibid. 128.

94 Ibid. 36.

95 Desmond, *God and the Between* 11; emphasis removed.

96 Ibid. 11.

97 Hart 66.

98 Given Colebrook's reconstruction of a passive vitalism, theological materialism still faces the question as to whether – with respect to worldly immanence, which God has given to be and become – every becoming presupposes a subject. To recall, Colebrook resists articulating becoming in terms of the becoming *of* some actual body because this occludes the molecular desiring processes that precede all bodies and which afford immanent creative transformations. This is a question I do not have space to address properly here. Moreover, I have not yet arrived at a position on this matter that I am reasonably satisfied with. However, minimally, it seems to me that a theological materialism would admit the idea of inherent tendencies and forms in nature; as Stephen Clark puts it: "All living creatures, like diamonds and snowflakes, exist because there are a limited (but very large) number of ways to be, to be beautiful, to declare God's glory" (14).

99 Colebrook, "Queer" 87.

100 Colebrook, "On Not Becoming Man" 78.

101 Howie.

102 Ibid. 85–86.

103 Ibid. 85.

104 Clark 284.

bibliography

Ahmed, Sara. "Open Forum Imaginary Prohibitions: Some Preliminary Remarks on the Founding Gestures of the 'New Materialism.'" *European Journal of Women's Studies* 15.1 (2008): 23–39. Print.

Alliez, Éric, Claire Colebrook, Peter Hallward, Nicholas Thoburn, and Jeremy Gilbert. "Deleuzian Politics? A Roundtable." *New Formations* 68 (Spring 2010): 143–87. Print.

Almaio, Stacy. "Trans-corporeal Feminisms and the Ethical Space of Nature." Almaio and Hekman 237–64. Print.

Almaio, Stacy, and Susan Hekman, eds. *Material Feminisms*. Bloomington: Indiana UP, 2008. Print.

Barad, Karen. *Meeting the Universe Halfway: Quantum Physics and the Entanglement of Matter and Meaning*. Durham, NC: Duke UP, 2007. Print.

Barad, Karen. "Nature's Queer Performativity." *Kvinder, Køn & Forskning* 1–2 (2012): 25–53. Print.

Barad, Karen. "Posthumanist Performativity: Toward an Understanding of How Matter Comes to Matter." Almaio and Hekman 120–54. Print.

Bennett, Jane. "The Force of Things: Steps Toward an Ecology of Matter." *Political Theory* 32.3 (2004): 347–72. Print.

Bennett, Jane. *Vibrant Matter: A Political Ecology of Things*. Durham, NC and London: Duke UP, 2010. Print.

Braidotti, Rosi. *Metamorphoses: Towards a Materialist Theory of Becoming*. Cambridge: Polity, 2002. Print.

Butler, Judith. *Bodies That Matter: On the Discursive Limits of Sex*. Rpt. London and New York: Routledge, 2011. Print.

Clark, Stephen. *Biology and Christian Ethics*. Cambridge: Cambridge UP, 2000. Print.

Colebrook, Claire. *Deleuze and the Meaning of Life*. London and New York: Continuum, 2010. Print.

Colebrook, Claire. *Gilles Deleuze*. London and New York: Routledge, 2002. Print.

Colebrook, Claire. "Introduction." *Deleuze and History*. Ed. Jeffrey A. Bell and Claire Colebrook. Edinburgh: Edinburgh UP, 2009. Print.

Colebrook, Claire. "On Not Becoming Man: The Materialist Politics of Unactualized Potential." Almaio and Hekman 52–84. Print.

Colebrook, Claire. "The Politics and Potential of Everyday Life." *New Literary History* 33.4 (2002): 687–706. Print.

Colebrook, Claire. "Queer Vitalism." *New Formations* 68 (Spring 2010): 77–92. Print.

Connolly, William E. *A World of Becoming*. Durham, NC and London: Duke UP, 2011. Print.

Coole, Diana, and Samantha Frost. "Introducing the New Materialisms." Coole and Frost, *New Materialisms* 1–43. Print.

Coole, Diana, and Samantha Frost, eds. *New Materialisms: Ontology, Agency and Politics*. Durham, NC and London: Duke UP, 2010. Print.

Deleuze, Gilles. "Immanence: A Life." *Pure Immanence: Essays on A Life*. Trans. Anne Boyman. New York: Zone, 2001. 25–33. Print.

Deleuze, Gilles, and Félix Guattari. *Anti-Oedipus: Capitalism and Schizophrenia 2*. Trans. Robert Hurley, Mark Seem, and Helen R. Lane. London and New York: Continuum, 2004. Print.

Deleuze, Gilles, and Félix Guattari. *A Thousand Plateaus: Capitalism and Schizophrenia 2*. Trans. Brian Massumi. London and New York: Continuum, 2004. Print.

Deleuze, Gilles, and Claire Parnet. *Dialogues II*. Trans. Hugh Tomlinson and Barbara Habberjam. London and New York: Continuum, 2002. Print.

Desmond, William. *God and the Between*. Oxford: Blackwell, 2008. Print.

Desmond, William. *Hegel's God*. Aldershot and Burlington, VT: Ashgate, 2003. Print.

Desmond, William. "On the Surface of Things: Transient Life and Beauty in Passing." *Radical Orthodoxy: Theology, Philosophy, Politics* 1.1 and 2 (2012): 20–54. Print.

Dolphijn, Rick, and Iris van der Tuin. "The Transversality of New Materialism." *Women: A Cultural Review* 21.2 (2010): 153–75. Print.

Eckhart, Meister. *The Complete Mystical Works of Meister Eckhart*. Ed. and trans. Maurice O'C. Walshe. New York: Crossroad, 2009. Print.

Edwards, Jason. "The Materialism of Historical Materialism." Coole and Frost, *New Materialisms* 281–98. Print.

Frost, Samantha. "The Implications of the New Materialisms for Feminist Epistemology." *Feminist Epistemology and Philosophy of Science: Power in Knowledge*. Ed. Heidi E. Grasswick. Dordrecht: Kluwer, 2011. 69–83. Print.

Hallward, Peter. *Out of this World: Deleuze and the Philosophy of Creation*. London: Verso, 2006. Print.

Hart, David Bentley. *The Beauty of the Infinite: The Aesthetics of Christian Truth*. Grand Rapids, MI and Cambridge: Eerdmans, 2003. Print.

Haynes, Patrice. "Immanence, Transcendence and Thinking Life with Deleuze and Eckhart." *Medieval Mystical Theology* 22.1 (2013): 5–26. Print.

Haynes, Patrice. *Immanent Transcendence: Reconfiguring Materialism in Continental Philosophy.* London and New York: Bloomsbury, 2012. Print.

Howie, Gillian. "Becoming-Woman: A Flight into Abstraction." *Deleuze Studies* 2 (2009): 83–106. Print.

Hull, Carrie. *The Ontology of Sex: A Critical Inquiry into the Deconstruction and Reconstruction of Categories.* London and New York: Routledge, 2006. Print.

Irigaray, Luce. *The Forgetting of Air in Martin Heidegger.* Trans. Mary Beth Mader. London: Athlone, 1999. Print.

Irigaray, Luce. *Speculum of the Other Woman.* Trans. Gillian C. Gill. Ithaca, NY: Cornell UP, 1985. Print.

Kierkegaard, Søren. *Journals and Papers.* 7 vols. Ed. and trans. Howard V. Hong and Edna H. Hong. Vol. 2, entry 1251. Bloomington: Indiana UP, 1967–1978. Print.

Lykke, Nina. "The Timeliness of Post-Constructionism." *NORA – Nordic Journal of Feminist and Gender Research* 18.2 (2010): 131–36. Print.

McMullin, Ernan. "From Matter to Materialism ... and (Almost) Back Again." *Information and the Nature of Reality: From Physics to Metaphysics.* Ed. Paul Davies and Niel Henrik Gregerson. Cambridge: Cambridge UP, 2010. 13–37. Print.

Nietzsche, Friedrich. *On the Genealogy of Morals.* Oxford: Oxford UP, 1996. Print.

Reader, Soran. "The Other Side of Agency." *Philosophy* 82.4 (2007): 579–604. Print.

Smith, Anthony Paul. "The Judgement of God and the Immeasurable: Political Theology and Organizations of Power." *Political Theology* 12.1 (2011): 69–86. Print.

Soper, Kate. *What is Nature?* Oxford: Blackwell, 1995. Print.

Stevens, Wallace. "Autumn Refrain." *Collected Poems.* London: Faber, 1954. Print.

Tanner, Kathryn. *God and Creation in Christian Theology: Tyranny or Empowerment?* Minneapolis: Fortress, 1988. Print.

> Every messianism, whatever the theoretical elaboration that constructs it, is first an empiricism.
> *Christian Jambet*

angels and nature, a double risk

There is a double risk running throughout this essay, for I will be wagering on two fictions to unveil something that remains real for the human, and to the creatural that is their shared immanent identity. These two fictions are angels and nature and it is by way of discussing a contemporary angelology and *naturphilosophie* that we will disclose a messianicity that runs through the immanental creature, separated from any God or any Master, and that resists death by living as if it were angelic, as if it were a Christ.

This essay is part of a larger ongoing project concerned with developing the practice of non-theology and builds off arguments made in three other essays. The first of those essays, "Too Poor for Measure: Working with Negri on Poverty and Fabulation," co-written with Daniel Colucciello Barber, lays out a general ontological theory of poverty as the fabulation of the immeasurable (which itself is a disruptive or inconsistent ontological formulation of Being when compared to the standard Greek philosophical conception). The second, "The Judgment of God and the Immeasurable: Political Theology and Organizations of Power," surveys the various forms that political theology takes in contemporary discourse and sketches out a political non-theology which would act as a practice with the ability or power to select from these antagonistic positions by short-circuiting the

anthony paul smith

NATURE DESERVES TO BE SIDE BY SIDE WITH THE ANGELS
nature and messianism by way of non-islam

underlying friend/enemy distinction upon which they are based. The short-circuit is found in moving beyond apophaticism to apoptosis, or a proliferation of forms of thought that have the power to pass away rather than attempting to become the immeasurable itself. In a third article, "What Can Be Done with Religion? Non-philosophy and the Future of Philosophy of Religion," these ideas were placed more rigorously within a non-philosophical practice and so the immeasurable comes to be another name for the One or the Real from which non-philosophy thinks (rather than thinking of the Real, as standard philosophy does). Non-theology then becomes the name for a non-philosophical unified theory of religion and philosophy, where religion is made relative to the Real and then treated as simple material that may, through the axioms of non-philosophy, be used in the construction of theories that work for the Human.

The ultimate focus in this essay is to add to that project by dealing with the second term in Spinoza's classic equation of equivalency, *Deus sive natura*, as we have already dealt with the first in "The Judgment of God and the Immeasurable." As I will show in this essay, this equivalency is also a choice, for Spinoza conveys in this axiom his choosing the whole of nature to practice his form of secular theology. Ultimately our own non-theological conception of nature will be more radically immanental and developed from the One-Real as a clone or name of the Real rather than as the substance of Being. As Spinoza is the Christ of the philosophers and his messianic act is located in his thinking immanence fully for the first time, I will also connect nature to messianism. However, I won't do so by the usual materials that Continental philosophy employs when it engages with religion, for, if we were to be honest, we would all have to admit that when one speaks of theology in Continental philosophy one almost always does so with a silent "Christian" before it, and this silent Christian almost always contains a silent "European" or "Western" before it. I hasten to add that honesty about this fact does not denote acceptance, but rather in this paper I will move away from this Christian-centric focus and engage with a conception of nature found in messianic Islam. This conception, found in the work of the tenth-century Ismaili philosopher Abû Ya'qûb al-Sijistânî, unites messianism and nature under the radical autonomy of the Oneness of God that is the religious mirror of the secular conception of the Real found in non-philosophy.[1]

We can locate in the Judeo-Christian tradition, which while real is also an abstraction, a pure homology between a theological understanding of nature and a secular one: in either case, where nature is either always the apparent as analogue with what is revealed of the transcendent God (Aquinas) or nature is what simply is (contemporary naturalism), nature is the site of human submission to transcendence. In the first case it is submission to God as the power within or underlying nature and in the second submission to nature as the determining power of the human. Against this has been set the gnostic refusal of nature, an absolute revolt against the whole of nature in the flesh, as it pursues the salvation of the exiled God that is beyond the dialectic of power in all its forms. This is what Christian Jambet and Guy Lardreau mean when they refer to the rebel becoming angelic. It is a rejection, in sum, of any mediation of the identity of the rebel through sexuality and the individual body.[2] The rebel is the person who is most truly human for Jambet and Lardreau and so the identity of the rebel unveils the identity of Man (as species-being). In the same way, by conceiving of a nature that is angelic, we will reject any mediation of nature through its reduction to matter or to the idea of matter. This leads to a non-philosophical thesis: nature is not reducible to matter and matter is not reducible to the idea of matter or the natural; rather, the real identity of both is to be found in their unilateral relationship to the Real.

Both standard conceptions of nature, the latter idealist or theological and the former materialist, are derived from what François Laruelle calls a philosophical decision. It doesn't seem necessary to describe at length Laruelle's theory of the philosophical decision, as the theory has been the focus of much of the anglophone reception of Laruelle's work, but in short Laruelle describes it as

> a cut – repeated or relaunched – with regard to an empirical singular, or more generally, some given and, at the same time, an identification with an idealizing law of this given, itself then supposed as real, a transcendence towards the veritable real. It is a relation and it modulates itself each time as a function of the real assumed as given and reduced, and the real assumed as attained and affirmed.[3]

Laruelle holds that this Real (which he doesn't capitalize in this early work) assumed as attained and affirmed is not in a reciprocal relation to philosophy but a unilateral one. When philosophy then takes itself to have attained the Real within the philosophical decision, always a splitting of some given, then it actually takes its own operation as the Real, though to varying degrees depending on the particularities of the philosophy. It takes what is actually foreclosed, or, in religious language, "inexpressible," and confuses its ground (either matter or the idea of matter) with its object (in this case the object is nature).

From the position of non-philosophy materialism is the stronger philosophy, but still remains idealist at its unacknowledged core. Non-philosophy attempts to radicalize materialism by rejecting it in the name of matter. Laruelle's critique of the "philosophies of difference," by which he means Nietzsche, Heidegger, Derrida, and Deleuze, is ultimately a criticism of their attempt to ground an "immanent materialism." He sums up his criticism this way:

> In the last instance, it continues to subordinate matter to the ultimate possible form of the *logos* (the *logos* or Idea of matter as such), rather than subordinating the *logos* of matter to matter, thereby engaging a genuinely dispersive becoming-real of ideality instead of a continuous becoming-ideal of the real. Thus, in order to remain faithful to its original inspiration and secure a definitive victory over idealism, materialism should first consent to partially eliminate itself as category and statement – to subordinate its materialist statements to a process of utterance that would be material, relative, or hyletic in itself, then stop conceiving of this utterance as an ideal and relative process. *The decline of materialism in the name of matter, and of matter as hyle in the name of the real.*[4]

To really be an immanent materialism, materialism as a kind of "*logos* of matter" must fade away as such; thought and matter must be in some sense identical without thereby rendering any discussion of their differences superfluous. Laruelle brings this about by rendering both matter and thought, and their attendant sciences of idealism and materialism, identically relative to something that in turn has no relation to them – the Real-One.[5] This is the fundamental posture of non-philosophy towards regional knowings, to take various philosophies and their objects (philosophy of X) as equivalent before the Real and thus as material that may be thought in a really immanental way, but more importantly this early attempt to make non-philosophy a practice of thought after the decline of materialism in the name of matter rendered non-philosophy thoroughly material without being a specular materialism. This is because each thought was taken as material to be used in lived immanence, rather than an Idea to be lived up to.

angeology, a theo-fiction

Recently the genre of fiction has become important for Laruelle as he continues to develop the practice of non-philosophy, no more so than in his most recent and massive work *Philosophie non-standard. Générique, quantique, philo-fiction*. Fiction is freed here from its philosophically forced relation to the imagination and treated instead as an aspect of gnosis, of the practice of science. The name philo-fiction refers to the practice of "making the best use" of the "material" derived from the superposition or unified theory of science and philosophy. In Laruelle's typical proliferation of names we find him also calling this Generic Science. For Laruelle, then, philo-fiction (or science-phiction) is the hermeneutics of Generic Science, the aspect of non-philosophy that is able to tell the story of the mutation of standard philosophy without falling into the specular narcissism of philosophy and to practice scientific thought without slipping into a sterile pure positivism, which would lead to no new scientific knowledge.[6]

Ultimately it is from this aspect of non-philosophy that messianism as religious material is treated.[7] In this way Laruelle opens up a space for a theo-fiction that would, as he says of "mystic-fiction," "universalize more radically the representations, images and existing concepts that it identifies-without-unifying-them or that it 'recalls' in/for the Logos" and ultimately it "works out a system of rules for the transformation of mystical [or theological] statements, it identifies them in-the-last-Humanity as Word [*Verbe*] of the Messiah."[8] Such is the way angelology is approached in non-theology.

When looking through the history of monotheistic theology one cannot help but be struck by the attention given by some of the greatest theological minds to angelology. From Aquinas and Bonaventure to Ibn Sina and Ibn Khaldûn, angels remain vital to their theological systems. While the specific angelology of each thinker varies importantly, Henry Corbin's comparative study of angelology locates one invariant aspect: angelology is necessary in order to avoid idolatry.[9] To speak of God, without merely falling into the silence of absolute negative theology, one can speak, without allegory, through the names and experiences of the Angels. Every theophany is an angelophany and vice versa.[10] Corbin claims that "It is impossible to secularize or socialize the Angel from theophanic visions,"[11] and we will assume he is right. Can, then, angelology, while remaining connected to theophanic visions, be secularized in its totality and, if so, as we will argue, what will it then do?

Angelology can be secularized radically by way of treating it as a theo-fiction. Without repeating arguments made in "What Can Be Done with Religion?," the religious material is made secular by making all religious material equivalent before the Real. In this way non-theology adds two axioms to the axioms already operative in non-philosophy: (1) the Real is foreclosed to authority and tradition and (2) what is true(-without-truth) in theology is what is most generic and thus what is most secular.[12] We can then denude Corbin's statement by locating the real identity of the *Deus absconditus*, mediated and relatively unveiled by the theophanic event of the Angel's appearance, in the gnostic dream of a radically other World. What is revealed in the desire to see the Divine is the desire for the complete and utter overturning of the failure of creation, the desire for the Divine is a desire for salvation, for liberty, and hoping for the Angel to come is nothing other than the mediation of salvation from what is purely other; it is the cry against violence and the proclamation that another world is possible.

Thus theo-fiction follows the same general rule that Guy Lardreau locates as shared by philosophical fictions and science fiction: "why not?"[13] Non-theological angelology is then a part of the wider non-philosophical thought experiment. Angels, why not? Provided they are transformed in the midst of theo-fiction into concepts that are in-the-last-instance immanent to Man. Because, more than a need to experience God, human beings everywhere desire to be free, they struggle with this World for the sake of the World: "In the beginning was the struggle, and the struggle was *with* the World and the World did not know it [...]"[14] It is because angels have been at the heart of some real theo-political debates and were important to groups seeking to overturn the very structures of this World that angelology may still be important today. For instance, at the theoretical level, angelology was the site of the struggle between the Spiritual Franciscans (who claimed that the time of the institutional Church and all other institutions of power had come to the end) and the Worldly power of the Papacy and its supporting structures. For the Spiritual Franciscans St Francis was, with his disregard for material wealth, for organized work, and the sexual body, an Angel of the Apocalypse.

Our angelology will not, however, be developed here in conversation with these medieval sources but rather derived from some already secularized angelologies, and so we will not follow the triadic formula of Christian angelology well known in Pseudo-Dionysius. This angelology follows the gnostic development of Christian Jambet and Guy Lardreau's Maoist Angeology in *L'Ange* and their subsequent self-criticism in *Le Monde* that is again submitted to criticism and *détournement* in their individual works, most notably Ladreau's *La Véracité* and Jambet's *La Grande Résurrection d'Alamût*. For their Angel is the name for the rebel who is in absolute revolt, the rebel who seeks to overturn the Master in all forms of mastery. In Jambet's later work he locates the messianic act of the Ismaili community of the Alamut mountain fortress in their overturning of the Law in the name of a liberty found in living the higher life of contemplating the divine: "The abolition of the law means we replace it as series of distinct obligations by a single one, which is that of the sabbath."[15] In other words, one lives the life of one divine rather than the life of survival.

So our angelology will be dualistic, there will be but two orders of angels. The first will be the Angel as the name of the rebel, the name of the masses in revolt seeking to overturn the Master. This Angel is polynomous, it manifests itself whenever the masses revolt in the plenitude of situations engendered by the World.[16] But this "polyangelism," or proliferation of different theories of angelic purity that necessarily lay at the heart of their angelology, may also give rise to the barbaric Angel of which we will say more below.[17] In each case this Angel is a negative name for a positive act; the creation of another world (the other of the other, in their terms) or living the resurrected life.[18] Then there will be another Angel, a passive transcendent angel; one that serves this World and guards the entrance to the other. This angel serves the twin rulers of this World, because why not also talk about gods? These gods are called Moloch and Mammon. The second is the demiurge of this World, the one that reduces all things to a price and all bodies to elements of economic exchange. The first, Moloch, is below him but far more cruel. For he demands the greatest sacrifice from the masses, he is the god of servile austerity, an austerity of inequality and the disjunctive synthesis, chaining the masses to the masters while keeping them in misery through a separation of value.

Overturning this World, and its two gods, in order to live the divine life rather than the life of survival is not only the dream of the ancient gnostics but also of every rebel that wants to participate in cultural revolution, or the revolution that dares to act decisively to overturn this World. The messianic act inaugurates a utopia here and now or immanentizes the eschaton (to positively reclaim a slur directed at every revolutionary act by the neo-conservative philosopher Eric Voegelin). But this messianic act, which is human in-the-last-instance, is haunted by another Angel: Benjamin's Angel of History. The threat that all human attempts to bring about a true revolution, a revolution that is one, is destined to be but one piece in the one single catastrophe that piles up before the Angel. That all human attempts at liberty are destined to become black masses, that the attempt to overturn the World ends in the continued reign of a single Master lurking behind many manifestations. Just as the Angel's eyes are staring, mouth agape, horror-stricken at the one single catastrophe that is human history and that it powerlessly is forced to watch, so are my eyes captured by the appearance of this Angel. This possession of my gaze, the posture of submission to the transcendent which it forces me to take, is the same as Benjamin's towards this Angel. All that Benjamin can see of this catastrophe, even of the wind blowing with such violence from the paradisal origin, all of it is seen as an image reflected darkly off the eyes of this impotent and sad Angel.

I am haunted by this Angel because everyone living today is haunted by it. This Angel is there every time a human community makes the attempt to live otherwise, to destroy this World and create something truly new, to create a future different from the apotheosis of catastrophe that is rushing headlong towards us, not in the name of progress but in the name of growth, often confused for progress, which is required for the status quo merely to subsist. Every time a human being attempts to be divine this Angel is there to hold back our hand and cry out to us "Messiah, Messiah!" And we foolishly respond as hostages, saying "Here am I." And this Angel says "Do not do anything, for now I know that you do not fear this god, raise up your eyes and see that Mammon has provided the ram for you." And we take hold of what this lying Angel says is the ram, blinded by the horror in its eyes and so unable to see that what we need to sacrifice, what lies before us on the altar for us to kill, is this Angel's other god, it is Moloch, the God of too much sacrifice itself, and that the ram this Angel claims has been provided for us, easy money, is our only child, the most costly sacrifice.

At least, though, we did not participate in progress, we didn't pile anything more onto the pile that is one single catastrophe, we did not do anything. Though the pile grows, we are innocent.

What we are told is a temptation is actually a wager. Let's wager that this Angel's eyes lie, that what its eyes reflect is not a single catastrophe but instead that there are two, always two, and that we can know the difference. There is the catastrophe that piles up continuously before this Angel and there is the catastrophe of those who bravely attempt but fail to end this single catastrophe. From this perspective this Angel belongs to the first catastrophe, for in its innocence, in its transcendence, it does nothing.

Then there is the Angel manifested on the Earth as the masses ("the masses don't need the Angel, for they are the Angel"), developed by Jambet and Lardreau in wild and intemperate fashion in *L'Ange*.[19] There they proceed by way of a gnostic wager that the World can be divided into two discourses: that of the Rebel and that of the Master.[20] This is not the friend–enemy distinction so close to the heart of twentieth-century political theology but is a more radical separation, one developed from gnosis rather than from the Statist form of life engendered by Christian orthodoxy, and so it is from the perspective of below rather than from that of the State, Society, or Empire (it matters little what the content of the organization is called; from the perspective of the Rebel it is all of the Master). This radical separation is an overturning of the measure of the friend–enemy distinction. It isn't a cutting away of some other or some group but a self-interrogation in the tradition of the most severe asceticism. It is a search for the enemy, or, more accurately, the adversarial Master within. But what are the specifics of this angelology? Is there any rigor to it?

The Angel is a pure negative name. Lardreau, who of the two is clearly more obsessed with the negative as philosophical method, writes in the introduction:

It is necessary that the Angel come. And so that he comes, being invisible, he must have been visible in his works, he must have been announced in history, he must have been there, not two objects of desire, that is where the Fathers were lost, but two desires. Or rather, a desire, that is to say a sexual desire, and a desire that has nothing to do with sex, not even the desire for God: rebellion. On the one hand pleasure, *jouissance*, and on the other not even beatitude. Something still unnamed, that we have called desire under the pressure of language, which we must force into delivering a name to us. But the Angel is anonymous, or polynomous. We only call it that by way of negative metaphors. That's how Pseudo-Dionysius wants to speak about that which is God. Negative theology. Speaking about the world before the break from which it will be born, we can say nothing except from the negative. I do not see how else to hold on to the hope of revolution.[21]

L'Ange is partly a polemic against the "revolutionaries of desire" (they discuss very briefly Lyotard, and Deleuze and Guattari) in ways that prefigure the now popular criticisms of Slavoj Žižek and Malcolm Bull. Namely, the revolution of desire is fully compatible with capitalism; it doesn't overthrow the Master but replaces him with a new form of the Master.[22] I'm not interested either in responding to this critique or in defending it; in fact, it often seems to me that *L'Ange* suffers from a certain inchoate rage directed at thinkers with whom they share a minimal difference. What is interesting to me is how this antagonism towards Lyotard as well as Deleuze and Guattari manifests as an anti-naturalism in Jambet and Lardreau.

For Jambet and Lardreau naturalism and anti-naturalism is the difference between two different forms of revolution. This dualistic theory of revolution is explored in the central chapter of *L'Ange*, written by Lardreau, entitled "Lin Piao comme volonté et représentation" [Lin Biao as Will and Representation]. There they posit yet another gnostic separation, this time between ideological revolution and the absolute revolt of cultural revolution.[23] This dualism isn't completely foreign to more familiar and popular forms of contemporary Marxism, like that found in Antonio Negri who traces revolutions in terms of the difference between constituted power and constitutive power. Like Negri in this respect, Jambet and Lardreau are concerned to uncover how it is that pure revolt against the Master behind every master, which is cultural revolution, becomes ideological revolution, a form of revolution that merely makes possible a new master as it is tied directly to historical processes like a new dominant mode of production.[24] In this chapter Lardreau undertakes an empirical case study of this dualistic struggle between the different forms of revolution by locating a form of cultural revolution in the early irruption of Christian ascetic monasticism and its accommodation within the Church. This early monastic movement is a form of cultural revolution just as the Great Proletarian Cultural Revolution of Mao's China is one.[25] This was a form of life that, even if it was called Christian, had nothing to do with the worldly Church of institutional Christianity that helped to found the "institution" of Europe. Instead, as a form of cultural revolution, it "presented itself as an anti-culture, a calculated inversion, systematic, of all the values of this world."[26] In fact Lardreau locates three essential themes of cultural revolution as an extreme path of "struggle alone": "the radical rejection of work, the hatred of the body, and the refusal of sexual difference – certainly not as a production of *one* indifferent sex or of *n* sexes […] but as the abolition of sex itself."[27]

Thus cultural revolution is "totally *contra-nature*."[28] This has two different but connected meanings. Firstly, it may mean the rejection of the idea that what *is* simply is. This is the form of nature that we located already at work in both the Christian theological tradition and contemporary naturalism. It is nature as the *sékommça*; nature as the "it's like that."[29] The second meaning has to do with death. The hatred of the fleshly body and the desire (for, whatever Jambet and Lardreau say, this is a desire even if it is, like Job, cried forth as a protest) for the subtle or spiritual body can give birth to the messianic act (what we may

name as the coming of Christos Angelos or the Future Christ) or to the barbaric Angel.[30] Lardreau is more direct about this in his own work of negative philosophy entitled *La Véracité*, where he argues for a Kantian sublime within politics defined as "a politics that makes a finality sensible to us completely independent from nature."[31] Lardreau again invokes the Angel in his development of the concept of the political sublime, this time as the "political name for the desire for death."[32] Within a negative philosophy this desire for death is limited; it is a desire for the self-referential play of the correlative images of the self and the other. In the terms laid out in our "The Judgment of God and the Immeasurable" it is the desire for the death of play of friend and enemy. For Lardreau, within a negative philosophy, this desire is checked by way of a negative presentation of the Real.[33] Death is always a form of transcendence as limit for philosophers, and Lardreau is no different.[34] The barbarous Angel, for Lardreau, comes when there is a positive presentation of the Real, a presentation that threatens to topple the sublime.[35]

Jambet and Lardreau come to fear this barbaric Angel in the interval between *L'Ange* and *Le Monde*. In *L'Ange*, writing in July of 1975, they declare "Our philosophy is then that of the Cambodians."[36] Over the next few years, as Pol Pot and the Khmer Rouge engaged in their own cultural revolution, aiming systematically for an absolute break with the traditional values of old Cambodia, the world witnessed the forced evacuations of the cities (in a way not unlike the flight of the desert fathers into the desert that Lardreau connects to the Christian cultural revolution) and the murder of educators and intellectuals. From that perspective the words of Lardreau concerning intellectuals found in *L'Ange* were regrettable (to say the least): "They [intellectuals], if they want to be the heralds of cultural revolution, must burn themselves, as in so far as cultural revolution is against everything that they are then cultural revolution can be lit up by their embers."[37] So this was how the theory of cultural revolution began with the Angel and ended (for a time) in a compromised position with the World, in abject horror at

> the transformation of an entire country into a work and extermination camp, a land that is without reserve living in terror. But what's this? That metamorphosis does not break in the name of an imperial desire, of a despotic possession, but in the name of a will to absolute purity, of universal emancipation. Immediately when the capital was occupied, the *Angkar* [the self-given name of the Khmer Rouge] proclaimed the desire to abolish exploitation, inequality and selfishness. And in order to realize a life devoted to goodness, kindness [*bonté*] and transparency, they have generalized violence, secrets, and darkness.[38]

Here we see why the Angel of History gets a hearing, why it always threatens us with inaction.

christ as generic subject

But the same Jambet who is horrified at the barbaric regime, the barbaric Angel, that dominated Pol Pot's Cambodia, also writes these words: "Despair is the greatest sin."[39]

So, how are we to stop our angelology ending in either despair or allegiance to the Angel of History? Is there a way to save cultural revolution from a form of nihilism found in the accelerationism of absolute deterritorialization without at the same time falling back into the simple capture of the power of cultural revolution by mastery? After all, the terror against intellectuals and the World that Lardreau advocates above, though understandable because there is a war, ends in "so many vicious circles and tendencies" that "mistake the whole of the phenomenon" for "the heretical struggle is not born from terror or the specular-whole, which it practically undoes, it is born from the being-separate of man that is in-Man."[40] In addition to the hatred that lies at the heart of Lardreau's negative philosophy, there is also salvation by way of gnosis. Gnosis knows that "the divine creation – the World – is a failure," but also that "the necessity for salvation is universal."[41] If the choice is really between the authority of the World or an arbitrary but absolute will of the people captured or manifested in State power become barbaric then there is no real choice. In each instance the human, or Man-in-Man in Laruelle's terminology, is turned into a subject, its real identity, as the inconsistent immanence of the One, is obscured within an idea of humanity given from an authority. And in each case we never stop rebelling, man nevertheless rebels, Man is in-struggle. Laruelle puts it this way: "*There is revolt rather than only evil*; nearly everywhere and always people do not cease to kill but they also rebel against the most violent powers as the most gentle."[42]

We have come here to the discussion of struggle-as-primary in Laruelle's *Future Christ*. It is from this empirical fact that Man is everywhere in revolt, that our unified theory of nature and messianism develops.

Laruelle differentiates three forms of human struggle: the philosophical as *agon* or war, the gnostic as an absolute rebellion against the Master, and the immanent struggle with the World as theorem of the Future Christ summed up in this mutation of the prologue to the Gospel of John: "In the beginning was the struggle, and the struggle was *with* the World and the World did not know it […]"[43] In *Future Christ* Laruelle thinks from the perspective of the murdered gnostics of history as a particular form of universally persecuted heresy. This is not a denial of the horrors of the Jewish Shoah and it is not in any way a justification for the many crimes committed against humanity by itself. Rather, it reveals something beneath the particularity of the name "Jew" or "Tutsi" or "Shi'a" (all names for peoples who have been murdered). It reveals that a human is murdered as a human. That the human endures crime. Laruelle puts it this way:

> The heretics reveal to us that man is in an ultimate way that being, the only one, who endures crime and is characterized by the possibility of being murdered rather than simply persecuted and taken hostage, exterminated as "man" rather than as "Jew". Why ultimate? *Because man is without-consistency, he is on principle, in contrast to*

other beings, able to be murdered, he is even the Murdered as first term for heretical thought and for the struggle that it performs.[44]

This focus on the *minority* status or radical individual identity, *precisely because it is without-Essence*, of the human distinct from the forms of unitary identity that are bestowed upon human-beings by the World discloses the radically foreclosed nature of the Real to authority and tradition. Instead, the Real-One is always a challenge to authority, always an "outside-memory" that is lost to the Western form of memory, but that is at the same time not lost because it is the essence of thought's non-consistency as always insufficient to think the Real.[45]

Thus, heresy is the privileged form of non-theological thinking, because it is in its immanence always inconsistent, always the shared inconsistency that marks the identity of the human. There are, of course, majoritarian or authoritarian forms of heresy, and concerning these Laruelle remarks: "What is more hopeless than a *Principle of Sufficient Rebellion*," but these can be differentiated from heresy as struggle.[46] Laruelle delineates this differentiation in *Future Christ*, tracing the differences between war, or the *agon* of philosophical absolute immanence, and the rebellion of historical gnostics. In the case of war and rebellion it is always a matter of an underlying authoritarian logic, a "because of." The rebellion of gnostics against Christian philosophy is always "a reaction of auto-protection against aggression."[47] While the non-theological point is always to raise as primary that which is not auto-protective, that which is an "(immanent) because," of that "revolt that commences and does not cease to commence in each instant, proletariat or not, exploitation or not. But if it has in itself sufficient reasons to start, it has only too many of them and cannot make a cause of them."[48] In other words, struggle, when separated from even rebellion as a minoritarian form of authority, is separated from the World in general. It is a generic practice as universal rebellion of which the Future Christ is the generic subject.

Christ may take on the character of a subject for the masses as well. Laruelle recognizes this when he writes:

> The Future Christ rather signifies that each man is a Christ-organon, that is to say, of course, the Messiah, but simple and unique once each time. This is a minimal Christianity. We the Without-religion, the Without-church, the heretics of the future, we are, each-and-everyone, a Christ or Messiah.[49]

It is in the positive religions that Christ is misunderstood: "Christianity is the limit, the whole content of which is a misinterpretation of Christ."[50] Gilles Grelet, a student of Laruelle, Lardreau, and Jambet, goes further and connects Christ with Jambet and Lardreau's Angel, by separating a "marshmallow" Christ ("The marshmallow offers the perfect image of relation between the 'fundamentally Christian' West and Christ, since we know that the soft and very sweet candy does not, in fact, contain any marsh mellow"[51]) from the *Christos Angelos* ("Angel of all the angels, the Gnostic Christ is the Envoy charged with delivering men from their enslavement in this world by liberating in them the knowledge of their origin and the means of getting back to the place from which they have been exiled: *Christos Angelos* frees by the knowledge which gives men the means of rebellion that they are, against all humility, fundamentally driven by"[52]).

So in order to understand Christ as generic subject we must understand him as radically separate from Christianity. What better way than to consider Christ from the perspective of a gnostic-Islamic Christology? In the editors' introduction to *After the Postsecular and the Postmodern* Daniel Whistler and I differentiated between a postsecular *event* and the appropriation of that event in the name of a theologization of philosophy or what we called "imperial secularism." The event marked a break with Western imperialism, which used Christian forms of thought to develop a post-Christian secularism in an attempt to separate the oppressed colonial subjects internally – a separation of the political and their religious identity, whereas the appropriation of the event is often an attempt to reinstate (at best) a war at the ideational level and (at worst) a new form of imperial war in the name of the clash of traditions.

The postsecular event, we claim there, was located largely in Islamic countries throughout the Middle East and North Africa, and though the response to the postsecular event is not an Islamic turn in Continental philosophy there should be more engagement with forms of thought outside of the Christian tradition. There are two clear non-theological reasons for this: (1) if the generic is to be located in a way that avoids the shortcomings of Hegelian philosophy and its continuing influence on the practice of philosophy of religion, where European Christianity comes to be the name for universalism as the only consummating historical religion, then it must take the infinite task of working with any material whatsoever in order to locate the power of the generic that lies there; and (2) non-theology always begins from the perspective of the murdered, and thus from the perspective of heretical material, which is to say that there is within non-theology a principle of minority or preferential option for the poor as immanent to generic humanity. With regard to the second, in a very real sense, a very bodily sense, a certain appearance of the power of poverty, what Negri calls the "force of the slave" in regard to Job, has coalesced around the name "Muslim." In Europe the Muslim has become the exception that grounds the law, both political law and the economic law of class difference. As this structural aspect in-person the Muslim is, as Mehdi Belhaj Kacem has argued, the contemporary form of pariah: "The pariah is at once captured and delivered, locked within its exclusion and banished by inclusion."[53] The reality of the pariah is manifested clearly in the collusion of the institutional Left with the establishment Right of Europe regarding these "places of the ban" (Belhaj Kacem makes a clever play on the name of the suburban ghettos of France, *les banlieus*, as *les ban-lieux*) as *problems* to be neutralized (and both speak in this language if with differing degrees of violence) while also referring to them as what negatively grounds their existence as government.

Islam as pariah is repeated within thought in the same way as it is found in the political field. Within a teleological-oriented philosophy of religion, which carries with it always a certain amount of servitude to the European project of expansion, Islam poses a problem because it arises historically after Christianity, which was to be the consummation of Spirit in the religious realm.[54] Islam is the religion that proves Christianity's true universalism, as an idea made concrete, while (as Toscano says) Islam "takes universalism too far" in its abstract passion for the real.[55] As such, it is both brought within the scope of the historical development of European spirit and excluded from it as a form of fanaticism which threatens the rational integration of people within the State. There is a ban on Islam in Continental philosophy of religion that grounds its practice within post-Christian secularism in so far as Islam is so dangerous as to be outside this form of the secular. This is why Islam must be material for the construction of a true non-theology, not in the name of an Islamic theologization of philosophy but because the event taking place amongst Muslims, both as postsecular event and as name of the pariah, have consequences for philosophy and may help free philosophy, practiced here as non-theology, from its capture as imperialist weapon.

the foreclosed one of non-philosophy and the paradoxical one of ismaili shi'a islam

Let us return to the question posed above: how do we save the angelism of Jambet and Lardreau from despair, a despair that comes from formulating the angel as a radical purity from all of nature? The wager here is that we do so by reconceiving nature, a reconception that places both the Angel and Rebel back on the Earth, that locates a radical nature, one that is necessary for the Angel and the Rebel but that does not over-determine them or require that they submit to the natural. To do that we have to conceive of a nature differently than nature is conceived in naturalism, even one differently conceived than we find in the attempted immanent materialism of Deleuze and Guattari. Nature must be conceived as radically immanent; the decline of naturalism in the name of nature.

To lay the groundwork for this conception we must consider the unilateral relationship between thought and the One. I will begin by briefly summarizing the non-philosophical conception of the One. From there I will show that the Ismaili conception of the One described by Jambet is closer to non-philosophy's conception than Christianity and can therefore be used as a kind of One "already-cloned" from the Real-One. This exploration of this paradoxical or fissured One of the Ismaili will provide a new conception of nature different from both the transcendent analogical conception and the conception of nature as subsumed into absolute immanence.

Non-philosophy aims to be "neither Greek nor Jew," as Laruelle puts it, meaning to think neither from the primacy of Being or Alterity.[56] It aims to think *from* the Real, which Laruelle also gives the ancient philosophical name of "the One" and even sometimes calling it the Real-One. The One for non-philosophy does not engender a problematic of the One and the Many because it makes everything in some sense in-One. Not subsuming everything into a One-All, but by making the claim that all things are in-One as identity. To understand this it is it is important not to confuse the One with substance, with Being, with even the Other as such, for all these things must be thought as if One. Being is in-One, the Other is in-One; in each case the One speaks to either the radical immanence of their identity or the non-thetic transcendence of that identity. There is then in non-philosophy a "realist suspension" that takes place from the mutated and foreclosed figure of the One.

The Real is pragmatically asserted through a variety of axioms, rather than circumscribed and represented. The realist suspension is a pragmatic style of thought that asserts the ultimately Real identity of all things. That all things are, in-the-last-instance, Real, while still remaining what they are, while at the same time the Real is itself foreclosed to the thought, are the two aspects of the realist suspension. So, real objects may be described and known while the Real is always the deductively known cause of these real objects, not ontologically, but as One. Let me remind the reader of the six corollary axiomatic descriptions of the Real summarized by Ray Brassier as found in Laruelle's *Philosophie et non-philosophie*:

1. The [R]eal is phenomenon-in-itself, the phenomenon as *already*-given or given-*without*-givenness, rather than constituted as given via the transcendental synthesis of empirical and a priori, given and givenness.
2. The [R]eal is the phenomenon as *already*-manifest or manifest-*without*-manifestation, the phenomenon-without-phenomenality, rather than the phenomenon which is posited and presupposed as manifest in accordance with the transcendental synthesis of manifest and manifestation.
3. The [R]eal is that in and through which we have been *already*-gripped rather than any originary factum or datum by which we suppose ourselves to be gripped.
4. The [R]eal is *already*-acquired prior to all cognitive or intuitive acquisition, rather than that which is merely posited and presupposed as acquired through the a priori forms of cognition and intuition.
5. The [R]eal is *already*-inherent prior to all the substantialist forcings of inherence, conditioning all those supposedly inherent models of identity, be they analytic, synthetic, or differential.
6. The [R]eal is *already*-undivided rather than the transcendent unity which is posited and presupposed as undivided and deployed in order to effect the transcendental synthesis of the empirical and the metaphysical.[57]

This is not, then, a "negative theology" of the Real that we find in Lardreau but rather takes the same posture that science does with regard to its own practices. That is, it takes the Real as the necessary "superstructure" for thought, rather than as that whose being or non-being negates the possibility of thinking in general.[58] In other words, the realist suspension, which can be found in science, is a relationship with the Real that thinks without any recourse to a transcendent self founding.[59] Non-philosophy is a practice of liberty from philosophy, from the structures of the World, and not an account of foundation.

A non-philosophical discussion of the One then comes to be the site where non-philosophy develops an axiomatic formalism of the Real. Where it experiments with thinking from the Real, or looking at its material from the vision-in-One, and so to understand non-philosophy's One is largely to formally understand the practice of non-philosophy. To begin with, since the Real-One is foreclosed to thought this comes to also be referred to as the One-in-One. Non-philosophy clones its transcendental organon from this One-in-One.[60] Or, in other words, it clones a (non-)One that will be used as an organon of selection when applied to its material and that will operate on the philosophical resistance to the foreclosed nature of the Real, formalized as non(-One). The dualism, as a thought, is in unilateral causal relationship with the One where one aspect of the dualism, the one taking the place of transcendence, will correspond to a non(-One) while the other, taking the place of a relative philosophical immanence, will correspond to a (non-)One. The non(-One) indicates that the transcendent element of thought is a kind of negation, a hallucinatory aspect of thought that arises from the foreclosed nature of the Real-One. It is that aspect of thought that responds to the trauma of the foreclosing by negating the radical immanence of the One, reducing it to some hallucinatory transcendence of Being, Alterity, Difference, etc., but this aspect is at the same time *actually transcendent* within that philosophical occasion, but only as rooted in the radical immanence of the One.[61] The (non-)One is the suspension of negation or the negative of philosophy and thus it does correspond to those conceptions of immanence, found, for example, in Henry and Deleuze, that resist in a philosophical way the philosophical negative, but they are radicalized here so that the (non-)One indicates its mutation of the radical immanence of the One. The last vestiges of philosophical transcendence have to be chased out from these philosophies *of* immanence in order to create an immanental style of thought. A thought that is, in its very practice, rigorously immanent.

This formalism is more easily seen in person when we turn to the Ismaili experience of liberty which was actually lived in the proclamation in the twelfth century of the time of Resurrection (*qiyâmat*), after the collapse of their Fatimid caliphate that ruled over the Islamic world. The story of the Ismaili of Alamût is fascinating and should be of interest to anyone interested in messianism, but the historical details are not of particular interest here.[62] Rather, it is the relationship between this messianic act and the One that is important. For Jambet locates a certain necessity of neoplatonism for the Ismaili, the theoretical structure of the One allowing them to think the messianic event as such:

> It seems to us that there are two simple enough reasons for this. First and foremost, the neo-Platonic schema of the One and the multiple permits the One to be situated beyond any connection with the multiple wherein it would be totalized or counted as one. The One is thought beyond the unified totality of its emanations in the multiple. On the other hand, freed from any link with the totality of the existant, and situated beyond Being, the One can signify pure spontaneity, a liberty with no foundation other than itself. In this way, the sudden messianic appearance of the Resurrector will be founded in the creative liberty of the originary One; thus, in the necessary reign of the existant, the non-Being that results from the excess of the One will be able to mark out its trail of light. But, conversely, this creative spontaneity will also explain the creation of the existant, the ordained and hierarchized formation of universes. Just as much as with the unjustified liberty, the One will be able to justify the procession of

the intelligible and sensible, and the gradation of the spiritual and bodily worlds. Avoiding dualism, all while thinking the duality between the One and the order of Being which it interrupts; conceiving, on the other hand, of the unity of order and creative spontaneity – all while preserving the dualist sentiment – without which the experience of messianic liberty was impossible: this is what neo-Platonic thought offered to the Ismaili.[63]

In short, the One allows the Ismaili to think the pure formalism of the Real – there is the non-thetic transcendence found in the negation of Being, interrupting the order of Being and beings, and the immanence of (non-)One or the existant that is beyond any totality, that is pure fissure itself.

The immanental aspect of the Real-One, which is carried in each One, simply cannot be reduced to a totality, to some kind of idea of number. It exists without any ground whatsoever, and this is its source of liberty or autonomy from any attempt to capture it within philosophical or theological structures:

> The Ismaili experience of liberty is not the discovery of the autonomy of consciousness or the political rights of the individual. It is the feeling of a different and powerful idea: liberty is not a moment of Being, and it is even less a piece in the game of the existant. Liberty is not an attribute, but rather a subjective affirmation without foundation. Liberty is not a multiple effect of the One, but it can be nothing but the One, disconnected from whatever network of constraints it engenders or by which, on the contrary, it would come to be seized. Liberty is the experience of this non-Being of the One, through which the One inscribes itself in the universe of both Being and beings as pure alterity.[64]

This reveals something important about the identity of immanence: immanence has no ground and is thus, in some real sense, the other to any form of thinking that searches for a transcendental or absolute ground from which to think. Immanence itself is fissured, it itself is the Real-One and thus every real thing is in-Immanence and is Immanence-in-the-last-identity. Not as subsumed into immanence as absolute substance, but as lived. This Ismaili One of absolute liberty as already-cloned from the Real-One will provide the necessary material for thinking a non-theological nature from this radical immanence.

nature as condition for unveiling, non-theological nature

There are two standard options when trying to think nature outside of the limits of naturalism and in relation to messianism: from an analogical conception or from a position of absolute immanence. Both end ultimately by making the messianicity of creatures impossible.

The first, characterized by St Thomas Aquinas, assumes that what is created by God is good because it contains in it some likeness of God. In this way the essence of God remains unknowable except by way of analogy with what is and what is then ultimately known through its relation to God. This analogical loop allows Aquinas to avoid making God too immanent, and thus not God, and too transcendent, and thus unknowable, while also giving relative dignity to creatures. It also has the consequence that what *is* is by necessity taken to be reflective of the essence of God and what *is* is the only way to gain access to an understanding of God. So, Aquinas' doctrine of analogy ironically suffers from its own version of the naturalistic fallacy. Analogy must proceed from what is in order to understand the nature of the divine. In doing so it lacks any kind of organon for selection and thus may select, as Aquinas himself did, an analogy of monarchy. A discussion concerning the failings of this selection is beyond the scope of this essay. Suffice to say that Aquinas is wrong when he writes: "[...] whatever is in accord with nature is best, for nature always operates for the best. But in nature government is always by one [...] Among the bees is one king bee, and in the whole universe one God is the Maker and Ruler of all."[65] Here, Aquinas proceeds not from an understanding of nature to a properly analogical understanding of God but proceeds from what human government is to a misunderstanding of what government in nature is and then to a conception of God's governance. Bees, we now know, do not have any one ruler as the queen of a particular hive does not direct the action of that hive; the hive, rather, proceeds in a way altogether unlike human government from monarchy to parliamentary democracy. Indeed, what is in nature may be best, because it is what is, but what is in nature is varied. Its organization is not reducible to any one organization and thus analogy may not find a secure position from any one part of nature and may not be able to think from the whole of nature in ways that allow it to remain within the fold of Christian orthodoxy.

The second option is found in Spinoza, where immanence is made absolute. We can read this as a response to the Thomist lack of an organon of selection, for instead of selecting some aspect of nature from which to think God, Spinoza selects the whole of nature (*Deus sive natura*). This is an ingenious solution to the Thomistic problem, but ultimately relies on a philosophy of substance where nature is reduced to being and so is unthought as such. In other words, this selection of nature as whole or "One-All" retains a transcendent shadow of a quasi-thing.[66] This allows for a certain liberty in nature, but such liberty is always limited as determined by its status as Being or what is. In both instances creatural messianicity is impossible because what *is* has already been consummated by the death and resurrection of the historical Jesus or, in less dogmatic terms, what *is* is already good and requires nothing more than right order or an ethical relation. In both cases nature comes to be a name simply for the *sékommça*.

Ya'qûb al-Sijistânî provides us with a proto-non-theological conception of nature that differs from both Aquinas and Spinoza. Whereas Aquinas occludes nature by making creation its proper apophatic name and Spinoza occludes creation within a subsumption of God and Nature into a One-All substance, al-Sijistânî places nature in the middle of six Creations that come from the uniqueness of the Creator for whom even essence is excluded.[67]

These are not seven distinct, linear creations, but seven cyclical Creations that are contained in each other as expressions of the manifestation of the unique nature of the One, which begins in creation and runs down through the created from universe to angels to peoples to prophets before culminating in the resurrection. In non-philosophical terms, they are clones of the foreclosed One.

Nature is the third Creation and is treated alone, while in the second, fourth and fifth Creations there are always two terms that move from one to the other. By treating nature alone in this way nature is raised to the same level as the Intelligence (from which the Angels are given their power and identity) and the Resurrector for al-Sijistânî. Al-Sijistânî raises nature to these levels by locating the real identity of nature as Earth rather than World:

> Do you not see that the human being, in whom the most subtle quintessence of the two universes has been concentrated, lives on the Earth? His subsistence is on the Earth. His return is a returning to the Earth, and his resurrection is a resurgence from the Earth. From these premises it follows that we have shown that the Earth is not inferior to heaven in dignity and merits the presence of the angels, since a great number of potentialities [*puissances*] are achieved in the Earth that are in harmony with the angels. Understand this.[68]

Jambet sums up al-Sijistânî's conception of nature by saying that it is not being or *physis* that allows for the appearance of every phenomenal existant.[69] Nature is then the condition for the appearance of what is totally different from the World, for what is the messianicity of creatures as the Angel rather than as Worldly.

The solution to the impasse between analogical transcendence and absolute immanence, where there can be no messianicity, is then a conception of nature as clone of the Real-One. Instead of trying to conceive of the relationship between the Absolute-God and Nature, which requires then some epistemological organon of selection, foreclose the One to thought as that which is beyond Being and Alterity, but which manifests itself as lived in-Person. In terms whose meaning is more directly understandable, instead of treating *Deus sive natura* as a relation between two terms, treat the equation as itself relative to the radical autonomy of the Real-One. This radicalizes the Spinozist response to the Thomist failure of selection, for instead of selecting the whole of Nature as the best way to think God, the non-theologian selects the whole of the dyad of God and Nature in order to think the cloned One.

What are the consequences of this choice? What does this choice do? And how, finally, does it bring together our angelology, which is ultimately a fictional way of thinking true liberation from this World or messianism, and nature?

Nature is no longer an object of knowledge nor is it the object of knowledge that comes to know itself, but itself is the condition for any such dialectic and is itself outside of any of this dialectic as radical immanence underlying the transcendental dialectic. Nature is identified with the Earth rather than with the World. As al-Sijistânî says, nature does not change state. Even if its parts were to be annihilated, it would still remain as nature, as the condition for the appearance of the messiah as divine potential.[70] Worlds may pass away, but their appearance and passing away depend on the Earth. Even when the Earth does pass away, nature as such will remain as *already*-inherent and *already*-manifest.

This choice then gives us a conception of nature that unifies a scientific stance towards nature as the One of what appears and the condition of that appearing and an ancient philosophical problem of nature that has all too often ended in a conception of an over-determining nature. Nature in this middle place between the One and the Future Christ as Resurrector does not provide any of the usual limitations to human and creatural liberty. Nothing in this conception is "unnatural," for nature is itself perverse here. As the condition for the appearance of messianicity of the human and other creatures it stands against what simply is, against the *sékommça*. And it is ultimately here, when nature can be turned against the natural, that we see the unified theory of messianism and nature. Yes, let everyone say with Jambet and Lardreau "let the Angel come!" but understand that the Angel can only come to the Earth, it can only overturn the World by overturning the absoluteness of either Being or Alterity. For the Earth, like the Angel, has no Master and is everywhere and always already in revolt.

notes

1 The title of this essay comes from al-Sijistânî's text entitled *Kashf al-mahjûb* [*Unveiling the Hidden*], which was translated into French by Henry Corbin as *Le Dévoilement des choses cachées* (in English the French would translate as "The Unveiling of Hidden Things").

2 Cf. Benjamin Noys, "The End of the Monarchy of Sex: Sexuality and Contemporary Nihilism," *Theory, Culture and Society* 25.5 (2008): 104–22. I also want to note that the reason I have chosen to focus on the angelology of Jambet and Lardreau, instead of more familiar names like Irigaray and Benjamin, owes to their particular gnostic orientation that is lacking in most Continental philosophy that engages with religious materials, as well as to Jambet's schooling in Islamic theology and philosophy. It should also be noted that while I do not deal with the sexual politics implied in Jambet and Lardreau's *L'Ange*, Noys' article does. There may be room here for a feminist critique, but in this instance when Jambet and Lardreau refer to the overcoming of sex they are making reference to a historical instance of this in the first century which included both male and female persons.

3 François Laruelle, *Philosophies of Difference: A Critical Introduction to Non-philosophy*, trans. Rocco Gangle (London and New York: Continuum, 2010) 198.

4 François Laruelle, "The Decline of Materialism in the Name of Matter," trans. Ray Brassier, *Pli* 12 (2001) 37. This is a translation of a small part of Laruelle's early work entitled *Le Principe de minorité* (Paris: Aubier, 1981).

5 Laruelle writes: "idealism and materialism are reciprocally relative, and both relative to or identical with the real – whilst the real is not relative to

them or distinguishes itself absolutely from them" (ibid.).

6 Cf. François Laruelle, *Philosophie non-standard. Générique, quantique, philo-fiction* (Paris: Kimé, 2010) 488–93.

7 Ibid. 493. I do not quote this passage directly as the meaning of it is dependent on understanding some difficult technical language that, to properly understand, would take us too far afield. In short, though, Laruelle locates an important connection between messianism and science. For a summary in English of this idea see François Laruelle, "A Science in (*en*) Christ," trans. Aaron Riches, in *The Grandeur of Reason: Religion, Tradition and Universalism*, eds. Peter M. Candler, Jr. and Conor Cunningham (London: SCM, 2010) 316–31.

8 François Laruelle, *Mystique non-philosophique à l'usage des contemporains* (Paris: L'Harmattan, 2007) 262, 261. (Unless noted otherwise, all translations are my own.)

9 Henry Corbin, *La Paradoxe du monothéisme* (Paris: L'Herne, 2003) 106.

10 Ibid. 105. As a corollary to this angelophany we find in Shi'ite Islam a certain necessity of Imamology (Corbin 114). In that discussion Corbin appears to back away from equating the two so directly, speaking of the Imams' spiritual capacity separate from their fleshly capacity, while still making the Angel that being who animates Prophets, those who speak for the unsayable in the political-cultural realm. This separation of the spiritual and the fleshly will remain important in the work of Christian Jambet (his student) and Guy Lardreau when they speak of the Angel.

11 Corbin 114.

12 These are developed in more detail in a forthcoming article entitled "Against Tradition to Liberate Tradition: Weaponized Apophaticism and Gnostic Refusal."

13 Guy Lardreau, *Fictions philosophiques et science-fiction. Récréation philosophique* (Arles: Actes Sud, 1988) 30.

14 François Laruelle, *Future Christ: A Lesson in Heresy*, trans. Anthony Paul Smith (London and New York: Continuum, 2010) 4.

15 Christian Jambet, *La Grande Résurrection d'Alamût. Les Formes de la liberté dans le shî'isme ismaélien* (Lagrasse: Verdier, 1990) 362.

16 Christian Jambet and Guy Lardreau, *L'Ange. Pour une cynégétique du semblant, Ontologie de la révolution I* (Paris: Grasset, 1976) 36.

17 Christian Jambet and Guy Lardreau, *Le Monde. Réponse à la question: Qu'est-ce que les droits de l'homme?* (Paris: Grasset, 1978) 188.

18 Ibid. 177.

19 Jambet and Lardreau, *L'Ange* 79.

20 Ibid. 22.

21 Ibid. 36.

22 Cf. Ibid. 213–24.

23 Cf. Ibid. 92.

24 Ibid.

25 Ibid. 84.

26 Ibid. 87.

27 Ibid. 100.

28 Ibid. 109.

29 Ibid. 20.

30 Cf. Jambet and Lardreau, *Le Monde* 187.

31 Guy Lardreau, *La Véracité. Essai d'une philosophie négative* (Lagrasse: Verdier, 1993) 237.

32 Ibid. 241.

33 Ibid.

34 Ibid. 243. Cf. Philip Goodchild, *Capitalism and Religion: The Prince of Piety* (London and New York: Routledge, 2002) 148–55.

35 Lardreau, *La Véracité* 241.

36 Jambet and Lardreau, *L'Ange* 233.

37 Ibid. 131.

38 Jambet and Lardreau, *Le Monde* 188–89.

39 Ibid. 181.

40 Laruelle, *Future Christ* 17.

41 Ibid. 39, 40.

42 Ibid. 6.

43 Ibid. 4.

44 Ibid. 34. I should note that, though this article is not the place to develop it, I don't share Laruelle's anthropocentric characterization of man as such

and consider it a form of philosophical determination of the Earth that has remained within his theory. My own work within non-philosophy, drawing again on theological material is dependent upon the radical immanence of the in-Creature rather than the in-Man, for, at the more fundamental level, the Creature is more generic than Man, especially if there is no Creator. This will be the focus of another article in this series on non-theology.

45 Ibid. 42–43.

46 Ibid. 4.

47 Ibid. 7.

48 Ibid. 4, 8.

49 Ibid. 117.

50 Laruelle, "A Science" 318.

51 Gilles Grelet, *Déclarer la gnose. D'une guerre qui revient à la culture* (Paris: L'Harmattan, 2002) 119f50.

52 Ibid. 119f49.

53 Mehdi Belhaj Kacem, *La Psychose française. Les Banlieues: Le Ban de la République* (Paris: Gallimard, 2006) 18.

54 Cf. Alberto Toscano, *Fanaticism: On the Uses of an Idea* (London: Verso, 2010) 164 and the entirety of the chapter "The Revolution of the East," which is an excellent examination and exposition of the weaknesses of the engagement of Hegel and Žižek with Islam, specifically with regard to the One of Islam.

55 Ibid. 153.

56 François Laruelle, *En tant qu'Un. La "Non-philosophie" expliquée aux philosophes* (Paris: Aubier, 1991) 253.

57 Ray Brassier, *Nihil Unbound: Enlightenment and Extinction* (Basingstoke: Palgrave, 2007) 128.

58 François Laruelle, *Philosophie et non-philosophie* (Liège: Mardaga, 1989) 176–77.

59 François Laruelle, *Théorie des identités* (Paris: PUF, 1992) 59.

60 See Eric del Buffalo, *Deleuze et Laruelle. De la schizo-analyse à la non-philosophie* (Paris: Kimé, 2003) 40.

61 François Laruelle, *Les Philosophies de la différence. Une introduction critique* (Paris: PUF, 1986)

215–19. See also 237–40 for an early formal schema of the One; and idem, *Principes de la non-philosophie* (Paris: PUF, 1995) 168–92.

62 See Jambet 33–49 for a compressed history.

63 Christian Jambet, "The Paradoxical One," trans. Michael Stanish, *Umbr(a): A Journal of the Unconscious* (2009) 141; idem, *La Grande Résurrection d'Alamût* 142; translation slightly modified.

64 Jambet, "The Paradoxical One" 142, 143.

65 St Thomas Aquinas, "On Kingship or The Governance of Rulers (De Regimine Principum, 1265–1267)," trans. Paul E. Sigmund, in *St. Thomas Aquinas on Politics and Ethics*, ed. Paul E. Sigmund (London and New York: Norton, 1988) 17–18.

66 Cf. Laruelle, "Decline" 41.

67 Ya'qûb al-Sijistânî, *Le Dévoilement des choses cachées* (Kashf al-Mahjûb), trans. Henry Corbin (Lagrasse: Verdier, 1988) 33–35.

68 Ibid. 81.

69 Jambet, *La Grande Résurrection* 210.

70 Al-Sijistânî 77.

The struggle over the contemporary theorization of art is structured by a series of interlocking and antagonistic positions. These can be summarized under: relations, objects, and immanence. The proponents of relations argue that they offer a linking, an interaction, that promises the displacement of the art object and the entry or dissolution of art in social relations.[1] This turn to "relational art" problematically risked dissolving antagonism and encouraging mere immersion into contemporary forms of neoliberal capital.[2] Objects, in the formulations of Object-Oriented Philosophy, offer withdrawal from this relational field and access to the world of the non-human.[3] This access seemed to exceed the world of capitalism, but at the cost of an aestheticization of this access that generated a deliberately *anti-political* aesthetics, which evades the very question of capitalist forms of value.[4] Immanence implies a superior plane, in the Deleuzian characterization, which can be reached through practices like art. Immanence immerses in order to exceed specification or determination. Relations and objects both reply that this immersion allows no differentiation, simply dropping us into flux and flow – another night in which all cows are black. Sartre castigated thinkers of immanence "in which everything works by compromises, by protoplasmic exchanges, by a tepid cellular chemistry,"[5] although he has in mind very different thinkers to Deleuze. Despite the difference of target, the Sartrean charge is echoed, unconsciously, in critiques of Deleuzian immanence today.[6]

This seeming impasse offers the opportunity to reconsider the problem of immanence and not simply in terms of the theorization of art, although this will be my focus here. Art

benjamin noys

THE ART OF THE ABSOLUTE
relations, objects, and immanence

throws into sharp relief the problems of an adequate conceptualization of immanence in the present moment. Immanence is a key term because it does not simply abolish relations and objects in some undifferentiated process, but it raises the question of the relation or link to immanence through relations and objects. This question of the link also raises the crucial political question, which structures these positions, concerning our relation to capital. If the form of immanence we most insistently encounter is the immanence of capitalism, as the "untranscendable horizon" of our time, then we are forced to consider how the metrics of value formation, the "geometry of rationalization," dictates our experience of immanence today.[7]

In question is the desire to break with this form of immanence and so to constitute some sort of alternative or horizon not subject to this metrics. The difficulty is that such a desire often constitutes itself in terms of a militant excess, whether coded as relation, object, or immanence, rather than, to use Jaleh Mansoor's phrase, a "militant fold."[8] In the case of militant excess the desire to escape is formed by or through some moment which exceeds all determination. Such a moment flares-up into existence, only then to fall back into the determinations of capitalism and the state. Contrary to such a consolatory but ephemeral moment the necessity is to think a militant fold, which would consider antagonism or contradiction secreted within the seemingly smooth and soft immanence of capital. Art, in this reading, becomes a site to consider the tendency to postulate a militant excess as solution to the riddle of the present moment and the possibility of thinking immanence in a different way, as site of contradiction.

The reason for this is that the tendency to turn to militant excess re-introduces transcendence into immanence. As we shall see, the desire to constitute an absolute immanence is, finally, indistinguishable from the desire for transcendence. The result is a problematic religious or theological register of militant excess. To counter this we can return to Deleuze's conceptualization of immanence as a problem of *relation*. The link to immanence is a moment which tends to become sublated in a theological register. To dispute this theological construal I turn to Deleuze's use of the early Sartre to dispute and put under pressure the concept of immanence. Here I want to add another term to the struggle over the theorization of art: the "absolute." While objects, relations, and immanence, form the hegemonic "master signifiers" (or, perhaps, little master signifiers, or even buzzwords) of our moment we don't have much of a taste for the absolute – associated, as it is, with the sins of totalization and (bad) Hegelianism. Sartre's thinking of art as "absolute," however, actually offers a means to undo the theological turn to militant excess and disrupts the interlocking positions that constitute our present moment.

To turn to the figure of the "militant fold" is to remain within a Deleuzian topology. My claim is that the occluded debate between Deleuze and Sartre might also put pressure on Deleuze's topology of the fold. This is to reinscribe the notion of immanence in a direction away from the Deleuzian emphasis on the expansive plane of immanence that absorbs all moments and towards the fold as moment of secreted contradiction and tension. Rather than the dissolution of all questions in the plane or "protoplasmic exchanges," I consider that we could reinscribe or redescribe the problem of immanence in terms of a tension of relations that engages the political, material, and objects. This would not only be relevant to the field of art. In fact, art could even be considered here as something of a detour to the issues of the political, materiality, and objects although, hopefully, without dissolving the specificity of art as a site in which these issue are posed. Art, or perhaps better the theorization of art, would therefore be a *necessary* detour to probe and rework the notion of immanence.

facing immanence

In one of his discussions of contemporary art, collected in *Chronicles of Consensual Times* (2005), Jacques Rancière remarks on the tension in modern art between an art of presence and an art of flatness.[9] This bifurcation shapes modern art, which operates between the piling-up of images and their purification, between the purity of images and the commerce of images. Rancière traces the origin of this tension back to the early Manet painting *The Dead Christ with Angels* (1864). In this painting the dead Christ stares at us as viewers:

> The dead Christ reopens his eyes, he resurrects in the pure immanence of pictorial presence and writes down in advance monochrome paintings as well as pop imagery, minimalist sculptures as well as fictional museums in the tradition of icon and the religious economy of the resurrection.[10]

Fig. 1. Edouard Manet, *The Dead Christ with Angels*. The Metropolitan Museum of Art, H.O. Havemeyer Collection, bequest of Mrs H.O. Havemeyer, 1929 (29.100.51).

Manet's painting stages "pure immanence," which coincides with the pure presence of Christ, in the flatness of the image. In this way presence and the image absolutely coincide.

The bifurcation of these tendencies, and their reconvergence, will shape, according to Rancière, the possibilities of modern and contemporary art. This art splits between the flatness of the image, radicalizing it in monochromes, and the iconic function of this flatness, in our fascination for cabinets of curiosities. The importance of Manet is that in this work he condenses both tendencies: flatness that is iconic. Rancière continues: "Their dream of immanence may only come about through self-contradiction: that of a discourse which transforms every piece of art into a little host, a morceau detached from the great body of the Word made flesh."[11] Immanence begins to coincide with its opposite: transcendence. The desire to achieve absolute immanence, Rancière suggests, cannot be extricated from its theological supplement.

It is this moment of transcendence or transubstantiation which interests me about this little scene of the staging of pure immanence in terms of pure presence, or the coincidence of image and presence. The self-contradiction of immanence is that its "flatness" recomposes grace or depth. The result is that immanence can never coincide with itself, and that this coincidence can only form as a relation of possible transcendence *within* immanence. It's not hard to suspect that within a point about the fate of contemporary art Rancière is also making a critical point about the work of Gilles Deleuze, as the premier prophet of immanence.

This tension between immanence and transcendence, flatness and the iconic, is also played out in Jorge Luis Borges's parable "Paradiso XXXI, 108."[12] This short text is a strange kind of commentary on Dante's lines: "'Segnor mio *Iesù Cristo, Dio verace*, or fu sì fatta la sembianza vostra?'" In Allen Mandelbaum's translation: "'O my Lord Jesus Christ, true God, was then / Your image like the image I see now?'"[13] The second line is line 108. What concerns Borges is a "broken and scattered god," a dispersion that he figures in the "irrecoverable face" of Christ.[14] In Dante the split is between the image of Christ then and our image of Christ, with this hiatus raising the issues of representation and truth. To know if we truly had the image of Christ would be, according to Borges, "the key to all parables."[15] The lost moment of presence would unlock all the enigmas of narrative and restore us to singular meaning.

The difficulty is compounded that while we don't have access to this image, the past moments of access are also deeply paradoxical:

> Paul saw it as a light which hurled him to the ground; John saw it as the sun when it blazes in all its force; Teresa of Léon saw it many times, bathed in a tranquil light, and could never determine the colour of its eyes.[16]

For Paul or John it is the excess of light which denies access to the image. For Teresa of Léon the image is perfectly accessible, but still she cannot determine the colour of his eyes. We have lost the image of Christ from the beginning.

Borges, or his narrator, suggests, in line with the opening of the parable, that the image of Jesus' face may be broken or scattered. Our loss of the infinite is its dispersion everywhere, which permits the possible recovery of the infinite, but only as a fragment. We may catch glimpses of the face in the world: "A Jew's profile in the subway is perhaps that of Christ; the hands giving us our change at a ticket window perhaps repeat those that one day were nailed to the cross by some soldiers."[17] Loss is recompensed by dispersion, with the iconic now appearing everywhere: "Perhaps some feature of that crucified countenance lurks in every mirror; perhaps the face died, was obliterated, so that God could be all of us."[18] We may, as the short narrative concludes, see the face of Christ in our dreams and yet the next day we may not recognize it.

Loss prefigures resurrection. The face or image of Christ appears now as a moment of transcendence in the immanence of the everyday. Borges's parable prefigures Rancière's parable of modern and contemporary art. In both cases what is lost in the singular is recovered in the plural, and immanence returns as dispersion and recovery of the sacred. Art today is torn between the singular and the dispersed, between objects and relations, we could say. What repairs this tear is the theological moment of immanence becoming transcendence, a relation that coincides with an object in an excess that escapes both.

I've taken these two examples to labour an essentially simple point. Immanence does not form itself into pure immanence and in forming immanence we find a dispersion into transcendence. The expelling of relations and objects, or what appears to be an expelling, leads to their return as moments of grace or, more politically, as moments of "militant excess." In this way a turn through immanence can resist the soft immanence of contemporary capitalism and disrupt the metrics of value formation. The difficulty is that this is only a temporary moment and one which then returns to immanence. Instead of escape we have a grace or transcendence conferred upon the forms of value, in exactly the way Marx traced in the commodity-form. The fate of art, in which these moments of transcendence generate new forms of value generation, is indicative of this tension.

relating to immanence

The question of constructing or producing immanence is not only a matter of thought but also of a practice, and often of art.[19] It is a matter of forming a relation to immanence. This is true of Deleuze's work on cinema. One of the roles of cinema is to generate or produce an immanence that is lacking. Again, this is an explicitly religious operation (shortly before this quotation Deleuze remarks on the Catholicism of many filmmakers):

> The link between man and the world is broken. Henceforth, this link must become an object of belief: it is the impossible which can only be restored within a faith […] The cinema must film, not the world, but belief in this world, our only link.[20]

The role of cinema is to regenerate our belief in the world, to establish the link to immanence as a gesture of faith. The link or relation is turned back towards the theological that now coincides with the immanence of the world.

This practice of reaching the plane of immanence is one *not* given to philosophy, but to experiment and practice. In *What is Philosophy?* (1991) Deleuze and Guattari argue that the plane of immanence is "pre-philosophical," and that to grope towards immanence requires

> measures that are not very respectable, rational or reasonable. These measures belong to the order of dreams, of pathological processes, esoteric experiences, drunkenness, and excess. We head for the horizon, on the plane of immanence, and we return with bloodshot eyes, yet they are the eyes of the mind.[21]

The relation to immanence is not given to philosophy, but must be formed elsewhere. What is crucial to note, however, is that we "return with bloodshot eyes" to thought or philosophy. The militant excess of immanence may be immanence itself, but only on the condition of thought grasping this excess.

Deleuze and Guattari define the plane as "the formless, unlimited absolute, neither surface nor volume but always fractal."[22] Deleuze, resolute if ambiguous opponent of Hegel, inscribes the plane of immanence as an "unlimited absolute." This absolute immanence is given by the fact of an immanence we relate to as inexhaustible and expansive, at once compact and without limits. The compression of immanence, in the same manner as we traced with the theological excess of art, generates an expansive and dispersed grace. Art is one way in which we can touch the plane, but the plane itself is a chaos that never stabilizes. This instability means that we cannot somehow rely on the plane of immanence, but that it must always be constructed or reached. That said, however, it forms an unlimited absolute that exceeds any particular determination – which allows immanence to evade reduction to relations, objects, or forms that might simply lie in congruence with capitalist immanence.

In his final text "Immanence: A Life" Deleuze invokes Sartre's early text *The Transcendence of the Ego* (1936–37) to buttress his claims to develop an impersonal transcendental field.[23] In Deleuze's modelling the field or plane of immanence exists in the absence of the subject or consciousness. For immanence to be immanence it must refer to nothing else: "Absolute immanence is in itself: it is not in something, *to* something; it does not depend on an object or belong to a subject."[24] The disappearance of consciousness from this field is a result of its speed: "as long as consciousness traverses the transcendental field at an infinite speed everywhere diffused, nothing is able to reveal it."[25] This peculiar "accelerationism" of thought displaces consciousness and the subject to reveal a relation to immanence that is delinked from both.[26]

What, then, guarantees the relation to immanence for Deleuze? This relation is formed by the generic "a life." Deleuze argues that "A life is the immanence of immanence, absolute immanence: it is complete power, complete bliss."[27] The first example of this non-relational relation is the character Rogue Riderhood in Dickens's *Our Mutual Friend* (1864–65). Rescued from death, Rogue lies in a coma between life and death. In this state he elicits a strange sympathy, but when he starts to awaken the onlookers realize that:

> The spark of life was deeply interesting while it was in abeyance, but now that it has got established in Mr. Riderhood, there appears to be a general desire that

circumstances had admitted of its being developed in anybody else, rather than that gentleman.[28]

The "separable"[29] spark of life is not so far from Agamben's later reflections on "bare life" – a "*life exposed to death*."[30] It is this strange moment of separable life that touches immanence in a relation that flickers away as actual life is regained, replaced by animosity to the dastardly Riderhood.

Obviously this "spark of life" is related to death, which is not affirmative enough for Deleuze. His other example is that of the child. "Small children, through all their sufferings and weaknesses, are infused with an immanent life that is pure power and even bliss."[31] What is striking is that this supposedly more affirmative incarnation of "a life" is still predicated on suffering and weakness, which is then transformed into unlimited potential. The religious language of bliss and beatitude, although Spinozan, again indicates how immanence is intimately linked to the religious, if not to the Christological. Immanence is here a relation to "a life," which persists and insists beyond the realm of subjectivity and consciousness.

The paradox I have explored is that it is precisely in invoking a *relation* to immanence that Deleuze still turns to a theological conception of this relation – in which we assume or inhabit the grace of immanence. Such a relation tries to insistently position an excess that cannot be reduced to philosophy, while all the while returning to it for its registration and evaluation. The continual attempt to displace immanence from simply agreement with what is, what we might call a "bad affirmationism," merely results in a "good affirmationism" that insists on excess that must return but can never fully return.[32] This surplus immanence forms the horizon of the theology of immanence.

under a blinding light

Certainly Sartre's analysis in *The Transcendence of the Ego* initially appears to conform to Deleuze's reference. Sartre, abandoning the transcendental "I" of Husserl, remarks, as a result, that "the transcendental field becomes impersonal; or, if you like, 'pre-personal,' *without an I*."[33] Yet Deleuze flattens Sartre's conceptuality in his desire to digest and absorb it within the conceptualization of the plane of immanence. Sartre, as I've stated, had little time for what he regarded as philosophies of immanence. The abandonment of the "I" is not the dissolution of consciousness into immanence or into the vitalism of "a life." Instead, Sartre – we should specify the early Sartre – is interested in using phenomenology to place us back within the field of objects and relations.

Sartre argues that abandonment of the transcendental "I" means that the ego or me (*moi*) "is outside, *in the world*."[34] In an earlier article, introducing Husserl's thinking, Sartre had argued that "The philosophy of transcendence throws us out onto the high road, amid threats and under a blinding light."[35] The category of intentionality, which Sartre took as crucial, throws us out into the world. We burst out towards things. We do not, however, ingest things in what he mocks as "digestive philosophy."[36] Instead, we place ourselves among things and relations – which have their own affects not dependent on us. "Husserl has put horror and charm back into things."[37] The result is a philosophy that places us in the actual world: "It is not in some lonely refuge that we shall discover ourselves, but on the road, in the town, in the crowd, as a thing among things and a human being among human beings."[38] It is this worldly philosophy that would be crucial for the entirety of Sartrean philosophy, although modulated and inflected in different ways across his career.

In *The Transcendence of the Ego* Sartre picks up and extends the centrality of intentionality as the means by which "consciousness transcends itself."[39] Consciousness is always consciousness *of* something:

> I am then plunged into the world of objects; it is they which constitute the unity of my consciousness; it is they which present themselves with values, with attractive and repellent qualities – but *me*, I have disappeared; I have annihilated myself.[40]

The "I" is annihilated, but only into a series of relations to objects and not altogether into immanence itself. Intentionality is a transcendence from the stream of immanence that throws us into relations and objects as a field of frictions and tensions. This offers a different emphasis from Deleuze or, at least, from certain moments in Deleuze.

What is true, and this is where Sartre does converge again with Deleuze, is that Sartre conceives of the ego or me as a blockage to the field of consciousness. In a remark that is eerily similar to Lacan, Sartre states:

> Everything happens, therefore, as if consciousness constituted the ego as a false representation of itself, as if consciousness hypnotized itself before this ego which it has constituted, absorbing itself in the ego as if to make the ego its guardian and its law.[41]

Sartre argues for the primacy of transcendental consciousness as "an impersonal spontaneity."[42] This would seem to converge with Deleuze's vitalism, in terms of a primary form of excess or freedom that is uncoded – precisely another version of "militant excess." Unlike Deleuze, however, for Sartre this spontaneity, this vertigo, does not throw us back into or onto an impersonal plane, but engages us with the world. These "pure spontaneities"[43] ensure we are not simply objects but also that this "absolute consciousness," while having nothing of the subject, conditions our existence. In fact it places us in contact with the world in a "relation of interdependence."[44] It places us in situations, to use the title of Sartre's collected essays.

Plunged back into the world we enter into politics as *friction* with the world. Idealists posit the "spiritual assimilation"[45] and consumption of the world that "never meets external resistances" and so "suffering, hunger, and war are diluted in a slow process of the unification of ideas."[46] Against this unification Sartre argues that transcendence places us within the tension of political (and other) forms of relation. Any assimilative philosophy, whether couched as idealist or materialist, simply absorbs the world under its own aegis, whereas transcendence does not allow us to escape, but places us *within*. This is a thinking of immanence against an immanence that would dissolve relations and objects into one plane. The return to Sartre allows us to problematize the "digestive philosophy" of Deleuze. While Deleuze was once proclaimed the "new Sartre,"[47] and heavily influenced by him, something Deleuze never denied,[48] I want to push Sartre *against* Deleuze. Sartre dissolves the ego into relations and objects, although not merely into that displaced world of immanence that is the non-human.

Tensions do remain. I've already noted Sartre's tendency to posit an originary freedom or spontaneity which is then compromised through insertion into situations. In this schema, as has recently been noted by Howard Caygill, a stress on decision and meaning tends to displace an account of the tensions and complexities of resistance and force.[49] While Sartre can be used to push against Deleuze, this also involves a pushing against Sartre. Rather than a Sartrean stress on disembedding, which recovers theological excess in the mode of Kierkegaard's anxiety of decision, I am suggesting that Sartre's "transcendence" can be read to imply an embedding that works on and in existent forces and potentials. The place of art would be one place of such a working.

art of the absolute

Sartre's articles "Calder's Mobiles" (1946),[50] on the work of Alexander Calder, and "The Quest for the Absolute: On Giacometti's Sculpture" (1948),[51] on Alberto Giacometti, offer us a means to grasp a situated phenomenology. Explicit in the title of the second article, both concern the absolute. This might be something of a surprise, considering a philosophy concerned with objects and relations. Sartre is concerned, as we will see, not with dissolving the artwork or object into a field, but on how it stays integral and absolute. This search for the absolute, in both cases, turns on movement. Taking the "static" field of sculpture, Sartre

Fig. 2. Henri Cartier-Bresson, *Alberto Giacometti's Studio, Paris 1960*. Henri Cartier-Bresson/Magnum Photos.

explores how such absolutes "capture true, living moments and craft [...] them into something."[52] Movement is the possibility of inscribing something living into an object, pushing it into relations. The absolute is not correlated with the static and complete, but with this mobility.

Calder's mobiles are obviously related to movement, taking the forces of nature to imbue themselves with sudden and unpredictable life. Sartre writes:

> A Mobile: a little local party; an object defined by its movement and non-existent without it; a flower that fades as soon as it comes to a standstill; a pure play of movement in the same way as there are pure plays of light.[53]

This transitory nature of the mobile, which fades and surges up, marks it out from the permanence associated with the artwork: "Sculpture suggests movement, painting suggest depth or light. Calder suggests nothing."[54] Sartre continues: "His mobiles signify nothing, refer to nothing other than themselves. They simply *are*: they are absolutes."[55] This self-referential nature *includes* relation. They exist for themselves, but as absolute within a field of relations that they engage with.

The mobile exists "halfway between matter and life."[56] The same might also be said of Giacometti's sculptures. For Sartre, Giacometti confronts the problem that "for three thousand years sculptors have been carving only corpses."[57] Again, the problem is to infuse movement and existence into inert matter through a mediation of the human and the stone. Sartre wonders: "I am not sure whether to see him as a man intent on imposing a human seal on space or as a rock dreaming of the human."[58] Giacometti abandons and reinvents the whole of sculpture from the beginning because he refuses the facile solutions of existing forms. He constantly probes the fact that "there is a fixed boundary to be reached, a unique problem to be solved: how to make a man out of stone without petrifying him."[59] Again, like Calder's mobiles, we turn on movement and the problem of space. Giacometti "knows space is a cancer of being that gnaws at everything."[60] The implication is that mobility gives us access to time and to a time that moves into the future. This dimension of the temporal, particularly in terms of mobility to move into the future, is crucial to Sartre in inscribing a force of freedom or rupture.

Movement is restored to sculpture through creating such sculptures as though the human were visible from a distance and in motion. These walking creatures elicit a reaction in us of movement through space, which is visible in Henri Cartier-Bresson's photograph of 1960, which mischievously doubles Giacometti striding forward with the similar pose of one of his sculptures. The blurred yet frozen image of Giacometti in movement captured by the photograph demonstrates, if anything, the greater mobility implicit in the sculpture. The two, the human and the sculpture, seem about to meet in a collision as the one actually moves and the other implies a virtual movement.

For Sartre, the solution of Giacometti to the problem of movement is to sculpt humans as if seen from a distance. Rather than the illusion of sculpture, which supposes we can view a sculpture from any distance and it remain consistent, Giacometti puts us at a distance. The fragile and elongated figures make us see them from a distance, from a particular viewpoint. The result is a refusal of the claim to neutral "wholeness" or integrity. Sartre writes: "By accepting relativity from the outset, he has found the absolute."[61] Instead of the absolute extracting itself from the relativity of relations, it is only by accepting this relativity that we can form the absolute. The absolute is not some neutral plane that escapes relation, but is formed in the relation of human viewer to the object. The object gains its "life" in the forcing of us into a relation to it. In this way the absolute is composed out of this particular relation with an object.

The absolute, the indivisible, is a *relational* effect. Sartre's suggestion is radically divergent from Deleuze's. Sartre claims that Giacometti "has quite simply suppressed multiplicity."[62] Deleuze, on the other hand, is always concerned with revealing multiplicity, even in the most unlikely of places.[63] The multiplicity of any particular "object" opens up that depth and fractal dispersion that touches upon the plane of immanence. In this way the object loses its integrity and is immersed into multiplicity, which also erodes the security of relations as well. The absolute is unlimited because this multiplicity means it can never be closed. On the contrary, Sartre argues that the absolute is found in the suppression of multiplicity and divisibility. We are forced into a relation, a particular relation, with a particular object. Instead of the dissolution of tension into "protoplasmic exchanges" the absolute forms a sharpening of tension and even conflict, such as we can intuit in the imagined virtual collision between Giacometti and his sculpture implied by Bresson's photograph.

In summary, the absolute, in the case of Giacometti, coincides neither with immanence nor simply with the integrity of the ever-receding object. As Sartre puts it: "Before him, artists thought they were sculpting *being*, and that absolute dissolved into an infinity of appearances. He chose to sculpt *situated* appearance and it turned out that one reached the absolute that way."[64] This is what I think might be crucial about Sartre's intervention, largely forgotten as it is; against the Deleuzian "unlimited absolute," the possibility of a "situated absolute" offers an alternative that places us amongst the stresses of relations and objects. Sartre's absolute, relative as it is, still has an echo of modernism that is not to contemporary taste. Also, Sartre's early philosophy or his art criticism is not unproblematic. The tendency to claim a primary spontaneity, the development of a transcendental field, converges with the thematics of militant excess I have been contesting. That said, this suggestion of a particular form of transcendence and a particular form of situated absolute unsettles the interlocking struggles into which the contemporary theorization of art has settled, and pushes art towards the problem of the militant fold. We placed back "on the road, in the town, in the crowd, as a thing among things and a human being among human beings."

the situated absolute

Sartre's situated absolute can undo the forms of militant excess that continue to bewitch contemporary thinking, without simply conceding to the defeat of uncontested immersion. Militant excess posits the theological excess that *always* escapes. From relations exceeding the limits of "cold" capitalist relations of value through the "warmth" of intimacy, to objects as instances of metaphysically excessive and irreducible moments, on to immanence as a superior plane, we are promised theological excess that consoles us against the penetration of capitalist abstraction. That these moments of excess remain, constitutively, in tension with falling back into those abstractions produces the contradictory tension of our moment between absorption and excess. This is the dialectic of recuperation, which posits an initial purity that is always threatened with recuperation by capitalist logic. While I am not saying recuperation never happens, such a modelling of purity and sin occludes the presence of capital from the start, as horizon, and consoles the creator or excavator of excess with a grace that can then be rued as it falls away. In this context the role of the theorist is to track, construct, or produce the excess that is merely latent, which also gives them an unwarranted power over the naïve. Art is saved and returned to the dignity of philosophical ontology, at the cost of grasping the fact that art is embedded in these contradictions from the start (and this is its *virtue*).

To signify this embedding by the term "fold" could be regarded as ironic, considering its Deleuzian provenance. Wouldn't Deleuze's own account of the fold imply that his analysis of immanence doesn't form a "militant excess" that is surreptitiously theological, but a folded or re-folded immanence? To briefly return to *The Fold* (1988) demonstrates, I think, the tension between the Deleuzian conception and what I am trying to reinscribe under this term. Deleuze argues that we have "the fold to infinity,"[65] which opens out a conception of the fold as fractal: embedded, yet infinite. This is, I'd suggest, another inscription of the "unlimited absolute." Also, unlike Sartre, the fold inscribes a horizontal "flow" that links together artworks in a common field of immanence.[66] What we could call the relative absolute of the particular artwork links to an unlimited absolute through the connective tissues of folding to form a new "diagonal."[67] In this way the resistant force of the fold inscribes another militant excess at the heart of the militant fold.

It is this conception I am disputing through a strategic turn to Sartre. Rather than the resolution of contradiction in the inscribed infinite the militant fold forms in the tensions and resistances of being thrown out into the world as the world of contradiction. The privilege of art, we could say, lies in its condensing of these moments of contradiction, its inscription within the forms of capitalist value and the immanent horizon of capital. The fold, then, gains militancy, in a certain traction of these forms of real abstraction that cannot be reduced or exceeded by the invocation of a militant excess. Art is, if we like, a kind of probe. The situated absolute, of course, places works in relations, immersing them in the field of objects and relations and so, as Sartre noted, in the political field as well. Political efficacy is not bought through an excess that transcends immanence, but by an action and effect within the immanence of relations. "Transcendence" here throws us out into these relations and contradictions, rather than rescuing us from them. In this way we meet "external resistances," which are now *internal* to the work of art and our experience of it. This permits an experience of resistances and stresses within these relations, which are folded into them, rather than at some transcendent point of redemption.

To return to Manet's *Dead Christ*, I want to conclude with another reflection on the tension encoded in this painting. Jean Clay argues that:

> Thanks to the lighting, to the viewing angle, to the daring frontal pose, and to the closing off of the represented space, the dead Christ, in the version on canvas, seems on the point of sliding toward us. His archaizing monumentality, however, holds him back. In any case, it is the "staging" that arouses our conflicting feelings.[68]

What interests me is this sliding off – movement that renders the absolute in relation and which is, at the same time, held back. I want to suggest, perhaps in a self-serving fashion, that this sliding shifts us from the attractions of immanence and militant excess into the more slippery and unstable place of the situated absolute and the militant fold.

Militant excess, in this little parable, would be a form of "archaizing monumentality" despite this excess presenting itself as a force of rupture and movement. It would be monumental in withdrawing from relations and objects to pose a friction-free moment or form of immanence that is at once singular and can encompass everything. In contrast, I am identifying the militant fold with the moment of sliding, in line with Sartre's thinking of the "relative absolute" as movement. The tension between these two moments or forces remains, and I think this speaks to the necessity of thinking in terms of the "relative absolute," which can retain this tension rather than dissolving it. The tension, or perhaps better contradiction, would then be a starting point for considering the forms and tensions of value, and the resistance to them, in our present moment.

notes

1 Bourriaud.

2 Bishop.

3 Harman, "Well-Wrought" 187–88.

4 Bromberg.

5 Sartre, *We Have* 5.

6 This charge is made by both Graham Harman and Peter Hallward – see Harman, *Prince* 6; and Hallward.

7 Mansoor.

8 Ibid.

9 Rancière 57–61.

10 Ibid. 60.

11 Ibid. 61.

12 Borges.

13 Dante 530.

14 Borges 274.

15 Ibid.

16 Ibid.

17 Ibid.

18 Ibid.

19 For a critical discussion of this thinking of art as access to immanence in Deleuze, see Hallward 104–26.

20 Deleuze, *Cinema 2* 171–72.

21 Deleuze and Guattari 41.

22 Ibid. 36.

23 Deleuze, *Pure Immanence* 32 n. 2; Deleuze and Guattari 47.

24 Deleuze, *Pure Immanence* 26.

25 Ibid.

26 For a critical discussion of "accelerationism" in Deleuze and more generally, see Noys, *Malign Velocities*.

27 Ibid. 27.

28 Dickens 442.

29 Ibid. 439.

30 Agamben 55; emphasis in original.

31 Deleuze, *Pure Immanence* 30.

32 For the critical use of the term "affirmationism," see Noys, *Persistence*.

33 Sartre, *Transcendence* 38.

34 Ibid. 31.

35 Sartre, *We Have* 6.

36 Ibid. 3.

37 Ibid. 5.

38 Ibid. 6.

39 Sartre, *Transcendence* 38.

40 Ibid. 49.

41 Ibid. 101. On the relation of Sartre to Lacan, see Jameson 131, 171.

42 Ibid. 98.

43 Ibid. 96.

44 Ibid. 106.

45 Ibid. 104.

46 Ibid.

47 Dosse 92–98.

48 See Deleuze, "He Was."

49 Caygill 2–5.

50 Sartre, *We Have* 146–48.

51 Ibid. 187–97.

52 Ibid. 147.

53 Ibid. 146.

54 Ibid. 146–47.

55 Ibid. 147.

56 Ibid. 148.

57 Ibid. 189.

58 Ibid. 188.

59 Ibid. 189.

60 Ibid. 191.

61 Ibid. 193.

62 Ibid. 194.

63 For example, Deleuze reads Proust as a writer of multiplicity, contesting the image of integration that has often dominated his reception. Deleuze does this by turning Melanie Klein's concept of the part-object against Klein's tendency to emphasize a fragmentation that refers to a whole; see Deleuze, *Proust and Signs* 109–10. It is ironic that Deleuze is not seemingly aware of Hanna Segal's articulation of Kleinian aesthetics, which takes Proust as the model of the re-creation of a lost world into an integrated artistic whole; see Segal 388–390.

64 Sartre, *We Have Only This Life* 195.

65 Deleuze, *The Fold* 122.

66 Ibid. 123.

67 Ibid. 137.

68 Clay 21.

bibliography

Agamben, Giorgio. *Homo Sacer: Sovereign Power and Bare Life*. 1995. Trans. Daniel Heller-Roazen. Stanford: Stanford UP, 1998. Print.

Bishop, Claire. "Antagonism and Relational Aesthetics." *October* 110 (Autumn 2004): 51–79. Print.

Borges, Jorge Luis. "Paradiso, XXXI, 108." *Labyrinths*. Harmondsworth: Penguin, 1981. 274–75. Print.

Bourriaud, Nicolas. *Relational Aesthetics*. 1998. Dijon: Réel, 2002. Print.

Bromberg, Svenja. "The Anti-political Aesthetics of Objects and Worlds Beyond." *Mute Magazine* 25 July 2013. Web. 3 Nov. 2013. <http://www.metamute.org/editorial/articles/anti-political-aesthetics-objects-and-worlds-beyond>.

Caygill, Howard. *On Resistance: A Philosophy of Defiance*. London: Bloomsbury, 2013. Print.

Clay, Jean. "Ointments, Makeup, Pollen." Trans. John Shepley. *October* 27 (1983): 3–44. Print.

Dante, Alighieri. *The Divine Comedy*. Trans. Allen Mandelbaum. Intro. Eugenio Montale. New York: Everyman's Library, 1995. Print.

Deleuze, Gilles. *Cinema 2: The Time-Image*. Trans. Hugh Tomlinson and Robert Galeta. London: Continuum, 2005. Print.

Deleuze, Gilles. *The Fold: Leibniz and the Baroque*. 1988. Trans. Tom Conley. London: Athlone, 1993. Print.

Deleuze, Gilles. "He Was My Teacher." *Desert Islands and Other Texts, 1953–1974*. Ed. David Lapoujade. Trans. Michael Taormina. Los Angeles: Semiotext(e), 2004. 77–80. Print.

Deleuze, Gilles. *Proust and Signs*. 1964. Trans. Robert Howard. London: Lane, 1973. Print.

Deleuze, Gilles. *Pure Immanence: Essays on A Life*. Trans. Anne Boyman. Intro. John Rajchman. New York: Zone, 2001. Print.

Deleuze, Gilles, and Félix Guattari. *What is Philosophy?* 1991. Trans. Graham Burchell and Hugh Tomlinson. London and New York: Verso, 1994. Print.

Dickens, Charles. *Our Mutual Friend*. 1864–65. Ed. and Intro. Adrian Poole. London: Penguin, 1997. Print.

Dosse, François, *Gilles Deleuze and Félix Guattari: Intersecting Lives*. New York: Columbia UP, 2011. Print.

Hallward, Peter. *Out of this World: Deleuze and the Philosophy of Creation*. London: Verso, 2006. Print.

Harman, Graham. *Prince of Networks: Bruno Latour and Metaphysics*. Melbourne: re.press, 2009. Print.

Harman, Graham. "The Well-Wrought Broken Hammer: Object-Oriented Literary Criticism." *New Literary History* 43 (2012): 183–203. Print.

Jameson, Fredric. *Antimonies of Realism*. London and New York: Verso, 2013. Print.

Mansoor, Jaleh. "Notes on Militant Folds: Against Weigel and Ahern's 'Further Materials Toward a Theory of the Man-Child.'" *Claudius App* V (2013). Web. 15 Oct. 2013. <http://theclaudiusapp.com/5-mansoor.html>.

Noys, Benjamin. *Malign Velocities: The Politics of Accelerationism*. Alresford: Zero, 2014. Print.

Noys, Benjamin. *The Persistence of the Negative: A Critique of Contemporary Continental Theory*. Edinburgh: Edinburgh UP, 2010. Print.

Rancière, Jacques. *Chronicles of Consensual Times*. 2005. Trans. Steve Corcoran. London: Continuum, 2010. Print.

Sartre, Jean-Paul. *The Transcendence of the Ego: An Existentialist Theory of Consciousness*. 1936–37. Trans. and Intro. Forrest Williams and Robert Kirkpatrick. New York: Hill, 2000. Print.

Sartre, Jean-Paul. *We Have Only This Life to Live: The Selected Essays of Jean-Paul Sartre, 1939–1975*. New York: New York Review of Books Classics, 2013. Print.

Segal, Hanna. "A Psycho-analytical Approach to Aesthetics." 1955. *New Directions in Psychoanalysis*. Ed. Paula Heimann and Roger Money-Kryle. London: Maresfield, 1977. 384–405. Print.

Index

Notes: Page numbers in *italics* refer to figures
Page numbers with "n" refer to notes

absolute 72, 73, 122; art of the 179–83; contingency 17–19; situated 182–3
"absolute profanation" 76
Adorno on Nature (Cook) 120
Adorno, Theodor 8, 89, 115, 118–19; *Dialectic of Enlightenment* 118; History and Freedom 122; immanence and transcendence 116; metaphysics 116, 117, 125n7; *Minima Moralia* 115, 120; *Negative Dialectics* 115–17, 120, 121; philosophy 122; terminology 117; vital need 124
affirmationism 5, 178
After Finitude (Meillassoux) 6, 17, 33, 34, 36, 37, 51, 57
After the Postsecular and the Postmodern (Smith and Whistler) 161
Agamben, Giorgio 5, 7, 19, 65–8, 75, 115, 119; *Infancy and History* 69; *Language and Death* 67; linguistic turn 79n7; philosophical corpus 72; political nihilism 79n9
Alberto Giacometti's Studio, Paris 1960 (Cartier-Bresson) *180*
aleatory materialism 17
al-Sijistânî, Abû Ya'qûb 154, 166, 167
Althusser, Louis 17, 103, 111n7
Anders, Günther 88
angels, and nature 153–5
angelology 9, 153, 156–7; non-theological 156; as theo-fiction 155–60
animism 18
Anthropocene 3
anthropomorphism 16, 18
anti-naturalism 158
anti-reductionism 17
anti-vitalism 19
Aping Mankind (Tallis) 20
apophaticism 143
Aquinas, Thomas, St 68, 70, 73, 165, 166
Aristotle 43n3, 67, 69, 70, 72, 77, 137; *Poetics* 18; *Politics* 119
art of absolute 179–83

Asma, Stephen 18
atheism 55, 57
Augustine 71
Avicenna 6, 34, 37–40, 42, 44n12, 44n14, 45n26

Badiou, Alain 6, 17, 86, 87, 90–3, 101; *Being and Event* 102, 104, 105; external theory of subjectivity 102; *Logics of Worlds* 87, 91, 102–3, 105, 106; materialist dialectic 8; *The Meaning of Sarkozy* 91, 92, 95; *Peut-on penser la politique?* 95; renaissance of materialism 94; theory 8, 107; *Theory of the Subject, Being and Event and Logics of Worlds* 8, 102–4; *Third Sketch for a Manifesto of Affirmationism* 93
Barad, Karen 3, 134–5, 147n32, 147n34
Barber, Daniel Colucciello 153
Baudrillard, Jean 4
Being and Event (Badiou) 102, 104, 105
Being and Nothingness (Sartre) 107
Benjamin, Walter 121, 126n37; "Critique of Violence" 115, 119
Bennett, Jane 16, 133–5
Bergson, Henri 6, 16–17, 20, 23–5, 26n41, 27n47, 136; Bergsonism 20, 25
Bernstein, J.M. 119–20
Blake, Charlie 3
blinding light 178–9
Bloch, Ernst 88
Boutroux, Emile 17
Braidotti, Rosi 136, 146n6
Brandom, Robert 19
Brassier, Ray 5, 6, 19, 20, 23, 163; "everything is dead already" 20
Bull, Malcolm 158
Burns, Michael O'Neill 8, 101
Butler, Judith 131, 134, 136, 146n5

Cacciari, Massimo 121
Canetti, Elias 89
capitalism 4, 5, 92, 123, 173; contemporary 108
Cartier-Bresson, Henri *180*

187

INDEX

causality: emergent 135; narrative 18
chauvinism 24
Christ 75, 174–6, 183; future 159–61, 167; as generic subject 160–2; nature of 71, 78
Christianity 57, 68, 70–1, 76–7, 154, 159–66; and Islam 9, 154, 162; philosophy of 161–2; theology of 75–6, 159, 162; *see also* angelology; religion
Christos Angelos 161
Chronicles of Consensual Times (Rancière)174
clinamen 17
Colebrook, Claire 9, 132, 133, 136–42, 144; *Deleuze and the Meaning of Life* 136–7
The Communist Manifesto (Marx and Engels) 4
conatus essendi 143, 145
Connolly, William 135–6
contemporary capitalism 108
contemporary materialism 7, 111
Continental philosophy 4, 15–17, 101, 111, 154; post-Continental philosophy 5; theory, affirmationism in 5
contingency: absolute 17–19; as actuality 37–9; as unreason 34–6; without unreason 39–41
"contingentism" 18
Cook, Deborah 120
Coole, Diana 133
Corbin, Henry 9, 156, 168n10
correlationism 20, 34–6, 122
cosmic thanatology 16
courage 103–6
Critique of Dialectical Reason (Sartre) 107, 111n7
Critique of Violence (Benjamin) 115, 119
cultural revolution 157–60; in Mao's China 159

damaged life 8, 115, 116–17, 118, 120–1, 124; *see also* ephemeral life; mere life
dark vitalism 16, 19
The Dead Christ with Angels (Manet, 1864) 174–5, *175*, 183
de Beauvoir, Simone 131
de Biran, Maine 20
De Chardin, Teilhard 19
De la contingence des lois de la nature (Boutroux, 1874) 17
Deleuze and the Meaning of Life (Colebrook) 136–7
Deleuze, Gilles 3, 5–6, 9, 17, 20–1, 23, 25, 42, 132, 137–9, 142, 176–7, 179
DeLillo, Don 19, 21
democratic materialism 87, 91
Derrida, Jacques 136
Desmond, William 143–4, 145, 146n15, 148n84
determinate affirmation 86, 93–4, 96
De Trinitate (Augustine) 71
Deus absconditus 156
Deus sive natura 154, 166, 167
dialectical materialism 138

Dialectic of Enlightenment (Adorno and Horkheimer) 118–19, 123
dialectics 7–8, 76, 86–7, 95–6, 120–1; Hegelian 87; materialist 8, 87, 91, 94–6, 97n13, 101, 138
Dickens, Charles 177
Dickinson, Colby 7
Difference and Repetition (Deleuze) 21
dimorphism, sexual 144
divination 40–3, 44n20, 45n24
divine agency 142
divine inexistence 17, 51
The Divine Inexistence (Meillassoux) 50, 55, 59
divine transcendence 142–3
divinology 52
dualism, Cartesian 132
dynamic monism 25

Eckhart, Meister 143
economic materialism 17
"emergent causality" 135
Engels, Friedrich 4, 88
enthusiasm 105
ephemeral life 8, 115, 118, 121–4; *see also* damaged life; mere life
"essential spectres" 50–5
Evans-Pritchard, E.E. 40–1
exaggeration 89; *exaggerating reading* 89, 90
existentialism 4
"exteriority-within-phenomena" 135

feminism 78, 131–6, 140, 144–6, 146n4, 146n23
Finlayson, James Gordon 117
The Fold (Deleuze, 1988) 182
formalism: of the Real 164–5; subjective 106; structural 107
Foucault, Michel 136
Frost, Samantha 133, 135
Future Christ (Laruelle) 160, 161; *see also* Christ

Gender Trouble and Bodies That Matter (Butler) 131
Genealogy (Nietzsche) 55
Giacometti, Alberto 179, *180*, 181–2
Goodman, Benny 25
Grelet, Gilles 161
Guattari, Félix 9, 25, 132, 137–45, 158, 177

Haraway, Donna 134, 136
Harman, Graham 6, 16, 21, 43n9, 123
Hart, David Bentley 144
Haug, Wolfgang Fritz 87
Haynes, Patrice 3, 8, 9, 131
Hegel, G.W.F. 43n5, 87, 95–6, 138, 162, 174; *Hegelian without Hegel* 96
Heidegger, Martin 19, 34, 66, 67, 72, 123, 134
hermeneutics, utopian 122
History and Freedom lectures (Adorno) 122
Honneth, Axel 120, 121, 123

INDEX

Horkheimer, Max 118–19
Howie, Gillian 144
humanism 8, 49, 108–11, 123, 132–3, 138–45;
  anti- 4, 109, 111, 138, 146n16; liberal 109;
  materialist 102, 109, 110; minimalist 108, 109;
  promethean 55; secular 141
hylomorphism 132
hyper-chaos 35, 37, 38, 39, 43n9
hyper-vitalism 141

idealism 3–4, 7–8, 87, 117, 155, 167–8n5;
  linguistic 131, 146n5; without idealism 7–8,
  86–7, 91, 94–6
immanence 3, 5–7, 9, 73, 118, 143–4; absolute
  161, 163, 164–5, 166–7; and art 173–83; facing
  174–6; linguistic 77; plane of 10n10, 138, 140;
  relating to 176–8; religious 49–60; and
  transcendence 73, 116, 135–6, 142, 145, 176
immanent ethics 58
immanentism 144
imperialism, Western 161
impersonalism 58
infancy 69–70, 72, 73–4, 77, 79n6
Infancy and History (Agamben) 69
interpretation: of the world, changing 87–90;
  changing, as philosophical act 90–4
Irigaray, Luce 131, 134
Islam, messianic 9, 152, 161–2, 164, 167n2,
  168n10, 169n54; *see also* religion

Jambet, Christian 153, 154, 156, 158–9, 161,
  162–3, 166–7, 167n2
Jameson, Fredric 93
Johnston, Adrian 102, 111, 111n2
Judaism 56, 60, 75, 160, 163; *see also* religion
Judeo-Christian tradition 154

Kacem, Mehdi Belhaj 162
Kant, Immanuel 5, 26n8, 34, 43n4–5, 117–18;
  Kantians 22
Kierkegaard, Søren 142
Korsch, Karl 87
Kraus, Karl 115
Kripke, Saul 19

Labica, Georges 87, 95
L'Ange (Jambet and Lardreau) 156, 158–9,
  167n2
language 4, 7, 104, 133, 143, 158; bodies and 91,
  92, 93, 95, 97n13; and existence of god 75–8;
  linguistic idealism 131; linguisticism 133;
  profanation of 70–5; relation to being-in-the-
  world 66–70
Language and Death (Agamben) 67, 68
Lardreau, Guy 9, 154, 156, 158–9, 160, 161
Laruelle, François 6, 9, 16, 154–5, 160–1, 163,
  167–8n5
Latour, Bruno 5, 21

La Véracité (Ladreau) 156, 159
Lectures on the Negative Dialectics (Adorno) 89
Lenin, V.I. 3
liberal humanism 109
life: damaged 8, 115, 116–17, 118, 120–1, 124;
  ephemeral 8, 115, 118, 121–4; mere 8, 115,
  116, 118–20, 121, 122; Stoic 120
linguistic idealism 131
linguisticism 133
"The Logic of Continuity" (Peirce) 38
Logic of Sense (Deleuze) 42
Logics of Worlds (Badiou) 87, 91, 102–3, 105, 106
*Ludwig Feuerbach and the End of Classical
  German Philosophy* (Engels) 95
Lyotard, Jean-François 5, 20, 158

Macherey, Pierre 95
Magnus, Albert 68
Malabou, Catherine 8, 16, 102, 107–9
Manet, Edouard 174, 175, *175*, 183
Mansoor, Jaleh 174
Maoist fashion 103
Marcuse, Herbert 7, 85, 86
Marx, Karl 4, 136
Marxian thesis 88, 90; on Feuerbach 87, 95
Marxism 138, 159; economic materialism 17;
  materialism 101, 103; orthodox 86; theory of
  dialectical materialism 138
Material Feminisms (Colebrook) 132
materialism 4, 5, 87; aleatory 17; contemporary
  7, 111; demand of 103; democratic 87, 91;
  dialectics of 8, 87, 91, 94–6, 97n13, 101, 138;
  humanism and 102, 109, 110; Marxist 17, 101,
  103; mathematical 17–19; monisms 6;
  non-reductive 132, 133; philosophy 90;
  post-Althusserian 101; resurgent 5; theological
  9, 133, 145; twenty first-century 102
mathematical formalism 101
mathematical materialism 17–19
matter 3, 6, 8–9; feminism and 131–46; vs.
  mobile 181; vs. nature 154–5
Matter and Memory (Bergson) 16, 23, 24
The Meaning of Sarkozy (Badiou) 91, 92, 95
"Meditations on Metaphysics" (Adorno) 116, 125
Meillassoux, Quentin 5–7, 17, 18, 22, 23, 33, 34,
  36, 40, 42, 43n3, 44n12, 44n14, 50, 54, 102,
  109, 110, 122; *After Finitude* 6, 17, 33–4, 36,
  37, 51, 57; audacious inventory 57; hyper-
  chaos 35; ontologico-ethical project 55;
  religion 56; universal justice 55
mere life 8, 115, 116, 118–20, 121, 122; *see also*
  damaged life; ephemeral life
metaphysics 17, 23, 51–3, 56, 70–4, 111, 115–8,
  124–5
mimetic practices 118
Minima Moralia (Adorno) 115, 120
modern societies 85; political 86
monism 6, 23–5

INDEX

Morgan, Alastair 8, 115
mysticism 65, 66, 70; postmodern 36

Nagel, Thomas 21
Napoleon 21
narrative causality 18
naturalism 106, 137, 158–9, 163, 165
nature 9, 17, 118–19, 121, 122–4, 140; angels and 153–5; laws of 36, 44, 52; and messianism 159, 160, 162–3, 164, 165–7; non-theological 165–7; of the real 56, 59, 161, 164; scepticism of 146n3
Negative Dialectics (Adorno) 115–17, 120, 121, 125
negative theology 143, 156, 158, 163
Negri, Antonio 78, 159, 162
Nelson, Simeon 10
Newtonian mechanics 17, 132
Nietzsche, Friedrich 7, 52, 53, 55, 58, 59, 133
nihilism 19–20, 40, 72, 75–7, 79n9, 91–2
Nihil Unbound (Brassier) 5
non-reductive materialism 132, 133, 141
Noys, Benjamin 9, 167n2, 173

object-oriented philosophy 173
Ó Maoilearca, John 6, 15
omnipotence 35, 57, 142; of chaos 35
ontology 55–6, 103, 104, 108; Hegelian 107; posthuman 132, 139; radical 50, 53, 54
Our Mutual Friend (Dickens, 1864–65) 177
Outdatedness of Human Beings (Anders) 88

Parnet, Claire 138
passio essendi 143, 145
passive vitalism 9, 132–3, 136–42, 145, 148n98
Peirce, Charles Sanders 38, 39, 41, 42, 45n24; "The Logic of Continuity" 38
Peut-on penser la politique? (Badiou) 95
Philosophie et non-philosophie (Laruelle) 163
Philosophy as Creative Repetition (Badiou) 91
plane of immanence 3, 138, 140, 174, 177–8, 181
Poetics (Aristotle) 18
point of existence 93
Point Omega (DeLillo) 19, 21
political nihilism 7, 79n9; *see also* nihilism
political society 85–6
Politics (Aristotle) 119
postmodern mysticisms 36
post-structuralism 4
Price, Charles S. 6
Principle of Hope (Bloch) 88
Principle of Ultimate Reality 36
profanation, language as 7, 65, 70–6, 77–8
profane attention 121
promethean humanism 55
Pseudo-Dionysius 156, 158

radical empiricism 3
radical ontology 50, 53, 54

Ramey, Joshua 6, 33
Rancière, Jacques 174–6
rationalism 56, 78
religion 6–7, 56, 77; immanence 49–60, 52, 58; as "manmade" phenomenon 50; modern critique of 50; philosophy of 6, 153, 162; *see also* Christianity; Islam, messianic; Judaism
renaissance of idealism (Badiou) 94, 96
renaissance of materialism (Badiou) 94
resurgent materialism 5
rethinking agency 134–5
revelation 7, 36, 65–6, 71, 75–8
reversing reading 88–90
revolution, cultural 157–60
rigor mortis 19, 23
Rogue Riderhood (character) 177
Ruda, Frank 7, 85
Ryle, Gilbert 22

Sartre, Jean-Paul 9, 106–7, 111n7, 177, 173–4, 178–83; *Being and Nothingness* 107; *Critique of Dialectical Reason* 107, 111n7; *The Transcendence of the Ego* 178
scepticism 22; of nature 146n3
Searle, John 23
The Second Sex (de Beauvoir, 1949) 131
secular humanism 141
Sein-zum-Tode (Heidegger) 19
Sellars, Wilfred 19, 23–4
sexual dimorphism 144
situated absolute 9, 182–3
Smith, Anthony Paul 9, 141–2, 153
solar catastrophe 5, 20
"Spectral Dilemma" (Meillassoux) 22, 50–5, 61n3
speculation 5–6, 23, 36; on the actual 41–3
The Speculative Turn 5
Spinoza, Baruch 5, 20, 58, 78, 134, 138, 154, 166, 178
spiritualism 17
Stoic life 120
Strawson, Galen 20

Tallis, Raymond 20–1
Tanner, Kathryn 142, 148n79
Taylor, Richard 133
"terrible deaths" 7, 22, 50, 53
terror 105
theo-fiction *see* angelology
theologians 53, 66–7, 75
theological materialism 9, 133, 143, 145, 148n98
theology 65, 68, 70–8; Christian 75–6, 159, 162; feminism and 78, 131–46; life and matter 141–5; negative/non- 143, 153–4, 156, 158, 162–3; veiled 71
theory of subjectivity 101–10
Theory of the Subject, Being and Event and Logics of Worlds (Badiou) 8, 101–4

INDEX

Theunissen, Michael 120
Third Sketch for a Manifesto of Affirmationism (Badiou) 93
A Thousand Plateaus (Deleuze and Guattari) 137
Toscano, Alberto 5
transcendence 5, 8–9, 67–9, 73, 115–25, 142–5, 164–6, 174–8
The Transcendence of the Ego (Sartre) 177, 178
transformative reading 88–90

universal justice 55, 59, 110
Urpeth, Jim 6–7, 49
utopian dream 74

veiled theology 71
Vibrant Matter (Bennett) 16
Vico, Giambattista 6, 42

The View from Nowhere (Nagel) 21
vitalism 16, 20, 132–3, 178, 179; anti-vitalism 19; dark 16, 19; passive 9, 132, 133, 136–45, 148n98
"vital materiality" 16
Voice 66, 71–4

We Have Never Been Modern (Latour) 21
Western imperialism 161
What is Philosophy? (Deleuze and Guattari, 1991) 177
What Should We Do with Our Brain? (Malabou) 107
Whistler, Daniel 161
witchcraft 40–1
Wittgenstein, Ludwig 66–7, 75, 77

Žižek, Slavoj 89–90, 158